RERUNS
ON FILE:

A GUIDE TO
ELECTRONIC
MEDIA
ARCHIVES

COMMUNICATION TEXTBOOK SERIES

Jennings Bryant — Editor

Broadcasting
James Fletcher — Advisor

RERUNS
ON FILE:

A GUIDE TO
ELECTRONIC
MEDIA
ARCHIVES

*Compiled by **Donald G. Godfrey***
Arizona State University

LEA LAWRENCE ERLBAUM ASSOCIATES, PUBLISHERS
1992   Hillsdale, New Jersey   Hove and London

9200005117

Lawrence Erlbaum Associates, Inc., Publishers
365 Broadway
Hillsdale, New Jersey 07642

(no loan)
P
96
.A722
U54
1992

Library of Congress Cataloging-in-Publication Data

Godfrey, Donald G.
    Reruns on file : a guide to electronic media archives / compiled
by Donald G. Godfrey.
    p.   cm.
    Includes indexes.
    ISBN 0-8058-1146-X. — ISBN 0-8058-1147-8 (pbk.)
    1. Mass media—United States—Archival resources—Directories.
  2. Mass media—Canada—Archival resources—Directories.   3. Mass
  media—Great Britain—Archival resources—Directories.   I. Title.
  P96.A722U54   1992
  302.23′02573—dc20   91-35707
                                                            CIP

Printed in the United States of America
10 9 8 7 6 5 4 3 2 1

To Christina, Floyd, Donald, Emma and Daniel, who gave their father time to enjoy old-time radio and who seem to enjoy the old mystery programs themselves — especially when they're camping alone in the woods.

and

To the memory of Professor Milo Ryan — a mentor to all who undertake the rewarding task of "phonoarchive" research.

Contents

viii

ACKNOWLEDGMENTS

Special thanks are extended to the Broadcast Education Association and particularly the members of BEA's Broadcast History Division. These individuals have provided invaluable assistance in the formulation of the original questionnaire and have guided this second edition from the outset. Special mention and thanks are due to Professors Steven Craig, University of Maine; Robert Tiemans, University of Utah; Larry Lichty, Northwestern University; Val Limburg, Washington State University; Pat Cranston, University of Washington; Ray Caroll, The University of Alabama; and Barbara Cloud, University of Nevada. Also Louisa Nielson, Executive Director, Broadcast Education Association and Fay Schreibman, Museum of Jewish Heritage.

The manuscript received the expert readings of Chris Lembesis of the Society to Preserve and Encourage Radio Drama Variety and Comedy; Marvin Bensman, Memphis State University; Richard Bartone, William Paterson College; and James Fletcher, University of Georgia. Christopher Sterling provided editorial feedback helpful in the Introduction. To these people I express my most grateful appreciation for their input and specific direction in the preparation of the final manuscript.

Special thanks are due the Walter Cronkite School of Journalism and Telecommunication, the College of Public Programs' Auxiliary Resource Center, and the Broadcast Education Association. Each provided assistance without which this project would still be in the stage of discussion.

FOREWORD

by Marvin R. Bensman

Few researchers and scholars made use of broadcast primary resources. Most often this absence of use is due to the lack of information on how to locate and the difficulty of obtaining the material. Most private collectors and institutional archives have not had sufficient funds to adequately catalog their materials which has made locating particular materials difficult. Audio materials are also not generally obtainable through interlibrary loan. These materials have also not been considered as trustworthy as print by traditional historical scholars. Historians prefer to rely on citations that are easily available to their peers. Many also question source reliability when in many instances the recorded incident is the primary documentation of that event.

Historians and other areas of scholarship have begun to focus on the development and outcomes of a variety of 20th-century issues. In this century it has been broadcasting and the electronic media that has most immediately documented our social and cultural history. Thus, scholars must go beyond print descriptions to the primary source material of our age. This can be accomplished by studying specific occasions or episodes, including the social and cultural impact of media itself. The primary broadcast of an occasion or a sequence of events rather than secondhand print descriptions of observers who place their own interpretation upon the episode is a yet untapped scholarly resource.[1] One of many examples would be studying the appointment by President Roosevelt of the liberal Hugo L. Black to the Supreme Court. There was strong opposition from the public and in the Senate because of Black's former membership in the Ku Klux Klan. The appointment was approved by Congress after Black went on network radio and gave a disarming speech explaining his membership. However, any researcher who relies on the written record of this event without listening to the recently discovered broadcast speech of October 3, 1937, does a disservice to the complete evidence now available and their understanding of the event.[2]

In this final decade of the 20th century, collecting examples of bygone radio and television programs has become considerably easier. Estimates vary —
but there may be at least 15,000 separate U.S. radio program series consisting of thousands more individual episodes circulating among private collectors.

Newly discovered radio broadcast material is constantly surfacing. A number of programs are in institutional archives that have not yet been released because of the terms of owner's agreements. Those institutional collections available to bonafide researchers usually require travel and often restrict copying. Various companies have commercially exploited broadcast program material as "nostalgia" by introducing some broadcast material to the general public via the technology of the audiocassette developed in 1961 and which became an audio home-recording standard in the 1970s.

Archives serve three major functions: (a) to store materials; (b) to exhibit, sell, distribute, transcribe, and catalog; and (c) to restore disintegrating materials and maintain those that remain in better shape. Any particular collection focuses on different functions depending on the missions of the collector or their host institution.

The Library of Congress began to collect and preserve programming in 1949 in its role as the copyright depository. The National Archives also collected and preserved programming from governmental sources and increasingly received donated event and news materials.

Despite the interest of private collectors and the growth of institutional archives the preservation of electronic media programming faces a crisis. The crisis is due to a combination of problems and the lack of public policy.[3]

The most basic problem is twofold — the discovery and increasing availability of programs, and the increasing rate of disposal and destruction of material. The way programs have been recorded — transcription to tape formats — poses problems for preservationists. As transcription turntables disappear and reel tape recorders are replaced with cassette recorders, the means for playing the material are being lost or exist only in museums. The need to transfer the older formats into new forms is a time and cost problem. Magnetic audiotape deteriorates over time as it is exposed to heat, humidity, and atmospheric pollution and is more subject to catastrophic loss of information than is print.

The policy problems are copyright obstacles and the lack of a national strategy among competing advocacy organizations.

The copyright issue is a conflict between competing interests: "Preservation without access is historical censorship," and "Access without copyright protection is theft."[4] The 1976 copyright law revision encouraged the scholarly use of material by permitting off-air taping of programs for scholarly and educational purposes as a "fair use." Institutions were protected from copyright infringement under an exemption in the *Copyright Act of 1976*, which came about as a result of Vanderbilt University taping network TV news broadcasts and coming under attack by CBS. Howard Baker, then Senator from Tennessee, was instrumental in getting this exemption into the law.[5] Under certain conditions specified in the law, libraries and other archives are authorized to photocopy or do other reproduction. The photocopy or reproduction is not to be "...used for any purpose other than private study, scholarship, or research." If a user makes a request for, or later uses, a photocopy or reproduction for purposes in excess of "fair use," that user may be liable for copyright infringement, but not the library or archive. The institution is protected if it gives appropriate warning about the possible infringement and withholds any copying for what might be an illegal use.[6] However, there are gray areas, such as how an archive may distribute the material and how much is "fair."

A market for old radio programming has developed in the industry. These potential markets have given owners an interest in protecting their copyrights. Because the copyright law is not clear, owners, if they even allow archiving, impose strong restrictions on institutional and private use of their material. Also, ownership of many programs is very complex and depends on contracts with directors, writers, performers, and rights holders of music and other materials used in the broadcasts. Private collectors who charge for duplication or selling programs are more susceptible to copyright problems than are institutions. Arch Oboler sued J. David Goldin for unfair competition over his selling of *Lights Out* which the court held as infringement under the copyright law.[7] In 1979, Jim Lewis, without a license, began leasing *Lone Ranger* episodes to radio stations. In 1982, Lone Ranger TV sued for copyright infringement and conversion. The court held that the *Copyright Act of 1909* provided valid copyrights in the underlying scripts that gave the company the right to control derivative works that had been infringed by Lewis. Under California law, Lone Ranger TV had an intangible property interest in the performances from the time of their recording and Lewis had taken something of value.[8]

Because programming is being archived by diverse institutions and individuals there is no unified policy of coordination in preservation. Funding to support institutional archives is as variable as the institutions preserving the available material. The UCLA Film and Television Archive discontinued the development of its radio archive that consists of 50,000 transcription discs and 10,000 tapes of radio from 1933 to 1983, to concentrate on film due to lack of funding. This shutdown is mostly academic, because the archive has never been open to the public.[9] Standardization of cataloging is haphazard and there is a basic lack of information as to what is available to be preserved, what has been preserved, in what condition and in what formats, and how the material can be made more accessible to scholars and the public. Without a national policy and a national advocacy organization there is no way to tell potential funders how to begin to address the problem of preservation. However, the material is "out there" and this is an effort to assist interested parties in locating what material is available.

Radio program collecting starts with the ability to preserve sound. On August 12, 1877, Thomas Alva Edison invented the first phonograph, which was patented on February 17, 1878. It worked with a revolving cylinder and did not produce very good sound. In 1886, Emile Berliner applied for a patent on the first flat phonograph disc.[10]

At the turn of the century, 78 rpm records became quite popular. In 1927, Thomas Edison had experimented with a long-playing record and achieved 20 minutes per side on a 12-inch disc, running at 80 revolutions per minute. Edison did not see a use for this improvement and left the recording industry soon thereafter. Columbia had excellent sound quality on a 10-inch 78 rpm disc, but the playing time was only 5 minutes. Commercial 78s with radio program matter were available to the public from 1928 on, the first being *Amos 'n' Andy* recording their WGN routines for use by over 30 radio stations when they were still known as "Sam 'n' Henry." The 5-minute playing time and noise level kept such recordings from being widely used by broadcast stations.[11]

In 1932, Victor introduced the "transcription" running at 33 1/3 rpm on a 10-inch disc. The standard Electrical Transcription (ET) running 15 minutes per side at 33 1/3 rpm on a 16-inch disc using a 1-mil needle was introduced shortly afterward and became a broadcast standard. The sound quality, even on those pressed for syndication, was quite high compared to the standard home 78 rpm record. ETs were also cut by the networks and their affiliated stations for rebroadcast of their programs at different times or for legal purposes. This type of ET was aluminum based, with a black vinyl coating. During World War II, when metal was scarce, many of these ETs were scrapped for their metal content. Wartime ETs were of a glass base and were extremely fragile. The networks destroyed many of these records as they moved operations and reduced storage costs. However, many affiliated stations, primarily on the West Coast, which had to record network programs because of the time zone difference, kept their recordings. Sources for older programs dating as far back as the 1930s were also engineers who had taken the ET discs home.

The tape recorder was theorized in 1888 by Oberlin Smith as a piece of string dipped in glue and coated with iron filings. In 1893, Valdemar Poulsen, a Danish engineer, used wire to store magnetic impulses that could reproduce sound.[12] In 1921, Nasavischwilly first proposed magnetic tape. But it required further electronic development such as the 1924 Western Electric Corporation patent on electrical sound recording. In the same year, the loudspeaker supplanted the use of headphones. In 1930, Germany's I. G. Farben industrial company created the first magnetic tape. When I. G. Farben was broken up after WW II for producing the gas used in the concentration camps, BASF — one of its pieces — continued to manufacture magnetic tape.

Major recording innovations were introduced in the second half of the 1940s. In 1943, both Optical Film and Wire Recorders were used to document the allied invasion of Europe at the Normandy beaches. When the war ended some people acquired home disc recorders. A small group of programs available today from the 1930s and early 1940s were originally recorded on these recorders using 7-inch discs that ran for 5 minutes a side. The home wire recorder was also introduced for home use in the 1940s. During the war years, the Armed Forces Radio Service (AFRS) preserved a great many programs for rebroadcast to troops overseas. The AFRS disc has a brightness and lack of distortion that is hard to find even among network disc copies. Home tape machines such as the Brush Soundmirror using Scotch 100 paper tape supplied by the 3M Company were beginning to appear in the consumer market, but fell far short of professional requirements.

In 1945, Armed Forces (U.S.) Col. John T. Mullin was part of a Signal Corps team investigating the military applications of German electronic technology. He was told by a British officer about a tape recorder at a Frankfort, Germany, radio station being operated by the Armed Forces Radio Service that had exceptional musical quality. There Mullin found German technicians working for AFRS using Magnetophone audiotape recorder/players. The technological improvements of a constant speed transport, plastic tape impregnated or coated with iron oxide and the employment of a very high frequency mixed with the audio signal to provide "bias" made these machines hi-fidelity.

The first two machines acquired were turned over to the Signal Corps and Col. Mullin disassembled two other machines and shipped them to his home in San Francisco. On his way home to be discharged Mullin stopped at Fort Monmouth, New Jersey, in November 1945, and was invited to Thanksgiving dinner by Lt. Col. Richard Ranger, a Signal Corp acquaintance. Mullin told Ranger of the Magnetophone. Ranger later went to Europe to probe the manufacture of the machine and the tape it used with the goal of manufacturing magnetic recorder/players. In 1946, Mullin rewired and reassembled the Magnetophone machines and went into a partnership with Bill Palmer for movie sound-track work, using those machines and the 50 reels of tape he had acquired.

In October 1946, Mullin and his partner Palmer attended the annual convention of the Society of Motion Picture Engineers (SMPE — now SMPTE). In his hotel room he demonstrated the machine to the sound heads of MGM, 20th Century Fox and the chief engineer of Altec Lansing. Arrangements were made for demonstrations at the movie studio sound departments. Ranger also attended the SMPE and accompanied Mullin and Palmer to the subsequent demonstrations. Concern was expressed by the movie technicians as to the future availability of recording/playback machines. Ranger stated his interest in making an American copy of the Magnetophone and its tape. Mullin-Palmer reached a verbal agreement with Ranger to share information in exchange for becoming his West Coast representatives when he got into production.

Mullin was then invited to an Institute of Radio Engineers meeting in May 1947 to demonstrate the German Magnetophone. It was there employees of Ampex saw and heard the tape recorder. Because of the agreement with Ranger, Mullin was not able to disclose to Ampex information he had learned beyond what he knew from his activities while in the Signal Corps and shortly thereafter Ampex began its own developmental project.

In 1947, the technical staff of the *Bing Crosby Show* on ABC arranged to have Mullin rerecord original disk recordings of the *Bing Crosby Show* on ABC onto tape and then edit them. Crosby had been with NBC until 1944, doing the *Kraft Music Hall* live, but did not like the regimen imposed by live shows. Since NBC would not permit recorded programs, Crosby took a year off and returned on the newly formed ABC network when his new sponsor, Philco, and ABC agreed to let him record. That process required transcription recording and rerecording (sometimes two or three generations) and quality of sound suffered. In July 1947, after the initial demonstration of editing, Mullin and Ranger were invited to give a demonstration of their respective equipment for Bing Crosby's producers by taping live side-by-side with transcription equipment the first show for the 1947-1948 season in August at the ABC-NBC studios in Hollywood.

Mullin recorded on the Magnetophone and Ranger brought in two prototypes he had built. The Ranger machines suffered from high distortion and background noise and the Crosby people were not satisfied with the Ranger demonstration. Ranger felt he had developed his machine to acceptability and was anxious to realize some return. Mullin terminated his agreement with Ranger and called Ampex with whom he had retained contact. Bing Crosby Enterprises then negotiated financing for Ampex for exclusive distribution rights and Mullin was employed to record the Crosby show on his original German equipment until the Ampex machines would become available. With the original German tape recorders and 50 rolls of BASF tape, Mullin's first recorded demonstration show of August 1947 was broadcast over ABC on October 1, 1947.

The 3M Company had contacted Mullin and the Crosby technicians and expressed an interest in making audiotape. Ampex was not interested, nor, at that time, capable of making tape for the machines. A number of different samples were developed and those that 3M thought would be superior to the German formula had unacceptable variable background noise. So a low grade oxide copy of the BASF tape to become known at Type 112 was put into production. Later it was determined that an adjustment to the recorder's bias circuit permitted use of the better formulation which became the standard Type 111. Finally in April 1948, Alexander Poniatov and his team of engineers at Ampex in Redwood City, California, introduced the first commercial audiotape recorder based on the Magnetophone as Ampex Model 200. The first two, Serial Numbers 1 and 2 were initially presented to Mullin and Numbers 3-12 went into service at ABC. To meet the contract requirements, Mullin gave his machines to ABC and later received Numbers 13-14 for his contribution. Mullin joined Bing Crosby Enterprises in 1948 and recorded his shows and others at ABC until 1951. Bing Crosby Enterprises, as the exclusive distributor for Ampex products, sold hundreds of recorders to radio stations and master recording studios.

In 1951, Mullin and other engineers were spun off as the Bing Crosby Electronic Division to handle development of audio instrumentation and video recording. In 1956, the Electronic Division became the Mincom Division of 3M where Mullin served as head of engineering and Professional Recorder Development Manager until his retirement.[13]

Because of the initial newness of audiotape equipment, the programs were at first transferred from a tape master to disc before being aired. In the late 1950s radio programs were aired directly from tape.

Serious recording and collecting of radio programs on home tape recording equipment began around 1950, after some 20 companies introduced an effective reasonably priced reel-to-reel recorder to the consumer market. This material, along with AFRS discs and a few network and syndicated discs, comprised the starting base of material which began to be privately traded in the 1960s.

In the 1960s, when radio as it had been almost was gone, individuals began to seek out other collectors and small groups began to form on both the east and west coasts to exchange material, information, and sources. People in the armed forces began to bring AFRS discs or tape recordings of AFRS programs home, and radio stations recordings became available as they began disposing of their stored material.

In 1954, Charles Michelson started the rebroadcast market by obtaining an umbrella agreement to license *The Shadow* to individual radio stations, LP recordings and home-enjoyment tapes. In 1965 he then acquired the rights to *The Green Hornet, The Lone Ranger,* and *Gangbusters.* The first aggressively marketed private seller of radio programs was J. David Goldin, a former engineer at CBS, NBC, and Mutual, who formed "Radio Yesteryear" and an album subsidiary, "Radiola," in the late 1960s. In 1988, Michelson's program rights were terminated and sold to "Radio Yesteryear."

Newsletters began to circulate on radio program collecting in the late 1960s. The most influential newsletter to set the standard was *Radio Dial* by the Radio Historical Society of America founded by Charles Ingersoll, then a 70-year-old radio buff. Carrying on the tradition, the leading newsletter today is *Hello Again* by Jay Hickerson, which began publication in 1970 and tied together over 100 of the most active collectors. Today, approximately 160 collectors comprise the mass of privately collected broadcast material available.

Following is a selected guide to some of the more useful sources for locating radio broadcast material. You must include a self-addressed postage-paid envelope in order to receive a reply from clubs or private collectors.

Finding Aids:

Marvin R. Bensman & Dennis Walker, *Sources of Broadcast Audio Programming* (ERIC Reports, ED 109 724; CS 501 094).

Robert Burchett and George Wagner, *Old-Time Radio Digest* (4114 Montgomery Road, Cincinnati, OH 45212).

Robert Burnham, *The Listening Guide Newsletter* (Box 2645, Livonia, MI 48151).

Leonard E. Chulev and Pamela M. Englebrecht (Eds.), *Dictionary Catalog of the G. Robert Vincent Voice Library* (Boston: G.K. Hall, 1975).

E. Roderick Deihl, "Using Media to Teach Broadcasting History — A Bibliography of Materials," *Communication Education*, Volume 25, No. 2, March 1976.

Janis DeMoss, *North American Radio Archives Newsletter* (5291 Jacks Creek Pike, Lexington, KY 40515).

H.L. Drake, "Special Report: Teaching Speech Communication with Recordings Including Old Radio Shows," *Central States Speech Journal*, Summer 1975.

Donald G. Godfrey, *A Directory of Broadcast Archives* (Washington, D.C.: Broadcast Education Association, 1983; 2nd edition, Lawrence Erlbaum Associates, forthcoming).

Ellen Reid Gold, "Recorded Sound Collections: New Materials to Explore the Past," *Central States Speech Journal*, Volume 31, Summer 1980.

James R. Heintze, *Scholar's Guide to Washington, D.C. for Audio Resources* (Washington, D.C.: Smithsonian Institution Press, 1985).

Jay Hickerson, *Hello Again Newsletter*; and *What You Always Wanted to Know About Circulating Old-time Radio Shows* (Box 4321, Hamden, CT 06514, 1986).

Lawrence W. Lichty, "Sources for Research and Teaching in Radio and Television History," *Performing Arts Resources*, Theatre Library Association, Volume 1, 1974.

Annett Melville, *Special Collections in the Library of Congress: A Selective Guide* (Washington,D.C.: Library of Congress, 1980).

Michael R. Pitts, *Radio Soundtracks: A Reference Guide* (Metuchen, NJ: Scarecrow Press, 1986).

Richard Prelinger & Celeste R. Hoffnar, *Footage 89: North American Film and Video Sources* (New York: Prelinger Associates, 1989).

Bonnie Rowan, *Scholar's Guide to Washington, D.C. for Film and Video Resources* (Washington, D.C.: Smithsonian Institutional Press, 1980; 2nd edition in progress).

Milo Ryan, *History in Sound* (Seattle: The University of Washington Press, 1963), and *History in Sound: Part II*, compiled and edited by Donald G. Godfrey (Seattle: University of Washington Press, 1974).

Chuck Shaden, *Nostalgia Digest* (Box 421, Morton Grove, IL 60053).

Radio Clubs (newsletters noted):

Golden Radio Buffs, Owen Pomeroy, 3613 Chestnut Drive, Baltimore, MD 21211 (*On the Air*).

Indiana Recording Club, William Davis, 1729 E. 77th Street, Indianapolis, IN 46240 (*Tape Squeal*).

Metropolitan Washington OTR Club, James Burnette, 6704 Bodensee Ln., Manassas, VA 22111.

Milwaukee Area Radio Enthusiasts, Ken Pabst, 4441 N. 77th Street, Milwaukee, WI 53218.

Old-Time Radio Club of Buffalo, 100 Harvey Drive, Lancaster, NY 14086 (*Illustrated Press*).

Radio Collectors of America, Bob Levine, 8 Ardsley Circle, Brockton, MA 02402.

Radio Historical Association of Colorado, Vicki Blake, Box 1908, Englewood, CO 80150 (*Return with Us Now*).

Revival of Creative Radio, Tim Coco, Box 1585, Haverhill, MA 01831 (*Wavelengths*).

Society to Preserve and Encourage Radio Drama, Variety & Comedy, Box 1587, Hollywood, CA 90078 (*SPERDVAC Radiogram*).

ENDNOTES

[1] Alan Havig, "Beyond Nostalgia: American Radio as a Field of Study," *Journal of Popular Culture*, (Vol. XII, No. 2, 1979), pp. 218-227.

[2] Hugo L. Black, Special address on his KKK membership, NBC Radio Network, October 3, 1937. Memphis State University Radio Archive, Memphis

State Library, Memphis, TN 38152, (Reel No. 0604, Cassette No. 1308, 1/4 hour).

[3] The same problems affect TV program collecting; see the Rapporteur Summary of the *Roundtable on Television Preservation*, Annenberg Washington Program, Communications Policy Studies, Northwestern University, 1455 Pennsylvania Avenue, N.W., Washington, D.C. 20004, May 19, 1989.

[4] *Ibid.*

[5] Title 17, USC, § 108, 201.

[6] Title 17, USC, § 201.14.

[7] *Oboler v. Goldin*, 714 F. 2d 211 (2nd Cir. 1983).

[8] *Lone Ranger TV v. Program Radio Corp.*, 740 F. 2d 718 (9th Cir. 1984).

[9] "Sounds of Radio Fading at UCLA Archive," *LA Times*, June 26, 1990, p. F 28.

[10] Orrin E. Dunlap, *Radio and Television Almanac* (New York: Harper and Brothers, 1951), p. 20.

[11] Erik Barnouw, "A History of Broadcasting in the United States," *A Tower In Babel*, Vol. 1 (New York: Oxford University Press, 1966), pp. 225-230.

[12] Mark Mooney, "The History of Magnetic Recording," *Hi-Fi Tape Recording* [N.D.], p. 2.

[13] John T. Mullin, "The Birth of the Recording Industry," *Billboard* (November 18, 1972); "Creating the Craft of Tape Recording," *Hi-Fidelity* (April 1976); Speech Communication Association Presentation, "History of Recorded Sound: Edison through Tape-Recording" (1976); Personal correspondence, 1975-79.

For more than half a century, broadcast recordings have reflected an important aspect of our culture and history. An increasing number of archivists and private collectors have restored and exchanged radio and television materials. Even Congress has mandated the establishment of a radio-television archive. However, despite the awareness of these primary resource materials, there is still some reluctance to utilize this aural and visual history resource. A part of this reluctance is due to the fact that little is known about the existence of many collections throughout the nation.

The archive work for many institutional, private, and commercial collections has grown beyond the hobby of collecting old radio programs. Producers, scholars, educators, and commercial enterprises are beginning to realize the value of these historical materials. It is hoped that this publication will facilitate the process of research and discovery within broadcasting. It is hoped that the traditional scholar who delves into the broadcast source will find such resources as attractive and accessible as print.

The project was undertaken for the purpose of providing a comprehensive directory of radio and television program archives in the United States and Canada. The project proposed to describe each collection, focus on its specialty, and thus provide a serious researcher with a knowledge of primary program resources. The project was simple and straightforward. A survey was mailed to all known collections: institutional, private and commercial. Each curator was asked to describe his or her collection in terms of its content as well as provide the usual organizational access information. Survey categories included requests for organizational proprietorship information, a general format description of the collection, a description of broadcast program types with the collection (indicating the number of recordings where possible), a general description of subject content and program types (variety, comedy, news — The 1920s, The Depression, World War II, etc.), related manuscript materials (scripts, etc.), special interests of the collection, and accessibility to the collection. The emphasis of the survey was on content.

As you can imagine the questionnaire received a varied response. Some archives took the time to provide a content analysis of their holdings as was requested. Others seemed to ignore the questionnaire and sent their already published materials. And there were some who did not respond. The editor conducted two survey mailings and followed up these mailings with extensive phone work to ascertain the information requested and to determine the extent of the collections. The information published reflects the respondents response to our queries. We have worked to maintain the integrity of the response feeling that the curator knows of the collection's specialty more than the editor. The "editor's notes" throughout the listings are based on the editor's evaluation of each collection as it relates to the total body of information available and is provided to help the researcher decide "is a trip to the collection going to yield the information desired?"

This guide is organized alphabetically by state and city. This is to facilitate any travel that the researcher might contemplate. The index provides the researcher with subject and location of any specific topics of interest within the body of the listing.

SUGGESTIONS FOR LOCATING
BROADCAST ARCHIVE MATERIALS

There are finding aids and catalogs unique to each individual collection. Each major collection generally has a published catalog, card file and or listing of its collection, a few are developing computerized access — which when developed will be invaluable to the researcher. This guide indicates the finding aids available for each collection surveyed. Contact with each collection will give you details on access, availability, and research aids for individualized collections.

There are a few publications that are invaluable to the sound and archive research process. Extracted from the Foreword listing, the following are recommended highly:

Marvin R. Bensman & Dennis Walker, *Sources of Broadcast Audio Programming* ERIC Reports, ED 109 724; CS 501 094.

> Professor Bensman has annotated a list of broadcast programs and commercial phonograph records available. He has computerized over 100 private collections and listed associations and companies that sell recordings, newsletters, and publications. This is the most extensive individual listing of private publications yet available, and by far one of the most valuable contributions to broadcast program research.

Richard Prelinger & Celeste R. Hoffnar, *Footage 89: North American Film and Video Sources* (New York: Prelinger Associates, 1989).

> A large and most extensive film-oriented catalog. Its emphasis is film and moving image, but you will also find radio and television listings. It is a bit expensive so check your library. Remember, a lot of films were broadcast and many such collections contain important papers, manuscripts, scripts, production materials, and video.

Milo Ryan, *History In Sound* (Seattle: The University of Washington Press, 1963). See also: *History In Sound: Part II* (microfishe) compiled by Donald G. Godfrey.

These publications/catalogs annotate the CBS-KIRO Milo Ryan Phonoarchive Collections now housed at the National Archives. *History In Sound* is an indispensable work regarding the news broadcasts of World War II.

The following Washington, DC-oriented publications are of great importance to the scholar who can visit the area:

James R. Heintze, *Scholar's Guide to Washington, D.C. for Audio Resources* (Washington, D.C.: Smithsonian Institution Press, 1985).

Annett Melville, *Special Collections in the Library of Congress: A Selective Guide* (Washington, D.C.: Library of Congress, 1980).

Bonnie Rowman, *Scholar's Guide to Washington, D.C. for Film and Video Resources* (Washington D.C.: Smithsonian Institutional Press, 1980).

Visiting the Collection

The researcher needs to contact each collection and check for details regarding availability, access, and updated information. Most collections are in an ever continuing process of cataloging, organizing, and serving researchers. Many restrict the use of their materials, especially private collectors. Each private collection is unique and while generally willing, curators are not always able to be as flexible as the institutional collections organized for research purposes. Call before you visit and be as specific as possible in your requests.

The Growing Importance of Private Collections

There are a growing number of private collectors throughout the world. These folks often have extensive collections and a networking system that although it may seem tedious at times, can be invaluable. Note the list of Radio Clubs in the Foreword. The largest of these private organizations with archive holdings include The North American Radio Archive (NARA), 33888 The Farm Rd., Lake Elsinore, CA 92330; The Society to Preserve and Encourage Radio Drama, Variety and Comedy (Sperdvac), P.O. Box 7171, Van Nuys, CA 91409-9712; and The Association for Recorded Sound Collectors (ARSC), P.O. Box 2086, Fairfax, VA 22031. ARSC puts out a valuable directory of this membership and notes the interests of each collector. Whereas ARSC membership includes a good many music enthusiasts, it also contains many broadcast collectors.

The Preservation of Recorded Sound

There are publications concerning the collection and preservation process. Many scholars have found themselves with valuable resources they continue to access after their initial research. Proper care and attention is important. The editor recommends the following:

Milo Ryan, "Preface," *History In Sound* (Seattle: The University of Washington Press, 1963).

Jerry McWilliams, *The Preservation and Restoration of Sound Recordings* (American Association for State and Local History, 1400 Eighth Avenue South, Nashville, TN 37203, 1971).

Association of Recorded Sound Collectors Journal, semiannual publication of the ARSC Association.

The Chronology of the Programs

There are two publications that are also helpful in setting the broadcast program within its historical chronology. These are:

Harrison B. Summers, Radio Program Carried on National Networks, 1926-1956 (Columbus: Ohio State University, Department of Speech, 1958). Printed by Arno Press, 1971).

Tim Brooks & Earle Marsh, *The Complete Directory to Prime Time TV Shows, 1946–Present* (New York: Ballantine Books, current edition).

Scholarship and Methodology

The introduction to this publication suggests varying methodological approaches to the subject of the electronic media. It includes citations and examples of both research and the research method. In addition, the following selected citations reflect the challenges of aural and visual research.

Cathleen C. Flanagan, "The Use of Commercial Sound Recordings in Scholarly Research," *Journal of the Association for Recorded Sound Collections* 11(1979): 13-17.

Donald G. Godfrey, "The Critical Analysis of Spoken Word Broadcasts," *Journal of the Association for Recorded Sound Collections* 14(1982): 19-32.

Donald G. Godfrey, "CBS World News Roundup: Setting the Stage for the Next Half Century," *American Journalism* 7:3(Summer 1990): 164-172.

Alfred Haworth Jones, "The Making of an Interventionist on the Air: Elmer Davis and CBS News, 1939-1941," *Pacific Historical Review* 42(February 1973): 74-93.

Michael Murray, "Behind the Murrow Myth: Radulovich Re-Visited," *Journal of CMU Studies* (Fall, 1990): 1-8.

Michael Murray, "Persuasive Dimensions of See It Now's Report on Senator J. R. McCarthy," *CMU Quarterly* (Fall, 1979): 13-20.

Milo Ryan, "Here Are the Materials — Where Are the Scholars?" *Journal of the Association for Recorded Sound Collections* 2(1970): 24-32.

INTRODUCTION

THE HISTORICAL METHOD AND THE ELECTRONIC MEDIA

The historical method is a method of research and discovery of growing importance within the discipline of mass communication. Yet, in the rush to the seemingly more glamorous, current, and dustless approach to quantitative data, the methods of historical research have often been overlooked. Popular mass media research texts all but ignore historical methods. Wimmer and Dominick's *Mass Media Research* has two pages on history, a discussion of the histogram.[1] Rubin and Rubin, in *Communication Research: Strategies and Sources*, also cover the subject in two pages and dismiss the purpose of historical research as merely "finding and describing."[2] Dominick and Fletcher provide a chapter on "Searching for Television's History," but the chapter is primarily a "prelude to a comprehensive location listing of existing television programs."[3] It contains little about the historical method or how one might handle the electronic media program materials as primary sources of evidence. Radio, television, and electronic media research in general certainly fit easily into the methodological disciplines of survey, experimental, content analysis, focus group, and all kinds of statistical and behavioral analysis. These methods dominate the published literature.

Contributing to the fact that comparatively little is being written about broadcast history is the fact that too little is being written [and taught] about the historical method itself. Broadcast historians seem to have accepted the view of the traditional historians, those who study Marxism, the Egyptian pyramids, and the founding of America, and so forth, that the aural and visual media have overwhelming limitations for historical research. Those familiar with broadcast research will note that even broadcasting's own history depends on printed sources and there are few program histories. The topic of broadcast history does, however, attract interest and publication: *Stay Tuned, The Modern Stentors, The General, In All His Glory, Rod Sterling, and Gunsmoke* have recently contributed greatly to the discipline.[4] However, only two research methods texts in mass communication deal substantially with the subject of the historical methods of mass communication research. Stempel and Westley's *Research Methods in Mass Communication* has two chapters, one on "The Nature of Historical Research" and a second on "The Method of History."[5] The most comprehensive contribution comes from Startt and Sloan, *Historical Methods in Mass Communication.*[6] Startt and Sloan are thorough and discuss the basic methods as well as a philosophical framework.

Although Startt and Sloan and Stempel and Westley's contributions are thoughtful, the unique challenges faced by the broadcast historian still need development and discussion. The purpose of this volume is to suggest ideas that the historian may consider in examining the broadcast record. This study discusses a traditional methodological approach to the topic of history and suggests parallels appropriate to the analysis of broadcast history. It also suggests some appropriate methods may be adapted to the challenges of broadcast history.

The Historical Method and Electronic Media Research

The Purpose of the Research. A purpose may be simple discovery, analysis, or the development of an argument. Broadcast historiography is a part of the discovery process that is most analogous to legal research and critical methodology. It is a process of systematic research undertaken for the purpose of "description, analysis, interpretation, and evaluation."[7] Historical research allows the analyst to compare the past with the present and to evaluate trends based on the historical record. It provides a basis for effective decision making. It provides a foundation of evidence from which societal, political, and business functions may be judged and directed. These are the purposes of most research whether the method of discovery is historical, critical, quantitative, or qualitative.

The examiner should not dismiss historical discovery by implying it is merely a process of sifting dusty facts. It is detective work. It is time travel. It is archeology. Historical research, as with other types, is about constructing an argument or, in other words, a factual image. It has a distinct and beneficial purpose for the reporter, for example, who examines past data to report the news, the corporate station executive who must analyze the record to establish future direction, the advertiser who must evaluate past performance to plan the new campaign. The politician must research legislative history to draft new law. The lawyer must research case history and the facts to determine precedent and present a convincing argument. Asa Briggs summarized the utility of history declaring that the purpose of historical research was to provide people with a "view of their own society, [a picture] arrived at by comparing themselves with their predecessors."[8]

Define the Object and Situation. Once a general purpose has been constructed, the second task to consider is the "object," or the focus of the study within its unique "situation," or environment. The object of historical analysis is not always easy to define. It often comes into existence in response to a situation within which the object exists. For example, the reporting of Edward R. Murrow becomes more important because of World War II. In this example, the object, Murrow, is given significance because of the situation, World War II. Similarly, an analysis of the 1970s television program series "All in the Family" gains significance because of the civil rights movement of the times. In contrast, the history of "The $1.98 Beauty Pageant" could be written, but its significance would be more challenging to justify — perhaps as an example or artifact rather than history. The definition of any object and the situation must be considered carefully. As in any thesis, the justification depends on the interrelationships of both the object and the situation. Once the object is clearly identified, do not forget the situation, a situation is defined for analytic purposes as "a complex of events, persons, objects, and relations presenting an actual or potential exigence" which can be understood through the analysis."[9]

This parallels the approach of critical theory such as is found in literary, rhetorical, and legal research methods. Historiography by its very nature is critical and reconstructive. Stevens and Garcia have called for the development of historiography, "Critical historiography [which] would stimulate ideas for other inquiries, reveal gaps in previous work, call attention to broadly applicable questions, and provide an impetus to theory generation."[10]

Let the Object Dictate the Method

Once the purpose, object, and situation has been brought into focus, the researcher can decide on the appropriate method. Dr. Allan Nevins, *Gateway to History*, indicated that there are few fixed methods in the historical research process.[11] Even though that statement is particularly true when dealing with the history of broadcasting, it is misleading. There are methods, but, as they relate to electronic media history, they remain necessarily eclectic, adapted from the methods of traditional history, rhetorical criticism, literary criticism, speech communication, public address, editorial journalism, film, drama, art, and so on. The historical scholar borrows from these related fields and must justify the tools of evaluation against existing methods as electronic media historiography evolves. For example, a researcher might use traditional historiography or the rhetorical method to analyze Murrow's 1945 Buchenwald broadcast. In contrast, the analysis of "The Cosby Show" would better utilize theoretical models of drama.

Adapting the Appropriate Method. Broadcasting is still comparatively young and there are very few traditional Likert-like scales or fixed rules. However, methods and patterns do exist. For example, Sloan organized his text suggesting there were three primary "schools" in mass communication history: developmental, progressive, and cultural.[12] The approaches within each of these schools represents differing subject and methodological insight.

The researcher will also find historical methods reflected in the periodical literature. The examination of pioneering stations may be measured in many ways: against the criteria established by Baudino-Kittross,[13] the analysis of congressional maneuvering against the rules of Cain, the movement studies against the criteria of Griffin,[14] or the documentary analysis may find the models of Murray or Bartone beneficial.[15] Broadcast news personalities may be examined following the examples of Leslie or Fang.[16]

Marwick suggested that the visual information of television was important to traditional historians.[17] The researcher may adopt the methods of Dondis or Zettl in the evaluation of historically important visuals.[18]

The literature of critical methodology is also adaptable to electronic media history. For example, Scott and Brock, in their discussion of rhetorical criticism, present and illustrate tradition, experimental, and eclectic methods of analysis.[19] Phifer's work in speech and theater suggests there are seven types of history: biographical, movement studies, regional studies, institutional studies, case histories, selected studies, and editorial studies.[20] Other works include Newcomb's *Television: The Critical View*, Primeau's *The Rhetoric of Television*, and Esslin's *The Age of Television*. All provide excellent approaches to the analysis of broadcast history and criticism.[21] Newcomb focused primarily on the criticism of the entertainment functions of television, and noted there are "no histories of television programming."[22] Primeau's oversimplified version of the Aristotelian method of analysis provides an excellent basis for beginning the historical analytic process. Esslin would argue that "the language of television is none other than that of drama," and no matter what the program genre, be it news or entertainment, Esslin contended the methods of dramatic analysis can be employed. Similarly, legal historians may wish to examine the works of Pember or Chamberlin for an approach to the historical and legal object. Pember's *Privacy and the Press* offers a basic text historical analysis of the privacy law. Chamberlin's and Brown's *The First Amendment Reconsidered* provides a collection of legal essays surrounding a variety of first amendment topics and differing methodologies. Both works provide excellent historical models.[23]

The citations mentioned earlier are by no means exhaustive; they represent a number of highly different approaches to a wide variety of historical topics.

For the most part, the historical methods as they relate to electronic media is still evolving. It is not always easy to find a clear-cut model or a mathematical scale that may be simply superimposed over the object. To this point little has been written solely about historical methods. As they are still evolving, they are lumped together and similarly dismissed. The electronic media historian is in the same position today as the television critic of the 1960s. Writing then about television criticism, Laurent commented:

> This complete critic must be something of an electronics engineer, an expert on our governmental processes, and an esthetician. He must have a grasp of advertising and marketing principles. He should be able to evaluate art forms, to comprehend each of the messages conveyed, on every subject under the sun, through television. And there's more.[24]

The historian, much like this critic, becomes the expert spectator adapting analytical models from the rich body of available historical literature.[25] However, as illustrated, there is no shortage of patterns or methods by which one may evaluate historical data.

Now, having defined the purpose, object, and situation, and decided on the methodological pattern, the researcher is faced with the unique challenge of applying these to the topics of electronic media history.

Dealing with Historical Resources:
Is the Broadcast Program a Primary Source?

Nevins listed six broad types of primary source materials and the broadcast program was not on the list. His list included: physical remains, orally transmitted materials, representative materials, handwritten materials, printed books and papers, and possibly motion picture film, phonographs and personal observation.[26] These sources, of course, are not mutually exclusive as it is important that "all available witnesses must be summoned."[27] However, broadcast materials were not listed for two reasons. First, Nevins was writing in 1938 and there were few broadcast materials available at the time. Second, and more important, Nevins' list reflects the reluctance of the traditional historians to accept the broadcast record as a primary resource. Nevins hinted at the acceptability of phonograph records and personal observation, but with unexplained reservations. Marwick, writing 30 years later in *The Nature of History* listed radio, film, and television in his list of primary source materials,[28] but then he added a final note of traditionalist skepticism, "It is all too easy to be bewitched by the attractiveness of visual sources of all sorts...."[29] Marwick was echoing the position of the mainstream historian, warning them of the deficiencies of radio, television, and film as primary sources.

Traditional Skepticism. The traditional nonmedia historian is rightly suspicious of the broadcast source because (a) traditionalists generally lack knowledge of the electronic media process; and (b) the increase over time of both commercialization and falsification within the media for sake of dramatic effect and profit, both of these distortions occurring at the expense of historical fact, have created the suspicion. For example, the fact that a recording that purports to be of Marconi's 1901 Signal Hill, Newfoundland, experiment exists does not make it authentic. Trace its roots and it can be located in the Canadian National Archives as a 1951 re-creation from radio studios of CFCF, Montreal, Quebec. It is a fine radio drama that even the novice must realize as a dramatic re-creation.[30] Its artistry is important, but the fact remains, it is a re-creation. The program itself cannot be taken firsthand as the broadcaster's "slight of hand,"[31] as Marwick called it, creates suspicion and question when electronic media programs are cited as primary historical documents of record. Evaluation of any broadcast record, therefore, requires the researcher to employ a wide "range of critical techniques... [and] technical skills"[32] often beyond the experience of the traditionalist. Marwick would not deny that the program is a valuable record, but his overall skepticism reflects the feelings of the traditional historian by pointing out that radio and television have been commercially exploited. The documentary has evolved into docudrama, news has all too often become the exploitation of the visual, and the "facts and their probability even plausibility are steadily ignored."[33] There are exceptions, of course: "World at War" produced by Thames Television being one of the most outstanding. Producers and researchers went directly to the primary source for their materials, even to the extent of advertising in European papers for pictures and old family film. "Victory at Sea," "Air Power," and the "20th Century" are others where the historical research was well done. However, such documentaries are rare within broadcasting's commercial line up.

Understanding the Roots. The skeptical perspective of the traditional historian toward primary electronic media source materials does not necessarily negate a program's historical value, but it does place a significant challenge in the path of the investigator who would utilize the program as a primary source. Those who would utilize the program as a primary source of information must look to the sources of that program as one would with any primary source and for additional supportive documentation. The investigator must understand the program developmental process, carefully documenting the evidence and its roots. The researcher needs technical skills to deal with the evidence and the medium. As information passes through the various stages of production, each step in the process must be analyzed in terms of the value of the information as evidence, and the effect that the process has had on the information presented. The investigator must hope some record of all this can be found.

Evaluating the Source. The historical researcher must understand the value designations placed on primary and secondary source materials. In addition to tracing the roots of the program evidence, the broadcast researcher faces the challenge of carefully documenting the authenticity of the information as a potential primary source. For example, by comparison, contemporary diaries and personal writings are far more important than the broadcast program as primary source materials. A similar problem occurs with the oral history interview and folklore records. The broadcast historian may learn from the oral historian and document a given program by adapting much the same procedure. The oral historian's interview, for example, may be substantiated through written accounts occurring within close proximity to the event. Bormann noted that the oral historian's challenge was similar to the news reporter's situation, "when the reporter writes of what he or she has personally observed, be it printed or broadcast, he or she becomes a primary source." However, the reporter is a secondary source when the information reported comes from "informed observers or sources close to the government, and 'undisclosed sources.'"[34] Herb Morrison's recording of the Hindenburg disaster, is clearly a primary source. Morley Safer, reporting on the evacuation airlift from Vietnam, is also a primary source. However, these same people reporting almost the same facts in retrospect become secondary source figures in their quotation of other participant observers. Thus, as reporters begin to intermingle their sources, and as time passes between the event and the record, it is often difficult to determine the authenticity of the story. Thus, it requires additional verification of the evidence. At one end of this challenge in broadcast history is the historian who deals with an eyewitness, the trained news observer; at the other, they have dramatic entertainment information, which at times seems to have passed through an endless evolving process of development. Despite the complexity of the media situation, the procedures of the oral historian may be used in establishing authenticity for the broadcast source. In historical research, all available witnesses must be summoned.

Authenticity of the Evidence. The most important differentiation to be made in determining broadcast primary and secondary materials is the authenticity of the source. This gains added emphasis within broadcasting because of the skepticism already noted. The authenticity of any primary document can always be called into question: Could the document be a forgery? Has someone tampered with the evidence for selfish purposes? These concerns are not new. Some letters attributed to President Abraham Lincoln have been called forgeries.[35] A forensic analyst was called in to examine early Mormon Church documents when it was discovered that a private collector was forging materials for commercial exploitation.[36] Although these examples may seem distant, even irrelevant, to the broadcast historian, they are not. In broadcasting, the skills of production, editing, and the recording of events have called into question the authenticity of historical resources. William S. Paley, longtime head of CBS, held tight to his early policy that his network would not record its radio programming from the 1920s into the 1940s. Programming, to be authentic, had to be live; to record a program called its authenticity into question. As producers today, this policy seems almost silly, but the question of historical authenticity remains a valid one. What part did others play in the formulation of the broadcast document: the unnamed writers, the editors, and technical people? These are all subject to the tests of authenticity if the record of their role can be uncovered.

The tests of authenticity include comparative witnesses, truthfulness, time and place of the observations, the point of view of the presenter, and the relevant influences of the production process. Comparative witness means factually verifying the information from other comparative and perhaps competitive sources. The broadcast historian must scrutinize the data and compare it to other known primary sources. The time, place, and proximity requirements of evidence can help assess the object and situation in relation to their environment. The further away from the event the record occurs, the more likely that external data influenced the record and the more complex the evaluation of authenticity. "The closer the time of making a document to the event it records," Gottschalk wrote, "the better it is likely to be for historical purposes."[37] The very nature of broadcast news reporting, where the immediacy is important, places a high value on the broadcast news resource. Thus, Edward R. Murrow's report of the allies capture of Buchenwald, April 12, 1945, the day the troops marched into the camp, is of more historic value than his well-known and colorful correspondence report that aired April 15, 1945. The further away from the event the record was made, the more the historical analyst bears the responsibility of summoning the additional witnesses to determine the value of the record. For example, how did other reporters view Buchenwald? What about a sound-bite that is used to reinforce a story a day or two later? Extended time decreases the primary value of the source. The time reference must also be considered along with other variables surrounding it, the total context, and the process. Lengthy periods of time and the extended production process of dramatic television make this a challenging undertaking. As Laurent noted, the broadcast critic and historian "learns quickly that the aphorism about 'two sides of a question' is a major understatement."[38] All aspects of the context and the process must be examined. Truthfulness and point of view, for example, obviously reflect on this context and the authenticity of the source. "Murrow on McCarthy," in the 1954 CBS documentary would be a useful illustrative case. If the reporter seems to toss editorial intonations into his or her delivery, the analyst must examine the value of the reporter as a source. Was the reporter biased? Was he or she in a position to observe the facts? Unfortunately, today the researcher also must deal with the ego of the reporter as an eyewitness. Did the reporter recount the facts, or did his or her actions affect the facts as they were presented? Are they reporting the news or are they the object of news? If there was distortion, it must be examined. There are serious ethical, as well as complex historiographical questions.

Radio and television are media of information and art. They do not fit easily into the test of critical, legal, and/or historical evidence. They are affected by economies and the law, technology and science, audience and entertainment, public trust and politics. The electronic media is itself a collection of dichotomies, nevertheless it deserves serious historical analysis. Nevins' analogy between historical research and the courtroom procedure is an accurate one, particularly in relation to a discussion of the authenticity of the primary source. The historian must distinguish among resources of documentation as a lawyer in the courtroom distinguishes between original evidence and rumor. The tests of evidence vary, necessarily depending on the object and circumstances of the trial, so it is with the process of historical discovery, the principles of evidence vary with witnesses and circumstances. Bormann indicated much the same in his analogy between the historical research and the news reporter. The reporter must "discriminate between statements of fact, statements of opinion, value and ethics ... the grounds upon which the historian makes a judgment ... in the end comes down to the facts that can be observed."[39]

Citing the Electronic Media Record as Primary Evidence. The citation of broadcast materials includes the necessary challenge of simple, yet thorough documentation. Nowhere in historiography is the footnote more important than when the researcher uses the broadcast program as a primary resource. This is the author's opportunity to note for the reader and future examiners the roots of the information and the authenticity of the source.

Examine the traditional content of any footnote style. There are five broad information divisions: (1) the author, the editor, the article; (2) the material cited, the article, the chapter, the book; (3) the location of the material, the publisher, the archive; (4) the date of publication; and (5) direct reference to the citation, page reference. In broadcast history, because the source is already suspect, any

xliii

omission of material weakens the argument, the credibility of the source, and the author. The footnote/documentation manuals may vary to facilitate different types of research style and method, but the subject elements of documentation remain basically the same. In developing the footnote for a broadcast program, these same elements apply, but the citation is probably going to look more like the citation of a library special collection as opposed to a simple book or article. Adapting the basic information requirements a broadcast program citation would include: (1) the author becomes the reporter, the editor, the writer, the creator, the actor...the primary disseminator of the facts; (2) the material cited becomes the program and/or the information context; (3) the location of the material becomes a combination of information about the production company or information sponsor responsible for the creation and the collection within which it is located. Just as with a print citation, there are unspoken hierarchies. For example, print material cited for *The New York Times* is considered more valuable as a source than a vanity press publication. Similarly, a broadcast program from an institutional archive becomes more valuable than the author's personal collection, and an unedited radio disc becomes more important than an audiotape recording. The citation becomes highly suspect and will need additional supportive documentation without the location information. It is valuable to the reader and to future research. (4) The date is the date of the original broadcast and station/network responsible for airing. This is the time reference of the citation. There are an increasing number of reference sources where the researcher can find the broadcast days of a program cited, and the newspaper's radio/TV logs can also provide this documentation. If the chronology of the broadcast time is important to the document, it can also be cited here without effecting the narrative flow. (5) The direct reference to the program includes the program number, the reel number, cuts where appropriate, and when available, the disc number and a direct reference to the collection from which the program was taken. The disc reference has special significance to the radio program citation. The glass and aluminum discs found in many broadcast archives represent the unedited live recording of many historical radio broadcasts. The fact that they were live and unedited increases the value of these records, the authenticity of the citation and source information. There is a significant body of information held in many programs recorded live on disc before the process of editing began. You cannot edit the aluminum and/or glass radio discs of the 1930s and 1940s as you can tape. Similarly, the authenticity of other works can be enhanced from evidence acquired within the film and video outtake files, and raw script materials that often accompany the larger broadcast archives. The footnote citation is the point where you verify this information without cluttering the narrative of the text. It is wise to add supporting documentation to any broadcast program citation. Questionable citations referencing primary programming documentation can be substantiated with the citation of other documenta-

xliv

tion evidencing the same conclusions. A program information source can be coupled with a parallel and supporting citation from *The New York Times*, a production script, the producers notes, etc. These supportive materials strengthen the validity of the presentation. A credible citation might look as follows:

(1) Edward R. Murrow, (2) "World News Tonight," (3) CBS News, June 1, 1941. (4) National Archives, Washington, D.C., CBS-KIRO Milo Ryan Phonoarchive, (5) Reel No. 1803, Disc No. 24, 1181a.

(1) Orson Wells, (2) "The Hitchhiker," (3) "Suspense," CBS Radio Network, September 2, 1942. (4) National Archives, Washington, D.C., CBS-KIRO Milo Ryan Phonoarchive. (5) Tape No. 5010, Discs No. (43) 2094A and (43) 4095B.

The broadcast program citation may initially look a little different in print, but the individual elements that comprise full documentation are essential to the validity of the source.

SUMMARY

Historical electronic media research must meet standards similar to print and traditional history. The researcher must learn to deal with the broadcast program as they would "think and write about books."[40] The process is about the same, although the task of proving the credibility and the authenticity of the broadcast source is paramount. Search the literature and carefully define the "object and situation" of analysis. Printed primary source materials will be considered throughout the initial literature search. Consider also the broadcast materials, as they are likely untouched sources of evidence. The materials surveyed constitute the body of evidence that the writer will subject to analysis in the construction of his or her argument. Search the literature and carefully select and/or adapt the methodology that is appropriate to the object. The electronic media represent a wide range of eclectic analytic opportunities. Writing history is about the analysis and reconstruction of an argument reflective of a "complex of events, persons, objects, situations, and relations." The evidence presented in constructing the argument must be subject to the same rigorous tests of authenticity as in any other historical, legal, or critical argument. The difference being that because of the skepticism toward the broadcast program as a primary source, and its commercial exploitation, the analyst must take extra care to support the documentation and the influence of the process on the evidential information. In this respect, the citation itself becomes increasingly important. It must reflect the rigors of documentation, the authenticity of the document, and will often require supportive documentation from a source to substantiate the broadcast evidence. The task of writing broadcast history is like that of any other analysis; it has as its purpose the goals of description, analysis, interpretation, and evaluation. History is a written reflection of how society views itself.

ENDNOTES

[1] Roger D. Wimmer and Joseph F. Dominick, *Mass Media Research: An Introduction*, Belmont, CA: Wadsworth Publishing, Inc., 1990.

[2] R.B. Rubin, A.M. Rubin, and L.J. Peile, *Communication Research: Strategies and Sources*, Belmont, CA: Wadsworth Publishing, Inc., 1985, p. 175.

[3] Joseph R. Dominick and James E. Fletcher, *Broadcasting Research Methods*, Boston: Allyn & Bacon, Inc., 1985. Chapter on history, "Searching for Television's History," by Fay C. Schreibman, pp. 16-41.

[4] Christopher H. Sterling and John M. Kittross, *Stay Tuned: A Concise History of American Broadcasting*, Belmont, CA: Wadsworth Publishing, Inc., 1990 (2nd ed.); Philip T. Rosen, *The Modern Stentors: Radio Broadcasters and the Federal Government, 1920-1934*, Westport, CT: Greenwood Press, 1980; Kenneth Bilby, *The General: David Sarnoff and the Rise of the Communications Industry*, New York: Harper & Row, 1986; Sally Bedill Smith, *In All His Glory: The Life of William S. Paley, The Legendary Tycoon and his Brilliant Circle*, New York: Simon & Schuster, 1990; Joel Angel, *Rod Sterling: The Dreams and Nightmares of Life in the Twilight Zone*, Chicago: Contemporary Books, 1990; SuzAnne Barabas and Gabor Barabas, *Gunsmoke: A Complete History*, Jefferson, N.C.: McFarland & Co., 1990.

[5] Guido H. Stempel III and Bruce H. Westley, *Research Methods in Mass Communication*, Englewood Cliffs, NJ: Prentice-Hall, 1989.

[6] James D. Startt and Wm. David Sloan, *Historical Methods in Mass Communication*, Hillsdale, NJ: Lawrence Erlbaum Associates, 1989. See also Wm. David Sloan, *Perspectives in Mass Communication History*, Hillsdale, NJ: Lawrence Erlbaum Associates, 1991.

[7] Barnet Baskerville, "Rhetorical Criticism," *Southern Speech Communications Journal* 37 (Winter 1971), 113-124.

[8] Asa Briggs, *Social History and Human Experience*, The Grace A. Tanner Lecture Series in Human Values, Cedar City: Southern Utah University, 1984, p. 9.

[9] Lloyd F. Bitzer, "The Rhetorical Situation," *Philosophy and Rhetoric* 1 (January 1968), 1-14.

[10] John D. Stevens and Hazel Dickens Garcia, *Communication History*, Beverly Hills, CA: Sage Publications, 1980, p. 31.

[11] Allan Nevins, *Gateway to History*, New York: Doubleday & Co., Inc., 1938, pp. 195-196.

[12] Sloan, *Perspectives in Mass Communications History*.

[13] Joseph E. Baudino and John M. Kittross, "Broadcasting's Oldest Stations: An Examination of Four Claimants," *Journal of Broadcasting* 21:1 (Winter 1977), 61-83.

[14] Leland M. Griffin, "The Rhetoric of Historical Movements," *Quarterly Journal of Speech* XXXVIII:2 (April 1952), 184-188. See Earl R. Cain, "A Method for Rhetorical Analysis of Congressional Debate," *Western Speech* 18 (March 1954), 91-95.

[15] Michael D. Murray, "Persuasive Dimensions of See It Now: 'Report on Senator Joseph R. McCarthy,'" *Communications Quarterly* XXIV (Fall, 1975), 13-20. See also Richard Bartone, "The Institutional Production Process as Determinant of Historical Presentation in 'Victory At Sea.'" Unpublished paper presented to Broadcast Education Association, April 1990.

[16] L.Z. Leslie, "Ethics as Communication Theory: Ed Murrow's Legacy," *Journal of Mass Media Ethics* 3:2 (Fall 1988), 7-19. Irving E. Fang, *Those Radio Commentators*, Ames: The Iowa State University Press, 1977.

[17] Arthur Marwick, *The Nature of History*, London: MacMillan Education Ltd., 1989, p. 323.

[18] Donis A. Dondis, *A Primer of Visual Literacy*, Cambridge, MA: The MIT Press, 1973. See also Herbert Zettl, *Sight, Sound, Motion: Applied Media Aesthetics*, Belmont, CA: Wadsworth, Inc., 1990.

[19] Robert L. Scott and Bernard L. Brock, *Methods of Rhetorical Criticism*, New York: Harper and Row, 1972.

[20] G. Phifer, "The Historical Approach," in C. W. Dow (Ed.), *An Introduction to Graduate Study in Speech and Theatre*, East Lansing: Michigan State Press, 1961, pp. 52-80.

[21] Horace Newcomb (Ed.), *Television: The Critical View*, New York: Oxford University Press, 1976. See Ronald Primeau, *The Rhetoric of Television*, New York: Longman, Inc., 1979; and Martin Esslin, *The Age of Television*, San Francisco, CA: W.H. Freeman and Co., 1982.

[22] Newcomb, 1st ed., p. xv.

[23] Don R. Pember, *Privacy and the Press*, Seattle: The University of Washington Press, 1972. See also Bill Chamberlin and Charlene J. Brown, *The First Amendment Reconsidered*, New York: Longman, Inc., 1982.

[24] Lawrence Laurent, "Wanted: The Complete Television Critic," in *The Eighth Art*, New York: Holt, Rinehart and Winston, 1962, pp. 155-171.

[25] Lawrence W. Rosenfeld, "The Anatomy of Critical Discourse," *Speech Monographs* 35:1 (March 1968), 50-69.

[26] Nevins, pp. 97 and 136.

[27] Nevins, pp. 224-225.

[28] Marwick, p. 209.

[29] Marwick, p. 325.

[30] "Marconi's Anniversary Signal Hill Broadcast," December 12, 1951, Public Archives of Canada, Sound Archives, Ottawa, Ontario, CFCF, 1973-16.

[31] Marwick, p. 319.

[32] Marwick, p. 313.

[33] Jacques Barzun and Henry F. Graff, *The Modern Researcher* (4th ed.), New York: Harcourt Brace Jovanovich, 1985, p. 120.

[34] Ernest B. Bormann, *Theory and Research in the Communication Arts*, New York: Holt, Rinehart and Winston, Inc., 1969, p. 173.

[35] Paul Angel, "The Minor Collection," *Atlantic Monthly* CXLIII (1929), 516-525.

[36] Linda Sillitoe and Allen Roberts, *Salamander: The Story of the Mormon Forgery Murders*, Salt Lake City, UT: Signature Books, 1988.

[37] Louis Gottschalk, *Understanding History: A Primer of Historical Method* (2nd ed.), New York: Alfred A. Knopf, Inc., 1969, pp. 150-155.

[38] Laurent, p. 161.

[39] Bormann, pp. 169-170.

[40] Professor Milo Ryan's material is quoted with permission of the Ryan Family Estate.

LISTING

OF THE

COLLECTIONS

ALABAMA

I. Organizational Information   Birmingham Public Library
2100 Park Place
Birmingham, AL 35203

Individual to Contact   Marvin Y. Whiting
Archivist & Curator of Manuscripts

Phone   (205) 266-3600

II. General Formats

450 16mm reels of WBRC film and 585 VHS; 400 16mm reels of WVTM film and 475 VHS.

III. General Program Types

WBRC and WVTM television news and commentary 1,910 recordings.

IV. Subject Content Description

The 1,910 recordings of the WBRC and WVTM Collections consist of television news and commentary for the years 1961 through 1985. WBRC and WVTM are local stations in Birmingham, Alabama.

V. Related Manuscript Materials

The **WVTM Collection** includes newscast scripts for the years of 1980 through 1982.

The Department of Archives and Manuscripts also has records of the Alabama Educational Television network for the years 1952-1976. The record consists of reports, minutes of meetings, correspondence, scrapbook of press releases and congressional hearings documenting the creation and development of the network.

VI. Special Interests

The Department of Archives and Manuscripts collects public and private records, personal papers, photographs and audio-visual material that relate to the political, social and economic history of Birmingham, Jefferson County, and the north central area of Alabama. Subjects covered include urban development, the iron and steel industry, coal mining, civil rights, education, local government, religion, civic organizations, postal history and women's history.

VII. Accessibility

The Department has a card catalog that provides a short description of all collections. All processed collections have an inventory of their contents. The Department has begun to enter descriptions of its collections onto the OCLC databases.

The **WBRC Collection** and the **WVM Collection** have not yet been fully processed, and no inventory or index of their contents is available at this writing. They have, however, been arranged chronologically.

Manuscripts, Linn-Henly Research Library, Birmingham Public Library. The cost is $5 plus postage.

See the *Guide to the Collections of the Department of Archives and Manuscripts, Linn-Henly Research Library, Birmingham Public Library.*

The Department is open from 9 a.m. to 6 p.m. Monday through Friday. Some collections are restricted. The researcher is encouraged to call ahead. Photocopying is available. Arrangements can be made for the copying of materials. The Department does not loan any of the material in its collections. Equipment for listening or viewing is available within the Department.

ARIZONA

I. Organizational Information

Hayden Library
Department of Archives and Manuscripts
Arizona State University
Tempe, AZ 85287-1006

Individuals to Contact

Robert P. Spindler
Curator of Manuscripts

Richard Pearce-Moses
Curator of Photographs

Marilyn J. Wurzburger
Special Collections

Phone

(602) 965-3145

II. General Formats

Limited archival broadcast materials, majority being video/film and audio, some never intended for broadcast. Materials range from wire-recordings to Beta Supercam formats.

IV. Subject Content Description

Four special collections contain archival material of interest to broadcasting:

The I.N. Shun Papers (MSM106) consist of correspondence and three radio scripts regarding the history of Chandler, Coolidge, and Willcox, Arizona. Shun was an employee of Advertising Counselors, Inc., of Phoenix, which produced the scripts on behalf of Valley National Bank for broadcast on KTAR radio in 1938. The **Shun Papers** are processed and readily available to patrons.

The Governor Howard Pyle Collection is unprocessed and runs approximately 115 linear feet. The preliminary inventory notes a number of radio scripts and other "scripts," but whether those materials were ever broadcast cannot be determined without a more detailed analysis of the collection.

Materials identified as radio scripts include: "Reaping the Red Whirlwind" by Frederick Ely Williamson, "Jennings and Thompson," and "Religious Readings Scripts for Radio." A number of file headings suggest documentation of the history of broadcasting, such as "CBS Church of the Air," "NBC and Timefinder," "Highway Commission—KOPO-TV," "Cavalcade of Broadcasting," and "Transmitter." The collection also includes a number of unidentified film reels and miscellaneous interviews and newscasts recorded on 18" record format. Because the collection is unprocessed, it is not currently available for research; however, it is possible to arrange for limited supervision examination of the material by contacting the Curator of Manuscripts.

The Tom Chauncey Collection contains some paper, film, video and audio materials relating to the early history of KOOL-TV of Phoenix. **The Chauncey Collection** is also unprocessed and subject to the same access restrictions as the Pyle Collections.

The George Everson and Philo Taylor Farnsworth Collection should also be of primary interest to the broadcast historian. Although this collection contains no broadcast materials, the relevance to the history of broadcasting is apparent. The collection centers around the material gathered by George Everson during the time he was associated with Farnsworth and the development of television. The collection is completely developed and accessible.

VII. Accessibility

The Department is open Monday through Thursday, 9 a.m. to 7 p.m.; Friday, 8 a.m. to 5 p.m.; Saturday, 1 p.m. to 5 p.m.

All materials must be used on site because the Department does not have equipment for viewing all formats it holds. An appointment is recommended as special arrangements for viewing may be required.

Patrons may access processed collections through the Libraries' on-line public access catalog (CARL) and through traditional finding guides. Reproduction charges are quoted on a case-by-case basis. A fee is charged for commercial reproduction.

Queries should be directed to the Curator of Manuscripts or the Curator of Photographs.

ARIZONA

I. Organizational Information

Newsweek Video Archive
University Libraries
Arizona State University
Tempe, AZ 85287-1006

Individual to Contact

Carol Moore
Special Collections

Phone

(602) 965-6519

II. General Formats

390 linear feet, videotape

III. General Program Types

Complete library prepared by *Newsweek Magazine*'s video department covering 1971-1982.

IV. Subject Content Description

The collection contains productions taped for network and cable programming, such as Newsweek Feature Service, Today's Woman, Cartoon-a-torial, Newsweek Woman, and others. The collection also includes some raw film footage, a portion of which is "effects only" film that contains location noises.

The collection also holds the accompanying press releases and scripts from Bureau Report, Cartoon-a-torial, Feature Service, Sports Week, Today's Woman, What's Cookin', You and the Law, and unanimated submissions for Cartoon-a-torial, those not chosen for animation (23 linear feet).

V. Related Manuscript Materials

Press releases, scripts, animated/unanimated materials for 1971-1982.

VI. Special Interests

Newsweek Magazine's videotapes.

VII. Accessibility

Not for commercial use—to be used only in the Special Collections area by faculty and students of Arizona State University for educational and informational purposes.

(The Newsweek Video Archive was a gift from Ted Slate, Library Director, *Newsweek Magazine*, in 1984, to the Walter Cronkite School of Journalism and Telecommunication and is housed in Special Collections Department of the University Libraries, ASU.)

ARIZONA

I. Organizational Information
Visual Literacy Collection
Department of Archives & Manuscripts
University Libraries
Arizona State University
Tempe, AZ 85287-1006

Individual to Contact
Edward G. Oetting
Visual Literacy Collection

Phone
(602) 965-3145

II. General Formats

Non-broadcast materials. The Visual Literacy Collection is a discrete research repository within the Department of Archives and Manuscripts. The VLC contains primary and secondary materials and collections in most formats.

III. General Program Types

Books and instructional film material on use of the visual. Provides indexes, guides, computer databases, and personal reference assistance to researchers. Dedicated to acquisition, cataloging, and processing for reference, dissemination, and preservation of materials. The VLC preserves and makes available unique resources necessary to the serious study of the field of visual literacy.

IV. Subject Content Description

Personal papers and collections from such significant individuals as John L. Debes and Dr. Joel Benedict.

Retrospective secondary source materials such as the Kodak retrospective collection that provides the solid base for VLC's clearinghouse operation.

VI. Special Interests

Actively solicits collections of manuscripts, personal papers, books, photographs, ephemeral, and other resource materials. Also interested in unpublished materials such as correspondence, diaries, photo collections, organizational records, scrapbooks, research files, financial ledgers, and minutes of meetings.

VII. Accessibility

Located on Level 4 of the Hayden Library. Open Monday through Thursday, 9 a.m. to 7 p.m.; Friday, 8 a.m. to 5 p.m.; Saturday 1 p.m. to 5 p.m.

Resources may be utilized in person as well as through modem access to the ASU's online computer catalog.

Photocopies of the resources of the VLC are provided consistent with its photoduplication policy, copyright, and donor restrictions.

Prints from the collection's graphic image collection are available. The VLC reserves the right to restrict or limit the copying of its materials based on the fragility of the materials.

Requests for nonresearch use of the VLC's primary source collections are handled on a case-by-case basis by the Head of the Department of Archives and Manuscripts.

Fees are charged for photoduplication.

ARIZONA

I. **Organizational Information**

Audio Visual Services
University of Arizona
Tucson, AZ 85721

Person to Contact

Carrie Russell

Phone

(602) 621-3282

II. **General Formats**

Film

III. **General Program Types**

Television commercials collection, approximately 500 from the 1960s.

VIII. **Accessibility**

Catalog (running log) with on-site facilities.

I. Organizational Information

Walt Disney Company
Walt Disney Archives
500 S. Buena Vista St.
Burbank, CA 91521

Individuals to Contact

David R. Smith, Archivist
Paula Sigman, Assistant Archivist

Phone

(818) 560-5424

Profit/Nonprofit

Profit

II. General Formats

All types (films, publications, music, publicity materials, photographs, character merchandise, production files, theme parks, oral histories, original artwork).

Several thousand LP - 16" ETs or 78s (discs); 861 audiotapes; 1,405 videotapes, approximately 50% are 3/4" tapes.

This is the total collection; radio shows account for only a small percentage.

III. General Program Types

The collections of the **Walt Disney Archives** are as varied as the activities of The Walt Disney Company. Some files deal with Walt Disney and the Disney family, but others cover such fields as motion pictures (live-action and animated), theme parks, character merchandise, publicity, promotion, publications, and recordings.

IV. Subject Content Description

Walt Disney. The **Archives** has all of Walt Disney's office correspondence files from 1930 until his death in 1966, along with some earlier files that date back to the days of the Laugh-o-Gram studio in Kansas City in 1922.

The collection includes gifts to Walt Disney, personal memorabilia, recordings and transcripts of speeches, office furnishings, and awards. There are over 8,000 photographs of Walt Disney, and a compilation of the history of the Disney family.

Films. Although the company film collection is housed elsewhere, the **Archives** assists in insuring that it is as complete as possible. The **Archives** has helped discover 30 prints of pre-Mickey Mouse titles, along with a number of war-time films made for government agencies or private companies. Some films are available on videotape for study.

Production Files. Scripts are available on all Disney live action films, along with cutting continuities and other production information. For animated films, drafts present the film sequence-by-sequence, with footage and animator noted. Some notable props and costumes are kept in the **Archives**, including such diverse items as the ornate books used in the opening scenes of *Snow White* and *Sleeping Beauty*, Annette Funicello's Mouseketeer outfit, Mary Poppins' carousel horse, a *20,000 Leagues Under the Sea* diving helmet, and the magic bedknob from *Bedknobs and Broomsticks*.

Oral Histories. Taped interviews have been held with many key Disney employees, covering many different topics. Included are interviews with Walt and Roy Disney, along with speeches that they made on various occasions. Typed transcripts have been made of most of the interviews and speeches.

V. Related Manuscript Materials

Scripts, production materials, personal papers of Walt Disney and others, and oral histories.

VI. Special Interests

Disney in all its forms, 1923 to date.

The **Archives** has prepared a number of special indexes, catalogs, and files to aid researchers. These include:

• Magazine article index—Disney stories indexed by subject and author.

- Annual reports—Complete collection of reports from 1940 to date.
- Photographs of Walt Disney—Arranged by subject and date.
- Biographies—Studio personnel and talent biographies arranged in alphabetical order.
- Attractions, shops, and food facilities—An alphabetical file of historical information for both Disneyland and Walt Disney World.
- Books—Cataloged by author, title, and illustrator.
- Phonograph records—Cataloged by title, performer, and film.
- Merchandise licensees—An alphabetical file giving inclusive years and items licensed.
- Employee newsletters—Complete collection of employee periodical publications from the Studio, Disneyland, Walt Disney World, Tokyo Disneyland, and Walt Disney Imagineering.
- Telephone directories—Complete sets for all parts of the company.
- Stockholder reports—Proxy statements, stock and bond offerings, 10-K reports, and related items.
- Insignia—Photographs of all military insignia produced by Disney, with a card index and original correspondence.

VIII. Accessibility

The **Walt Disney Archives** was established in 1970 to collect and preserve the historical materials relating to Walt Disney and the company he founded, and to make these materials available for researchers. The **Archives** is open to all Disney employees and by advance appointment to qualified students, writers, and other members of the public working on specific projects.

For additional information about material available for study and regarding regulations for the use of the **Archives**, contact in advance.

CALIFORNIA

I. Organizational Information

Warner Bros. Features
Warner Bros. Library
4000 Warner Blvd, Building 69
Burbank, CA 91522

Individual to Contact   Martin Fox

Phone   (818) 954-6000

Profit/Nonprofit   Profit

II. General Formats

35 mm film; some 70 mm.

III. General Program Types

General footage of broadcast music, talk entertainment, information talk/news/commentary.

V. Related Manuscript Materials

None.

VI. Special Interests

General stock footage from Warner features and television programs.

VII. Accessibility

Card catalog and computer access; no published catalog. On-site facilities—generally send footage out for viewing; tape fees: standard prices. **Hours:** Monday through Friday, 8 a.m. to 5 p.m.

CALIFORNIA

I. Organizational Information

Fox Hills Video
c/o Media Home Entertainment
5730 Buckingham Parkway
Culver City, CA 90230

II. General Formats

VHS.

III. General Program Types

Sports

IV. Subject Content Description

Greatest moments and unforgettable games in NFL history. Every Super Bowl ever played. Profiles and behind-the-scenes coverage. Heartstopping victories. Heartbreaking defeats. Team highlights. Humor. Sports history. Special team histories. The teams, players, and coaches that make America's pro football.

VII. Accessibility

Sales catalog available.

Editor's Note: VHS consumer release material such as one would acquire by calling 1-800. However, for the sports enthusiast there is a lot of information available.

CALIFORNIA

I. Organizational Information

Westwood I, Inc.
Attn: Div. of Business Affairs
9540 Washington Blvd.
Culver City, CA 90232

Phone

(213) 840-4000

VII. Accessibility

Restricted, no access.

CALIFORNIA

I. Organizational Information

Classical Recordings Archive of America
P.O. Box 1112
El Cerrito, CA 94530

Phone (415) 235-7179

II. General Formats

Disc (LP - 16" Ets or 78s): 350 - 16" ET
Pressing: 2,000
Audiotape: 4,500
Videotape: 400

III. General Program Types

Broadcast Music: about 50,000 recordings/programs.

VI. Special Interests

The collection consists of broadcast recordings of classical music by orchestral and instrumental artists from the period 1930-1970. Included are most of the artists active and broadcasting during this period including large collections by conductors, instrumental soloists (piano, violin, cello) as well as rehearsals. Included is much non-broadcast material derived from "inside" sources, mostly one-of-a-kind and therefore unique.

VII. Accessibility

Lists are available by artist; no published catalog.

Materials are available upon application and payment of dubbing fees.

CALIFORNIA

I. Organizational Information   Cal State University - Fresno
Armed Forces Radio and Television
Service Script Library
Department of Telecommunication
Fresno, CA 93740-0046

Individual to Contact   R.C. Adams

II. General Formats

Scripts of recordings are being cataloged, will be accessible to researchers on a "library-type" basis. No actual recordings.

CALIFORNIA

I. Organizational Information

Chabot College
Learning Resource Center
25555 Hesperean Blvd.
Hayward, CA 94545

Individual to Contact

Stanley Lichtenstein

Phone

(415) 786-6813

II. General Formats

Audiocassettes and records.

IV. Subject Content Description

General History of Radio, Announcers, News & Newscasters, Sports, Children's Shows, Comedians and Comediennes, Anthologies of Comedy, Comedy Drama, Comedy Variety Programs, Situation Comedy, Overview of Radio Comedy, Music and Variety Programs, Radio Drama, Western Drama, Detective Series, Mysteries and Horror, Police Drama, Soap Operas, Commercials.

Editor's Note: There is an 11-page mimeographed listing of the holdings. The collections appear to be small, but broad-based. Apparently they originated from programs held at Memphis State University. A call to obtain a listing prior to on-site inspection is recommended.

CALIFORNIA

I. Organizational Information Filmography of Anthony B. Chan
1154 Boulder Creek Drive
Hayward, CA 94544

Individual to Contact Dr. Angela W. Djao

II. General Formats

Videotapes (3/4" or 1/2"); 40 documentaries on producer/director/ writer Anthony B. Chan.

III. General Program Types

News/Commentary, 75 news packages; 40 documentaries, 22-24 minute shows.

VI. Special Interests

Documentaries of broadcast quality previously aired on commercial television in the United States, Canada, and English channels in Hong Kong. Topics include Asia (China, Hong Kong, Korea), Asian America, Canada, and the United States.

Specials on U.S. investments in Hong Kong, Textiles and Protectionism, Hu Yaobang, Asian American women, etc.

VII. Accessibility

Catalog: *Filmography of Anthony B. Chan*

Published research: Asian American documentaries for rent or purchase on 3/4" or 1/2" tapes.

CALIFORNIA

I. Organizational Information Hollywood Newsreel Syndicate, Inc.
Hollywood Newsreel Syndicate
1622 North Gower Street
Hollywood, CA 90028

Individual to Contact Mike Spaller

Phone (213) 469-7307

II. General Formats

Videotape and 16 mm film, standard speed, linear and 3/4" tape, 5 million feet of film tape.

III. General Program Types

Broadcast music, variety, drama, human interest, talk entertainment, information talk, news/commentary, documentary, politics, commercials, sports, comedy, Hollywood starts, newsreels, archives (i.e., NASA).

V. Related Manuscript Materials

Production materials (sound effects, music); limited oral histories.

VI. Special Interests

Interviews with stars; Academy Award footage; general stock footage; time lapse photography; nature; pollution.

VII. Accessibility

Card catalog; computer access; numerical listing, data. No published catalog. On-site facilities only; next-day tape availabilities; $45/hr w/$450 minimum fee. **Hours:** 9 a.m. to 5 p.m. Monday through Friday.

CALIFORNIA

I. Organizational Information

Sherman Grinberg Film & Libraries, Inc.
1040 North McCadden Place
Hollywood, CA 90038-2486

Phone

(213) 464-7491
Telex: 269950 SGFL LA

III. General Program Types

The Libraries offer the most comprehensive news coverage of the 20th century, dating from 1896 to the present, representing ABC Network News, Pathe News and Paramount News, covering world events, personalities, human interest, sports, entertainment, fads, fashions, science, technology, and so forth.

IV. Subject Content Description

The Pathe News Library spans the years 1896 through 1956. The original backing is 35 mm. B&W negative and is stored in Hollywood. The Paramount News Library dates from the mid-1920s to 1957. The original backing is 35mm. B&W negative; however, 17 years (1940-1957) have been transferred to both 1/2" and 3/4" videotape. The original negatives are stored in New York. Research for Pathe News or Paramount News may be done in either our New York or Hollywood offices on microfilm or in the index card files.

In 1963, we became the sole representative for ABC Network News, storing and cataloguing ABC's entire output of worldwide news coverage. From 1963 through 1967, ABC shot 16mm. B&W, switched to 16mm colore in 1967 and shot 16mm color until 1976. In 1976, ABC began shooting 3/4" videotape and is currently shooting either 3/4" or BETA-CAM. The ABC Library is stored in New York. The library is fully computerized with research terminals in either our New York or Hollywood offices.

In terms of production stock footage, we believe our collection is one of the largest. We represent the stock footage libraries of both Twentieth Century Fox and Turner Entertainment Co. (former Metro-Goldwyn-Mayer stock library). These vast collections are primarily 35mm. color and B&W outtakes from almost every feature and television show these studios ever produced. The film and complete catalogs are in Hollywood with some guides in New York.

Also represented is Home Box Office (HBO), I.T.C., Allied Artists, WGHB's "Nova" series, PBS, "Odyssey" series, ABC's "American Sportsman" series, Time-Life's "Wild, Wild World of Animals," the BBC's Natural History Collection, "Wildstock," and many other production libraries and collections too numerous to mention.

VII. Accessibility

Policy: The footage supplied by the Sherman Grinberg Film Libraries, Inc. is without representation or warranties other than that of title. Licensee assumes all risks and shall be solely responsible for obtaining any and all necessary clearances, payments or waivers. All footage furnished is on a non-exclusive basis. The use of the image or voice of ABC News personnel and/or principal actors/actresses is strictly prohibited. Further, we reserve the right to limit the amount of stock or news footage provided from any one subject or production.

Footage furnished by this library is authorized for use only in the production specified on the license agreement and for that one production only. Footage furnished may not be sold, rented, licensed, re-used or re-cut into any other production. It is also understood that footage furnished by this library is not purchased, but rather, license rights are granted on a limited basis. Footage is not authorized for use, nor are license rights granted, until license is duly signed and returned fully paid to this library.

All laboratory/transfer charges, shipping costs, wires, messenger fees, telephone calls, telexes, copies, etc., will be paid by the customer.

We reserve the right to view the licensee's completed production and it is agreed that a viewing copy will be made available upon request.

If, after a licensee has been issued, additional rights are requested, the original license fee will not be deducted.

Charges for the use of library facilities are payable at the time they are incurred.

Ordering of Material: Please consult with a librarian about package rates or quantity discounts.

Editor's Note: Film stock library; commercial; ABC Network News of special interest.

CALIFORNIA

I. Organizational Information

Music Collection, 0175Q
Central University Library
Univ. of California - San Diego
9500 Guiman Drive
La Jolla, CA 92093-0175

Individual to Contact

Garrett Bowles

Phone

(619) 534-2759

II. General Formats

1/4" tapes; 200 7" reels

III. General Program Types

Broadcast music—opera and symphony.

VI. Special Interests

Mostly opera and symphony broadcasts during 1960s.

VII. Accessibility

Listings.
For on-site use only, open to the public.

CALIFORNIA

I. Organizational Information

UCLA Film & Television Archives
Research & Study Center
46 Powell Library
Univ. of California - Los Angeles
Los Angeles, CA 90024-1512

Individuals to Contact

Steven Ricci, Manager
Andrea Kalas, Assistant Manager

Phone

(213) 206-5388

II. General Formats

All types; concentration television, 16mm; 3/4" and 1/2" cassettes.

III. General Program Types

All types; concentration television drama.

IV. Subject Content Description

1947 to present. Hallmark Hall of Fame, The Alcoa Hour, Story Theater, Texaco Star Theater, The Jack Benny Show, The Smothers Brothers Comedy Hour, Colgate Comedy Hour.
Most all Emmy Award-winning programs.
Politics include: Kennedy and Stevenson, Murrow's "See It Now" series, and March of Time.

VII. Accessibility

On-line database: UCLA Library System. Large viewing facility, over 70 monitors for on-site viewing only.

Editor's Note: One of the nation's preeminent collections. Very accessible and encouraging for researchers.

CALIFORNIA

I. Organizational Information

University of Southern California
Cinema-Television Library and
Archives of Performing Arts
USC - Doheny Library
Los Angeles, CA 90089-0182

Individual to Contact

Anne G. Schlosser
Head of Library

Ned Comstock
Archives Assistant

Phone

(213) 743-6058

Profit/nonprofit

Nonprofit

II. General Formats

Radio recordings and TV films (16mm)

III. General Program Types

Variety, drama, human interest, information talk, comedy.

Started in the early 1930s, the holdings of the Cinema-Television Library include over 18,000 volumes of books and periodicals on all aspects of film and television: history, aesthetics, criticism, biography, films and TV programs, production techniques as well as business and legal aspects of the entertainment industry. With its strong foreign language coverage, the library has extensive resources on the East European cinema. Subscriptions to 211 periodicals and annuals are available. In addition to its bound volumes, the library offers on microfilm back runs of such early trade periodicals as *Photoplay, Bioscope, Motion Picture Herald*, and *TV Guide*.

IV. Subject Content Description

Radio's golden age, World War II, Cold-war radio, television's golden age, Vietnam War era.

V. Related Manuscript Materials

Clipping files, scripts, photographs, pressbooks.

VI. Special Interests

Special research collections include:

- Clipping Files (over 60,000) on films, TV programs, personalities, production companies, studios, associations and organizations, and general subjects.
- Scripts, both film and television, from classic as well as contemporary productions. Over 10,000 titles are included.
- Stills/Photographs of personalities and from films and television programs.
- Pressbooks (over 8,500) from major U.S. films.
- Audiotapes from USC cinema classes with professionals in the industry, including producers, directors, writers, cinematographers, composers, etc.
- Videocassettes and discs of over 1200 theatrical films and a special collection of selected television documentaries.

The archives contain over 202 collections of personal papers and studio resources. Included are such varied materials as scripts, productions records, memos and correspondence, stills, pressbooks, scrapbooks, sketches and drawings, music scores, editing notes, and much more reflecting the diversity of artistry in the fields of film and television. Some of the notable collections included are:

- King Vidor (director), Robert Wise (director), Arthur Freed (producer), Dimitri Tiomkin (composer), Boris Leven (art director), Edward G. Robinson (actor), Fay Wray (actress).
- Studio resources include scripts and production records from Twentieth Century-Fox (1919-1967), Universal (1930-1960), Hal Roach (1916-1950s), and Metro-Goldwyn-Mayer (1919-1958). Also available is the Warner Bros. Archives.

VII. Accessibility

See library/archival description as published in *Motion Pictures, Television and Radio, a Union Catalogue of Manuscript and Special Collections in the Western United States* (Boston: G.K. Hall, 1977).

Reference Service: Full-time staff is available to assist you with your information needs from 10 a.m. − 6 p.m., Monday-Thursday, 10 a.m. − 5 p.m., Friday and Saturday. A large collection of reference books is in the reading room. They are for room use only.

Books: Books are listed in Homer, and the card catalog in the Cinema-TV Library. Check main catalog on first floor of Doheny Library for anything you do not find (titles cataloged before 1977). Most books circulate for 2 weeks.

Because the book stacks are closed, materials are paged by our staff at the Circulation Desk. Ask at the Reference Desk for anything you cannot find.

Periodicals: Check USC Union List of Serials to verify location and holdings available. Periodicals do not circulate.

Current issues and some back issues are in the reading room. Additional back volumes are in the stacks. Ask at the Circulation Desk if you cannot find what you need.

Reserve Materials: Listed in Homer. Ask at Circulation Desk by call number for a book, or by call number and course number for a reading.

Videos: Listed in the Video Notebook on the Index Table. Videos do not circulate. Reserving time on the video players is necessary; ask at Circulation Desk. A valid USC library card is required.

Scripts: Listed in the script catalog and in the Union Catalog of Scripts. Request General scripts and Boyle scripts at the Circulation Desk by title and call number if available. All Archival scripts must be requested at the Reference Desk. The reference staff will assist you in locating scripts.

▸▸ Scripts do not circulate, they must be read in the Collections Room. Scripts may not be xeroxed, photographed, or duplicated in any manner. ◂◂

Clipping Files: No index available, please request at Circulation Desk by name, title, subject. Room use only.

Audiotapes: Listed in the audio catalog by name or title. Request at Circulation Desk. Tapes do not circulate; they may be listened to on the library's audio players.

Stills/Photographs: Listed in the Stills Notebook by the Reference Desk. They do not circulate and must be consulted in the Collections Room. Inquire at Reference Desk.

Archival Collections: Available for scholarly and research purposes on an appointment only basis. Inquire at Reference Desk about holdings and access.

USC Library Card: A valid USC library card is required to use most materials. A current driver's license is required to study special resources.

CALIFORNIA

I. Organizational Information

Pacific Pioneer Broadcasters
Post Office Box 4866
North Hollywood, CA 91617

Individual to Contact

Martin Halperin
Director of Acquisitions

Phone

(213) 461-2121

II. General Formats

60,000+ 16" ETS and pressings, 33 1/3 and 78s; 8,000+ audiotapes, 3 3/4, 7.5, 15.

III. General Program Types

All types, only partially cataloged.

Purpose is to preserve irreplaceable material of historical interest. PPB has accumulated one of the largest collections of quality transcriptions and radio programs in existence. Additional kinescopes, scripts, photographs, music scores, publications, equipment, give-away premiums, and other memorabilia and artifacts are sought. The club's growing collection is stored in vaults provided by Home Savings of America on the site of the famed NBC studios at Sunset and Vine, Hollywood.

IV. Subject Content Description

In addition to the large number of recordings (both disk and tape) of radio broadcasts, the collection has a great many scripts, photographs, books, miscellaneous print materials, equipment and artifacts pertaining to the broadcast industry and history. The material covers the period from the early 1930s to the late 1960s. At this time there is no accurate inventory of the collection but this project is underway.

The collection deals primarily with national programs and broadcasts and covers all categories (e.g., drama, soaps, music, comedy, news, etc.).

Special subjects include 1920s, The Depression, Radio's Golden Age, World War II, Cold War Radio, and Korean War Era.

V. Related Manuscript Materials

Some 2,000 scripts and many production materials, personal papers, and oral histories.

VI. Special Interests

Photographs, equipment, magazines, and books. The collection has a few kinescopes but generally does not collect TV materials.

VII. Accessibility

Listings and some indexes. Personal assistance available.

No copying. On-site facilities with restricted access.

The collection is available for research purposes by appointment.

Editor's Note: The collection is a large one. As it is only partially cataloged, the researcher is advised to inquire prior to travelling.

CALIFORNIA

I. Organizational Information

Pacifica Foundation
Pacifica Radio Archives
3729 Cahuenga Blvd. West
North Hollywood, CA 91604

Individuals to Contact

Bill Thomas
Director

Lucinda Wong
Special Projects Director

Roger Bowerman
Archivist

Phone

(818) 506-1077

Profit/Nonprofit

Nonprofit Foundation — Pacifica Foundation

II. General Formats

Cassettes, reel-to-reel audio. 35,000+ programs.

III. General Program Types

Program recordings from the Pacifica stations — "40 years of new ideas and social involvement."

Broadcast music 10%; drama 20%; information talk 25%; news 10%; documentary 20%; politics 15%.

IV. Subject Content Description

Primarily U.S. public affairs since World War II with an emphasis on progressive causes.

Programming represents a broad spectrum of information, culture and the arts. It is reflective of the purpose of Pacifica which is to "make a better climate for peace and understanding among people through broadcast programming." Collection includes materials on The Depression, Cold War Radio, Vietnam War Era, and other topics.

VI. Special Interests

Third World; national and international politics; philosophy; minority issues; women's issues; environment; civil rights movement; anti-war movement; drama; poetry; avant-garde music; media; health; interviews; families; education; arts.

VII. Accessibility

Catalog of popular cassettes is available. The bulk of Pacifica's collection has been cataloged on microfiche. A microfiche listing of over 20,000 programs, cross-referenced according to the Library of Congress standards, is available for $30 at this writing.

The archive is available for on-site research by scholars, writers, and media producers, allowing full use of Pacifica's resources.

The programs are offered for nonprofit, non-broadcast, and may not be duplicated, published, or transmitted to any other party without the written permission of the Pacifica Radio Archive.

There is no fee for on-site auditing. Both cassette and reel-to-reel tapes can be purchased, with some restrictions for copyrighted materials. Fee depends on program length and format (e.g., 30' cassette, $13; 60' cassette, $15; 90' cassette, $17).

Facility open for research by appointment, Monday-Friday, 10 a.m. to 5 p.m.

CALIFORNIA

I. Organizational Information

City of Sacramento, History and Science Division
Museum and History Division
551 Sequoia Pacific Blvd.
Sacramento, CA 95814-0229

Individual to Contact   Charlene Gilbert

Phone   (916) 449-2072

Profit/nonprofit   Nonprofit

II. General Formats

16mm film, 9-10 million feet; very few videotapes.

III. General Program Types

Primarily news, few entertainment.

VI. Special Interests

KRCA's news footage; local NBC affiliate; local news station coverage.

VII. Accessibility

No published catalog. On-site facilities; availability on case-by-case basis; restricted access.

Call for information concerning facilities and hours.

CALIFORNIA

I. Organizational Information

Harry Sweet Film Collection
4305 Dennis Way
Sacramento, CA 95821

Individual to Contact

Harry Sweet
Private Collection

Phone

(916) 487-9827

Profit/nonprofit

Profit

III. General Program Types

Human interest, news, politics, documentaries, sports.

IV. Subject Content Description

News/commentary (1 reel 16mm—1 hour of 1970s in KCRA-TV files series of five 5-minute reports+), public affairs, politics, sports, religion.

Charles Kuralt Human Interest People, Places & things, "On the Go" series; several thousand 16mm mini-documentaries limited to 6 minutes; California legislative politics. Locally produced state and national sports.

The Harry Sweet Film Collection has just received a 45-minute reel of "An Interview with Earl Warren," in mint condition, color/opt sound, reel 2 of 2 reels.

Editor's Note: Difficult to ascertain specifics of collection. Call prior to travel. Mr. Sweet is the former archivist for KCRA-TV Film Collection housed at the Sacramento Museum of History.

CALIFORNIA

I. Organizational Information

KCRA-TV
News Department
3 Television Circle
Sacramento, CA 95814-0794

Individual to Contact   Bill Brooks

Phone   (916) 444-7300

Profit/Nonprofit   Profit

II. General Formats

16mm film; 3/4, M2 (Panasonic) videotape.

III. General Program Types

Information talk and news/commentary.

IV. Subject Content Description

News, 1955—present; most information on Ronald Reagan in country.

VI. Special Interests

Footage on former President Ronald Reagan.

VII. Accessibility

Card catalog and in-house computer search. Availability on a case-by-case basis. Tape available for purchase, non-broadcast use only, $50/story. No on-site facilities; most film kept at Sacramento History Center.
Hours: By appointment only; call first.

CALIFORNIA

I. Organizational Information

Priceless Sound Productions
Post Office Box 1661
Salinas, CA 93902-1661

Individual to Contact

Tom Price (Private Collection)

Phone

(408) 753-2558

II. General Formats

Audiotape record on open reel masters, a 3 3/4 ips cassette production.

III. General Program Types

All types — over 10,000 programs. All programs "are sound rated" and set in four major categories: Children's Programs; Comedy; Drama, Mystery, and Variety; and History, News, and Documentary.

IV. Subject Content Description

See **Program Index**. Individual programs are listed with page numbers directing user to collection.

V. Related Manuscript Materials

Several Fibber McGee and Molly original scripts.

VI. Special Interests

920 Fibber McGee and Molly programs; 880 suspense programs; 1,200 Lum & Abner programs. Mr. Price has written four publications which may be of interest: *Fibber McGee's Closet: The Ultimate Log of Performance by Fibber McGee and Molly, 1917-1987*; *Scripts of Smackout and Fibber McGee and Molly*; *Radio Program Timelines: 1920-1980*; and *The Ultimate Log of Suspense: CBS's Radio Thriller, 1942-1962*.

VII. Accessibility

Catalog available at $9.95 + 6% tax. Tapes are available by mail order from the catalog.

Editor's Note: The collection is a large one. The collector has rated the sound quality of the shows. The catalog is well worth the price.

CALIFORNIA

I. Organizational Information

San Francisco State Univ. Library
San Francisco Bay Area Television News Archives
1630 Holloway Avenue
San Francisco, CA 94132

Individuals to Contact

Helen Whitson
Meredith Eliassen

Phone

(415) 338-1856

Profit/Nonprofit

Nonprofit

II. General Formats

Videotapes (600+); 106 1/2", 2 hr VHS; 500 3/4" varying lengths; 16mm (approximately 10 million feet).

III. General Program Types

KPIX and KQED (PBS station) station collections; news/commentary and documentary (approximately 10 million feet). Our local Emmy Award winners collection contains approximately 300 of a variety of award winning programs in all of the aforementioned categories. The **News Archives** contains news and documentary film.

IV. Subject Content Description

News/commentary, public affairs, and politics from: The Cold War Television, Television's Golden Age, Korean War Era, Vietnam War Era, and Contemporary programming (music, variety, human interest, news/commentary [from both stations], public affairs, politics, sports, religion).

VI. Special Interests

Collections cover a wide range of topics covering San Francisco Bay Area daily life, history, culture, and events from 1949-1980. They include all of the aforementioned topics with an emphasis on news and documentary footage (e.g., rehearsals of the San Francisco Opera).

VII. Accessibility

Card catalog; on-site facilities (VHS 3/4" tape player, Cinescan Film Viewer. Restricted to research/study use, not for entertainment, do not hold copyrights. **Hours:** Monday through Friday, 1-5 p.m.

CALIFORNIA

I. Organizational Information

University of San Francisco
KUSF Archive of Recorded Sound
2130 Fulton Street
San Francisco, CA 94117-1080

Individuals to Contact

Steven C. Runyon
General Manager

Melissa S. Metz
Program Director

Phone

(415) 386-5873

Profit/Nonprofit

Nonprofit

II. General Formats

12,000 78s; 35,000 LPs; 2,500 45s; 1,000 CDs; 1,000 audiotapes, and 100 other.

III. General Program Types

Classical/popular music, old radio transcriptions; KUSF programs, and miscellaneous spoken-word materials.

IV. Subject Content Description

About one-third is classical music and the rest is popular music. The collection contains about 100 hours of old television programming and commercials, most on 16mm film, for use in USF Mass Media Studies Program classes.

VII. Accessibility

The collection has not been cataloged except for about 10% of the classical music on LP material. The collection is only available presently to KUSF staff for radio programming. It is hoped that, at some time in the future, the collection will be cataloged and limited access made available to researchers.

CALIFORNIA

I. Organizational Information

San Jose Historical Museum
635 Phelan Avenue
San Jose, CA 95112

Individual in Charge	Leslie Masunga
Individual to Contact	Nancy Valby, Curator of News Files
Phone	(408) 287-2290
Profit/Nonprofit	Nonprofit

II. General Formats

16mm news film; 16" ETs; wax cylinder pressings; audiotapes (not part of archives); videotapes ("hold" some tapes, not part of collection).

III. General Program Types

Broadcast music, information talk, and news/commentary.

IV. Subject Content Description

Sizeable general collection of music, though not archival; news/information, broken run—not a complete collection of news clips from news station.

V. Related Manuscript Materials

Silent film scripts; Channel 11 newsfilm, log books; pamphlets, programs, photographs.

VI. Special Interests

Local news film; Channel 11 newsfilm; general background information on first radio station in San Jose: KQW.

VII. Accessibility

Radio card catalog; no access to newsfilm, not catalogs. On-site facilities; no loans; no way to view films. **Hours:** Open Wednesdays from 1-4 p.m, two Saturdays a month; all other times by appointment.

CALIFORNIA

I. Organizational Information

Henry E. Huntington Library
Manuscripts Department
1151 Oxford Road
San Marino, CA 91108

Phone

(818) 405-2203

Profit/Nonprofit

Nonprofit

II. General Formats

Scripts

III. General Program Types

Entertainment (adventure).

IV. Subject Content Description

Radio/TV scripts for "Gunsmoke."

V. Related Manuscript Materials

317 radio scripts and 60 television scripts for "Gunsmoke."

VI. Special Interests

English and American literature and history.

VII. Accessibility

Handlisting of the "Gunsmoke" Collection. Facility open to registered readers only, Monday-Saturday, 8:30 a.m to 5:00 p.m.

CALIFORNIA

I. Organizational Information

Archive of Recorded Sound
Braun Music Center
Stanford University
Stanford, CA 94305

Individual to Contact

Barbara Sawka
Archivist

Phone

(415) 723-9312

II. General Formats

All types — ranging from wax cylinders to compact discs. Commercial 78 rpm and LP discs and private tape recordings comprise the largest portion of the holdings.

III. General Program Types

Music, drama, literature, history, and communications.

IV. Subject Content Description

The Archive houses more than 200,000 recordings of classical and popular music, literature, drama, interviews, public addresses, and radio broadcasts. Special collections within the Archive include the Department of Music concert tape collection, the Stanford Speech Collection, the Pryor Collection of early World War II newscasts; the Richard Crooks Collection, the Kirsten Flagstad Collection, the Benjamin Lincoln Jazz Collection, Project South (interviews with participants in the civil rights movement), the Monterey Jazz Festival and Carmel Bach Festival tape archives, the Djerassi Foundation tape archives, and the Stanford Program for Recordings in Sound literary series.

The Archive maintains an extensive reference collection of books and periodicals on the history and development of the sound recording industry and its major figures. Original record manufacturers' catalogs and photograph and clippings files are available to researchers as well.

VII. Accessibility

The sound recording collections are housed in closed stacks; the reference collection is shelved and available to users in the Archive's public reading area. Sound recordings are handled by only the Archive staff to ensure proper care and their correct playback for researchers. The audio room is equipped to handle playback of the many formats in the collections and can accommodate several listeners, including small classes or seminars.

Archive staff can prepare tape copies of Archive materials for faculty or students to borrow for prolonged study or classroom presentation.

Prior inquiries are necessary concerning policies governing copy requests for other than Stanford academic use.

The Archive is open to the public Monday-Friday, 1-5 p.m., or by appointment. Telephone reference is available weekdays, 9 a.m. to 5 p.m. Listening appointments are encouraged, and researchers planning extended work in the Archive should give the staff advance notice whenever possible.

Please consult the staff about policies and fees covering tape duplication of Archive materials not under copyright or other restrictions. All duplication requests are handled by the staff. Users may not bring personal recorders into the Archive or do their own recording on Archive equipment.

The Archive also offers for sale copies of some of its holdings in disc and facsimile reprint formats. The Archive staff or the Publications Sales Office in Green Library, (415) 723-0461, can provide further information.

A photocopy machine is available in the public reading area.

Wheelchair access to the Archive is possible by means of an elevator in the adjoining Music Library.

CALIFORNIA

I. Organizational Information

Thousand Oaks Library
American Library of Radio & Television
1401 E. Janss Road
Thousand Oaks, CA 91360

Individual to Contact

Marvin E. Smith
Director of Library Services

Ruth Leonard
Special Collections Librarian

Phone

(805) 497-6282

Profit/Nonprofit

Nonprofit

II. General Formats

The Library's primary focus is on papers, manuscripts, photographs, and other textual material.

5,000 discs; 500 audiotapes; 100 videotapes.

III. General Program Types

Broadcast music, variety, human interest, talk entertainment, information talk, news/commentary, documentary, politics, comedy.

IV. Subject Content Description

The Depression (variety, 1,000); Radio's Golden Age (music 25, variety 2,500, comedy 500, talk entertainment 50, human interest 25); World War II (talk information 100, human interest 100, news/commentary 1,000, public affairs 300, politics 100); Cold War Television (news/commentary 100).

V. Related Manuscript Materials

Approximately 5,000 scripts (not included in personal collections), production materials, personal papers (10 personal collections).

VI. Special Interests

The American Library of Radio and Television: A collection of original and important published materials related to the history of American broadcasting, with special emphasis on radio. Coverage of television dates from its beginning to about 1965. Primary formats collected are papers, manuscripts, photographs, and other textual materials.

The Library has the following: Rudy Vallee Collection, Carleton E. Morse Collection, Fletcher Markle Collection, and CBS/KNX Collection.

VII. Accessibility

Computer access; on-site facilities; must present Thousand Oaks Library card or two forms of identification.

Hours are 5-9 p.m. Monday and Tuesday; 1-5 p.m. Wednesday-Saturday.

CALIFORNIA

I. Organizational Information

Ken Weigel
7011 Lennox Ave., #126
Van Nuys, CA 91405

Individual to Contact

Ken Weigel (Private Collection)

II. General Formats

Cassette tapes.

III. General Program Types

Old-time radio collection (2,800 hours), uncategorized.

IV. Subject Content Description

Mysteries/crime detective (e.g., Inner Sanctum, Suspense, Sealed Book, Sam Spade, Richard Diamond, Green Hornet, The Shadow, The Whistler, Escape, I Love a Mystery); comedies (e.g., Jack Benny, Lum & Abner, Fred Allen, and Fibber McGee and Molly); science fiction (e.g., X Minus One and Dimension X); and juvenile adventure serials (e.g., Dick Tracy, Speed Gibson, Magic Island, Jungle Jim, Hop Harrigan, Superman, Captain Midnight, Jack Armstrong, Ann of the Airplanes, Jerry of the Circus, Chandu the Magician, Tom Corbett, and Space Patrol).

The collection has samplings of variety, documentaries, and drama which make up a negligible part of the collection. From the 1920s, there are only two or three Amos & Andy shows. Most of the collection dates from the 1940s; the 1930s and 1950s are about equally represented.

V. Related Manuscript Materials

About two dozen radio scripts; the video serial collection has about 65 serials with about the same number of movies on video, most of them mysteries. The pop culture/entertainment book collection runs to about 175 books, mostly on radio, movie and comic strip histories, and encyclopedias.

VI. Special Interests

Emphasis on radio productions and histories. Does not collect TV shows.

VII. Accessibility

A not-for-sale radio tape catalog, 200+ single-spaced pages of individual shows/series, is exchanged with traders; book list is 54 pages long.

CALIFORNIA

I. Organizational Information   The Society to Preserve and Encourage
Radio Drama, Variety, and Comedy (SPERDVAC)
P. O. Box 7171
Van Nuys, CA 91409-9712

Individual to Contact   Larry or John Gassman

Phone   (213) 947-9800

Profit/Nonprofit   Nonprofit Public Benefit Corporation

II. General Formats

SPERDVAC is dedicated to preserving the history of radio broadcasting. We provide members access to our lending libraries, available on both open reel and cassette formats. Our printed materials library has copies of radio program scripts and logs.

SPERDVAC has two audio libraries. Our General Library features over 4.000 hours of popular old-time radio shows from a variety of sources. The Archives Library is a collection of over 1,300 hours of broadcasts recorded exclusively from original sources. These program come to us on loan or through donations of transcription discs or master tapes.

III. General Program Types

Broadcast music, variety, drama, human interest, talk entertainment, news/commentary/documentary, politics, sports, comedy, oral histories of radio pioneers.

IV. Subject Content Description

- The 1920s (variety)
- The Depression (music, variety, drama, comedy, news/commentary)
- Radio's Golden Age (music, variety, drama, comedy, talk entertainment, human interest, news/commentary, sports, religion)
- World War II (music, variety, drama, comedy, news/commentary, sports, religion)
- The Cold War Radio (music, variety, drama, comedy, human interest, news/commentary, public affairs, politics, sports, religion)

- Korean War Era (music, variety, drama, comedy, news/commentary, sports, religion)

See **Program Index**. Individual programs are listed with page numbers directing user to the catalogs.

V. Related Manuscript Materials

7,000 scripts; personal papers, (miscellaneous acquisition letters, correspondence); radio magazines, and chronological logs.

VI. Special Interests

Original disc and tape collections include Cecil B. DeMille's Lux Radio Theater, recordings from Dana Andrews, June Lockart, Alan Young, Edward Everett Horton, Art Paul, Vincent Price, Olan Soulé and Lyn Murray. Other collections include extensive holdings from The Lone Ranger, Sgt. Preston of the Yukon, Wild Bill Hickok, Red Skelton, Space Patrol, and The Mutual Hollywood Shows. Scholarly research by appointment is encouraged.

VII. Accessibility

Lending libraries are available to our members. Two catalog listings, indexes. Catalog is part of the membership package. On-site facilities, no regular hours. Materials cannot be removed from premises. **Hours:** By appointment.

We offer a monthly newsletter, *The Radiogram*.

Editor's Note: Membership in SPERDVAC is worth the price. The collection is one of the nation's largest. People are most helpful. As with all large collections, there is a good deal of uncataloged work in progress. Call before you travel.

COLORADO

I. Organizational Information

Colorado Historical Society
The Colorado History Museum
1300 Broadway Street
Denver, CO 80203

Individual to Contact

Stan Oliner
Curator of Books/Manuscripts

Phone

(303) 866-2305

Profit/Nonprofit

Nonprofit

II. General Formats

Disc (LP - 16"ETs or 78s): 100
Audiotape: 50
Videotape: Not yet cataloged

III. General Program Types

News/commentary, human interest, talk information.

IV. Subject Content Description

Cold war radio (talk entertainment 90, human interest 10); cold war television (news/commentary 14,000 cans 16mm film); Vietnam War era (news/commentary); contemporary programming (news/commentary).

V. Related Manuscript Materials

Scripts: 1970+ for TV, 1922 for radio; oral histories of Colorado broadcasters, photographs.

VI. Special Interests

Any Colorado radio, television, or community access station since 1922 is included. Stations include KOA Denver, KREX Grand Junction, KCNC-TV, KLZ-TV (now KMGH).

VII. Accessibility

Card catalog, log book index. **Hours:** Tuesday-Saturday, 10 a.m.-4:30 p.m.

COLORADO

I. Organizational Information

Jim Harvey's - OTR
P.O. Box 3524
Grand Junction, CO 81502

Individual to Contact

Jim Harvey

Phone

(303) 434-9167

II. General Formats

Pressing: 650 (4400 to 4500 hrs)
Audiotape: Approx 600 = approx 4,000 hrs

III. General Broadcast Types

Variety, 10%; drama, 55%; information talk, 5%; commercial messages, 1%; sports, 4%; comedy, 25%.

IV. Subject Content Description

Almost all programs are from very late 1930s to the very early 1960s.

VII. Accessibility

Collection filed on 7" reels by subject: comedy, detective, sci-fi, adventure, etc., then by show name, such as Jack Benny, Red Skelton, etc.

Collection kept in file cabinets in radio room.

Editor's Note: Call before travelling.

CONNECTICUT

I. Organizational Information

Old Time Radio
P.O. Box 4321
Hamden, CT 06514

Individual to Contact

Jay A. Hickerson
Private Collection

Phone

(203) 248-2887

II. General Formats

8,000 audio recordings 3-3/4 ips.

III. General Program Types

All types.

IV. Subject Content Description

Golden Age of Radio, 2,200 series with about 50,000 titles.

VII. Accessibility

Private collections, trades, and circulates. Catalog available — organized alphabetically.

Use Conditions: Trading use only.

Comment: A newsletter, *Hello Again*, is published bimonthly, $12 per year, for collectors and traders of old time radio shows. Mr. Hickeson is founder of the Friends of Old Time Radio. The newsletter, *Hello Again*, is an old time radio newsletter of merit.

Editor's Note: This is an extensive private collection. Call and make arrangements before you travel, but it is worth attention.

CONNECTICUT

I. Organizational Information

The Wesleyan Cinema Archives
301 Washington Terrace
Wesleyan University
Middletown, CT 06457

Individuals to Contact

Jeanine Basinger
Corwin-Fuller Professor of Film Studies
Curator and Founder

Leith Johnson
Associate Curator

Claire LaPila
Administrative Assistant

Phone

(203) 347-9411 x2259

II. General Formats

All types

III. General Program Types

Film emphasis with a variety of collections valuable to the history of TV and motion pictures.

IV. Subject Content Description

The Ingrid Bergman Collection is a complete record of her professional and personal life, beginning with her baby pictures and childhood diaries and continuing through her Hollywood years, her international stardom, and on to the end of her life. The collection includes scripts, awards, portraits, photos of family and friends, scrapbooks, costumes and clothing, legal papers, financial records, stills, clippings, negatives, memorabilia, and excellent correspondence files that contain letters from friends such as Hemingway, Garbo, Steinbeck, Hitchcock, Selznick, and Cary Grant.

The Frank Capra Collection is a complete record of his life and career, from his childhood throughout his active directing years, his WWII service, his work with the Directors Guild, the Motion Picture Academy, and on to his years as an author and lecturer.

The Clint Eastwood Collection consists of scripts, stills, photographs, correspondence, production records and documents, costumes, and what Mr. Eastwood refers to as "a few pink slips." It is the documentation of a working professional life, from early stardom through international success, with particular emphasis on items that are professional in nature and which shed light on the business of filmmaking. The films of Clint Eastwood are held and preserved by the Department of Film of the Museum of Modern Art.

The Kay Francis Collection, a gift from the Museum of Modern Art, consists of her private diaries, her personal leatherbound scrapbooks, and a small correspondence file.

The William Hornbeck Collection complements Wesleyan's Frank Capra Collection, since the two men collaborated on "Why We Fight" as well as several other films. Materials include storyboards, photos, editing plans and analyses, and memorabilia such as celebrity Christmas cards and an excellent group of autographed photos of stars and co-workers spanning the silent era to the 1970s. This unique hobby was begun by Mr. Hornbeck as a child in Los Angeles.

The Elia Kazan Collection is one of the outstanding collections in American film and theatre. The collection includes scripts, correspondence (personal and professional), journals, directorial notes and analyses, books, manuscripts, production documents, film stills, family photographs and scrapbooks, art direction materials, diaries, and more.

The Robert Saudek/Omnibus Collection includes a complete set of kinescopes, negatives, and study copy videotapes of every Omnibus show ever made, making it one of the few total records of any pioneer television show available in the United States. The collection also includes original scripts, contracts, editing materials, photographs and stills, correspondence, and full production documentation. The quality of Omnibus was such that this collection represents a broad international spectrum of the greatest contemporary figures and institutions in the arts and sciences from its era: Gene Kelly in "Dancing is a Man's Game" ... James Agee's "Mr. Lincoln" (the unofficial first miniseries) ... the first televised performance of the Metropolitan Opera ... the first Jacques Cousteau undersea documentaries

... Leonard Bernstein on "The Art of Conducting" ... Bob and Ray ... and appearances by T.S. Eliot, Grandma Moses, Ernest Hemingway, Agnes DeMille, Helen Hayes, and more.

The Raoul Walsh Collection contains scripts, papers and production documents, scrapbooks, correspondence, film stills and personal memorabilia, including the original draft of Walsh's autobiography, *Each Man in His Time*.

The John Waters Collection, an ongoing acquisition from the career of a young filmmaker, will ultimately be one of the most complete records of any filmmaking career that exists. It currently includes a detailed clipping file which covers all aspects of Waters's work to date, with stills, photographs, correspondence, scripts, production materials, posters, costumes, and selected memorabilia to follow.

The Cinema Archives Special Collections contain a wide variety of material relating to film and television history ... from scripts from the hit television show "Growing Pains" to the first draft of the miniseries, "The Murder of Mary Phagan" ... from studio blueprints for the sets of "Arch of Triumph" to detailed architectural renderings by well-known film theater designer, Boyce Nemec.

VII. Accessibility

Visits by appointment. **Hours:** 9 a.m. - 5 p.m., Monday through Friday.

Researchers and visitors may call or write to schedule appointments and to inquire about the materials. Each collection is held under separately established guidelines for usage, and researchers are asked to adhere to those restrictions and to follow established archival methods of security and protection. All inquiries are welcomed, including requests to establish or donate a collection.

Editor's Note: See the **Robert Saudek Collection.** Mr. Saudek is the creator of the "Omnibus" program that ran from November 9, 1952 to April 16, 1961. This is an important collection.

CONNECTICUT

I. Organizational Information

The Yale Collection of
Historical Sound Recordings
Yale University Library
Box 1603A Yale Station
New Haven, CT 06520

Individual to Contact

Richard Warren, Jr.
Curator

Phone

(203) 432-1795

Profit/Nonprofit

Nonprofit

II. General Formats

Recordings, all types.

III. General Program Types

Primarily music (classical, jazz, and theater) from all eras.

Sampling of broadcast material as it has been commercially released covering all eras.

Recordings of authors reading their own dramatic works.

IV. Subject Content Description

Broadcast material emphasis is drama and politics.

VII. Accessibility

Finding Aids: Work in progress on the index of performers; to be extended to authors/composers and works as time permits. **Catalog:** None. **Use Conditions:** On-site listening weekday afternoons by appointment.

CONNECTICUT

I. Organizational Information

Robert E. Smith Record Library
University of Hartford
Hartt School of Music
200 Bloomfield Ave.
West Hartford, CT 06117

Individual to Contact

Linda Blotner

Phone

(203) 243-4492

II. General Formats

20,000 78s; 10,000 LPs; 250 audiotapes.

III. General Program Types

Broadcast music 100%.

IV. Subject Content Description

Robert E. Smith hosted two shows on radio station WTIC, Hartford. The shows, "Your Box at the Opera" and "Your Theater of Melody" ran for 25 years.

Comment: Primarily opera vocal with some orchestral and a smattering of popular and jazz.

DELAWARE

I. Organizational Information

Johnson Collection
Division of Historical
and Historic Sites
102 S. State Street
P.O. Box 1401
Dover, DE 19903

Individuals to Contact

James Stewart
Administrator

Kristin Presta
Site Supervisor
Kent County Sites

Phone

(302) 739-3262

II. General Formats

Disc — 20,000+; pressing — 1; speed — 78 RPM.

III. General Program Types

Broadcast music — first broadcast 1925, WEAF and 13 other stations.

Variety — vocal, instrumental, opera.

Drama — musical comedy, lyric drama, comic opera, romantic operas (languages: Italian, German, French, English).

Human interest — musical plays, fairy operas.

Talk entertainment — conventions, expositions.

Information talk — education, sales promotion.

News — magazines, newspapers, dealers, offering a quality product in catalogs, store displays, demonstrations.

Documentary — contract of artists, portraits; trade mark "His Masters Voice," autographed photos of Artists for Victor.

Politics — Recordings of speeches, noted bands, school bands.

III. General Program Types

The 1920s:

Vaudeville and variety — entertainment and specialties on education. Boston & Philadelphia Symphony Orchestra.

Politics and news — Camden Plan Expansion, free courses in Practical Salesmanship; World War I. Education Department for studying wireless.

Talk — Red Seal School to promote sale of Red Seal records. Dealers and distributors signed up for the school.

The Depression:

Fuel curtailed, instrument productions reduced. Extra excise tax because music a semi-luxury. Factory converted to assist war making aeroplanes, gun stocks, and metal parts.

Music variety — had scouts to go around the country and buy anything that would play, great demand for current popular numbers, talented artists. Back orders for about 50,000,000 records.

Drama — conventions was entertainment by the company's artists both Red and Black Seal records. Victor orchestra, Philadelphia orchestra, social activities.

Radio's Golden Age:

1925 pick up acoustical and electric motor, earphones.

Music variety — music was a variety of mixed vocal, male chorus, orchestras, bands, jazzy bands, dance bands.

Drama — 1926 Orthophonic Electrola and Radio; 1927 Automatic Record Changer by Victor Talking Machine Company, Camden, New Jersey.

News — *Saturday Evening Post*, double pages to advertise in black and white; double pages in color, newspapers, magazines, dealers displays.

Politics — engraved invitations were sent to important people in music, politics, publishing, word of mouth, publicity was tremendous.

World War II:

Cold war television and radio is RCA period, Korean War, Vietnam War.

VII. Accessibility

Card Catalog: 3-way card — performer, numerical, and alphabetical.

Index: Accession listing.

Other: Catalogs, books, files.

On-site facilities: Very good, original playback machinery, duplicating capabilities. Second floor and storage basement restricted to public.

Tape Availabilities: Unrestricted when supply own tape to be recorded.

Published Catalogs:

Eldridge Reeves Johnson: Pioneer ($1).

Guide to News Stories, E.R. Johnson & Victor Talking Machines Company ($5).

Caruso Discography.

DISTRICT OF COLUMBIA

I. Organizational Information

Broadcast Pioneers Library
1771 N Street, NW
Washington, D.C. 20036

Individual to Contact

Catharine Heinz

Phone

(202) 223-0088

Profit/Nonprofit

Nonprofit

II. General Formats

Disc (LP - 16" ETs or 78s): 1,560

Audiotape (5,431, including 2,300 Westinghouse Broadcasting Company Washington News Bureau news tapes, 1945-1981; and 1,061 BMI Program Conferences, 1951-1957).

64 videotapes.

III. General Program Types

The collection of oral histories, manuscripts, scrapbooks, photos, sound recordings, and rare books and periodicals has become an invaluable privately funded resource open to anyone who has wanted to make use of it. The **Broadcast Pioneers Library** also has become widely known as a definitive referral center to other sources of broadcast history.

V. Related Manuscript Materials

Scripts: 1,900 scripts including "Sky King" (full run), "Your Show of Shows," "Journeys Behind the News," Frank Blotter Scripts.

Production materials: "Wisdom."

Personal papers: 550 record group listings by donor (including 78 collections of personal papers; i.e., Edythe J. Meserand, Joseph E. Baudino, Robert E. Lee, Elmo N. Pickerill, Irene Beasley).

Oral histories: 850.

VII. Accessibility

Hours: 9 a.m. to 5 p.m., Monday through Friday, by appointment.

Research Services Fee Schedule:

Academic Institution: $75 per year
Faculty: $50 per year

- Staff research at $30 per hour. Maximum: 6 hours per quarter.
- One telephone reference call per month (up to 5 minutes) at no charge.
- *BBL Reports*, a quarterly newsletter at no charge.

Student: $25 per year

- Staff research at $15 per hour. Maximum: 3 hours per quarter.
- One telephone reference call per month (up to 5 minutes) at no charge.
- *BBP Reports*, a quarterly newsletter at no charge.

Nonmember

- Preliminary research per subject $65.
- Staff research at $80 per hour (advance deposit of one-half of fee required).
- Library visits where user does own research: $75 per day or $20 per hour.

Research Aids:

Listings of audiotapes and cassettes; Hedges Collection. **Card catalog** by author/title. **Index** of Westinghouse Broadcasting Company Washington News Bureau news tapes, 1945-1981.

Editor's Note: This is one of the nation's most important broadcast history resources. It covers a wide range of topics as well as references to other depositories.

DISTRICT OF COLUMBIA

I. Organizational Information

House Broadcasting System
House of Representatives
Office of Records and Registration
1036 Longworth House Office Bldg.
Washington, D.C. 20515

Individual to Contact

Charlotte Voorde

Phone

(202) 225-1300

Profit/Nonprofit

Nonprofit

II. General Formats

Audio and video.

III. General Program Types

House Proceedings

VII. Accessibility

Library of Congress
Recorded Sound Section, G-152
Jefferson Building
Washington, D.C. 20505
(202) 287-5509

DISTRICT OF COLUMBIA

I. Organizational Information

Human Studies Film Archives
Smithsonian Institution, NHB E 307
Washington, D.C. 20560

Individual to Contact   Wendy Shay, Curator

Phone   (202) 357-1300

II. General Formats

Film and video

III. General Program Types

Reference film and video of all formats. Primarily non-broadcast.

IV. Subject Content Description

The Human Studies Film Archives was established to collect, preserve, and make available anthropological film and video records for research. The primary works are of a reference nature although there are a few television broadcasts.

Subjects are organized geographically: Africa, Asia, Oceania, North America, Central and South America, Europe, and International.

Broadcast programs are of anthropological interest. For example, WOI, Ames, Iowa documentary about the Fox and Sak Indians on the Tama Indian Reservation, "Whole Town's Talking," 1952; KTUL-TV, Tulsa, Oklahoma, documentary presenting the history of Indian treaties which led up to the Supreme Court decision on April 20, 1970 stating that 96 miles of the Arkansas River belonged to the Cherokee, Choctaw, and Chickasaw Indian tribes, produced 1971; Auburn, Alabama television interview with Harold Huscher, produced 1959.

VII. Accessibility

An appointment, made at least 48 hours in advance, is required. The Archive is open 9 a.m. to 5 p.m., Monday through Friday, except for national federal holidays.

Editor's Note: Unique anthropological resource of limited interest to broadcast research.

DISTRICT OF COLUMBIA

I. **Organizational Information**

The Library of Congress
Washington, D.C. 20540

Individual to Contact

Samuel Brylawski
Reference Librarian

Phone

(202) 707-7833

- - - - - - - - - -

The Library of Congress
Motion Picture, Broadcasting
and Recorded Sound Division
Washington, D.C. 20540

Individual to Contact

Robert Saudek
Chief

Phone

(202) 707-5840

- - - - - - - - - -

Reading Rooms:

Recorded Sound Reference Center
Room LM 113, James Madison Memorial Bldg.
Library of Congress
101 Independence Avenue SE
Washington, D.C. 20540

Phone

(202) 707-7833

Motion Picture and Television Reading Room
Room LM 336, James Madison Memorial Bldg.
Library of Congress
101 Independence Avenue SE
Washington, D.C. 20540

Phone

(202) 707-1000

II. General Formats

Discs (broadcast)	600,000
Discs (non-broadcast)	800,000
Audiotape	250,000
Film & videotape	80,000

III. General Program Types

Film, television, and sound recordings.

IV. Subject Content Description

Radio

Radio programs in the collections of the Library of Congress number over 500,000. In view of the size of the collection and the fact that holdings are not completely cataloged, it is impossible to provide the subject breakdowns requested. Instead, a brief overview of the Library's radio collections is offered.

The radio collections at the Library of Congress comprise many "special collections," donations from radio networks, performers, writers, and producers. The two largest radio collections are those of the National Broadcasting Company (NBC) and the Armed Forces Radio and Television Service (AFRTS).

NBC. In 1978, NBC donated 175,000 sixteen-inch lacquer discs to the Library. The collection spans the early 1930s through the late 1960s. The recordings are available for listening by qualified researchers once they have been transferred to audiotape by the Library's Magnetic Recording Laboratory. As of 1990, over 21,000 hours of programming is available for use. Most of the programs transferred to tape thus far fall between the years 1938 and 1949. These include all genres of radio, including comedy, drama, public affairs, music, interview, news, and international shortwave broadcasts. Bibliographic access to the recordings of NBC radio broadcasts is provided by the published guide to LC radio collections, *Radio Broadcasts in the Library of Congress, 1924-1941* (now out-of-print), a dictionary card catalog, and an online PC-based finding aid.

Because discographic access to the NBC Radio Collection is not yet comprehensive, the best available source of information about contents of the discs is the card catalog compiled by NBC for nearly 40 years. It lists the credits and plots of tens of thousands of programs and indexes radio contributions by as many actors, musicians, politicians, government officials, writers, and directors. It also provides a complete outline of almost every news and propaganda program broadcast by NBC's two radio networks. The files in and of themselves are the single most complete written record of American broadcasting content in the collections of the Library of Congress.

The Recorded Sound Reference Center houses a microfiche copy of NBC's catalog, approximately 1,400 fiche. The fiche include "Recording Index Cards" (in three sets: 1930-1949, 1950-1959, and 1960-1969) — a limited index of names and programs found on the recordings. Note, however, that thousands of programs were recorded but not indexed on the "Recording Index Cards." Also included in the microfiche documentation is an index of radio 'artists,' that is, performers; and radio 'personalities.' 'Personalities,' as termed by the index, are nonperformers, such as writers, politicians, businessmen, or government officials. There is a separate 'personality' file for each year, 1930 to 1959. Other files in the index list and/or describe news broadcasts, sponsored programs, sustaining programs, and 'title segments,' the latter a list of adaptations of literary works, by title of the original work. With persistence, most researchers writing on a personality have been able to locate the programs of interest to them. Subject access to the NBC Radio Collection is very limited.

Copies of sound recordings in the collections of the Library of Congress can be made by the Magnetic Recording Laboratory if one is able to obtain the written authorizations of all proprietary right holders in the recordings. To obtain copies of recordings in the National Broadcasting Company Collection at the Library the written authorizations of NBC and the Museum of Broadcasting are required. Address requests to NBC Law Department, Rights Permissions and Clearances Attorney, National Broadcasting Company, Inc., Room 1022, 30 Rockefeller Plaza, New York, NY 10022.

AFRTS. The Armed Forces Radio and Television Service Collection at the Library of Congress is made up of over 300,000 sixteen- and twelve-inch electrical transcriptions, representing AFRTS production from 1942 to the present. Programming on the recordings is limited to those productions distributed from the AFRTS Los Angeles headquarters. No news broadcasts or local programs, such as DJ broadcasts as heard in Vietnam, are included in the collection. AFRTS discs at the Library of Congress fall into three categories: programs produced by the commercial networks 'recycled' for AFRTS use, programs produced by AFRTS, and music library discs. Access to the collection is provided by a partial inventory of titles held on 16" (pre-1959) discs and other finding aids.

Contractual arrangements with the Department of Defense stipulate that the following parties must give written authorization before an AFRTS program may be duplicated: SESAC, Inc., the American Federation of Musicians, the National Music Publisher's Association, the American Federation of Television and Radio Artists, the American Society of Composers, Authors, and Publishers, Broadcast Music, Inc., and AFRTS.

Other Collections. While the NBC and AFRTS Collections are the largest radio special collections in the Library of Congress, the Motion Picture, Broadcasting and Recorded Sound Division holds many other rich resources for the study of broadcasting. Several other radio networks have made major gifts of broadcasts to the Library of Congress.

Soon after World War II several thousand instantaneous lacquer discs representing propaganda broadcasts made by the U.S. Office of War Information were transferred to the Library of Congress. Most of this collection has since been copied onto tape and is available to researchers. The collection includes over 8,000 programs in English, in addition to broadcasts in many other languages, including French, German, Portuguese, Spanish, Swedish, and Greek.

The Library is the sole Western Hemisphere repository of the British Broadcasting Corporation Collection of archival long-playing discs, an annually selected group of the most important broadcasts made by the BBC. The collection numbers over 6,000 LPs.

National Public Radio has made gifts of their arts and cultural programming tapes dating back to NPR's formation in 1971. The archive consists of several thousand reels of jazz, opera, symphonic music, chamber music, folk music, radio drama, and poetry. NPR news and public affairs tapes are deposited with the National Archives and Records Administration.

The Motion Picture, Broadcasting and Recorded Sound Division also holds nearly 30,000 sixteen-inch vinyl electrical transcriptions. These ETs are comprised of popular music subscription services, U.S. Government programs, and a variety of syndicated dramatic series.

Among the other radio broadcast collections held are those devoted to a single performer (often donated by that performer) or company. These include: personal arbitrator A.L. Alexander; the Boston Symphony Orchestra; Arthur Godfrey; commentators Raymond Clapper, Raymond Gram Swing, and H.V. Kaltenborn; singer Jessica Dragonette; accordionist Basil Fomeen; soap operas and variety programs sponsored by the General Foods Corporation; captured Nazi-Germany broadcasts; soprano Frieda Hempel; conductor Andre Kostelanetz; interviewer Larry King; Library of Congress chamber music series broadcasts; talk programs of Mary Margaret McBride; ETs producer by the C.P. MacGregor Company; anthropologist Margaret Mead; *Meet the Press*; Moral Re-Armament, Inc; poetry and literature series *New Letters on the Air,* the *Original Amateur Hour*; Pacifica Radio; Edwin T. Randall and Friendly World Broadcasting; conductor Wilfred Pelletier; Phil and Evelyn Spitalny's All-Girl Orchestra; soprano Helen Traubel; and Voice of America music programs. In the 1950s the Library obtained air-checks from CBS and NBC. CBS radio is represented by complete programming from May 13 through May 26, 1957; NBC by October 31 through November 6, 1955. In addition, CBS made periodic gifts of public events radio broadcasts to the Library throughout the 1960s.

The most recent major radio collection to be acquired by the Library of Congress is that of WOR-AM, New York City. In 1984 RKO General, Inc. donated the complete archives of the flagship station of the Mutual Broadcasting Network. Included in the donation are several thousand sixteen-inch instantaneous transcription discs, the paper archives of WOR and an outstanding group of materials relating to the radio career of writer-producer Phillips H. Lord. Lord created and produced such radio series as *Gang Busters* and *Counterspy.* WOR acquired physical properties and intellectual rights to the series from Lord in the 1950s. Among the materials included in the WOR donation are copies of the FBI files from which *Gang Busters* scripts were derived, correspondence between Lord and the FBI, multiple drafts of production scripts, and disc transcriptions of the final broadcasts. The manuscript portion of the WOR donation is held by the Library's Manuscript Division where the collection is currently being processed for use by the public.

Print Resources. The Library of Congress Manuscript Division holds several important broadcasting-related collections in addition to the papers of WOR-AM, including a collection of over 5,000 CBS Radio scripts, donated to the Library in the 1960s; major collections of scripts representing the careers of Goodman and Jane Ace and Fred Allen; and the series

Amos 'n' Andy and *Vic and Sade*. Also, it is through the Manuscript Division that one gains access to radio scripts depositive for copyright between the mid-1920s, when such deposits began, and 1977, the last year the 1909 Copyright Act was in effect. Card indexes to pre-1978 copyright deposits are located in the Copyright Office, room LM 459, James Madison Memorial Building. Most radio scripts deposited for copyright have been placed in the category of talks or unpublished dramas by the Copyright Office. The indexes to these deposits are large, but often incomplete so searches through the card files by several different access points are often required in order to successfully locate items. For instance, scripts not indexed by title might be listed by radio network, advertising agency, and/or writer. Be sure to ask the Copyright reference librarian on duty for assistance when seeking unpublished copyright deposits of radio scripts. Post-1977 copyright deposits of scripts are thoroughly indexed and are accessible through COPICS, the Copyright Office online-database.

The Library of Congress has also assembled an extensive collection of books and serials about broadcasting. Some of the monographs held by the Library are listed in two bibliographies compiled by Don C. Smith in the *Journal of Broadcasting* (volumes IX(4) and X(1), 1965).

Television. The collections of the Motion Picture, Broadcasting and Recorded Sound Division include approximately 80,000 television programs. Television programs have been acquired by the Library of Congress since 1949, primarily via copyright deposit. (Major exceptions, described later, include the NBC Television Collection and the NET Collection.) Copyright technicalities have led to an emphasis on the registration of primetime entertainment series, as opposed to such programs as musical variety specials, talk shows, or game shows. Approximately 14,000 of these programs are listed in a recently published guide, *Three Decades of Television: A Catalog of Television Programs Acquired by the Library of Congress 1949-1979*. This guide, by Sarah Rouse and Katharine Loughney, is available from the Government Printing Office for $51 (stock # 030-000-00185-1). It includes only television programs acquired by the Library of Congress *before* 1980 and excludes commercials and nightly news broadcasts. Entries provide synopses of fiction and nonfiction programs, genre and broad subject terms, cast and production credits, and copyright and telecast information.

Scope. The vast majority of the programs listed in *Three Decades of Television* have been received as copyright deposits. Their copyright registration provenance has influenced the nature of the Library's holdings. Primetime series predominate in the catalog. Also documented is an apparent reluctance to collect television programs in the early years; only 13 selections from copyright registrations were made in 1950, compared with over 3,000 in 1980. The catalog includes two major series received as gifts: *Meet the Press* and the *Original Amateur Hour*. *Meet the Press* television and radio materials have been donated by Lawrence E. Spivak, producer of the long-running program (first broadcast on radio in 1945). Television programs (1949-present) exist mostly in 16mm kinescope negative and print, with videotape formats beginning in May 1974 (new programs continue to be received). Reference prints exist for about 250 of the pre-1978 shows. Card entries are filed alphabetically by guest in the Film and Television Catalog under *Meet the Press*. Extensive documentation was also donated. The *Original Amateur Hour* (550 kinescopes, 16mm, November 1948 through 1968), a long-running radio and television series hosted by Ted Mack, was donated to LC in 1970 by Lloyd Marx. There are only eight pre-1951 programs. Card entries in the Film and Television Catalog list holdings chronologically but do not identify contestants. Both the *Meet the Press* and *Original Amateur Hour* gifts to the Library of Congress include the programs' complete radio runs.

Television news documentaries, special coverage, and other productions of network news divisions are listed by title in *Three Decades of Television* and in M/B/RS Division catalogs. M/B/RS holds nearly complete weeknight broadcasts of ABC's *Evening News* (April 1977-present) and scattered issues of *Nightline* (beginning 1987) are held; nearly all CBS news programs have been registered since January 1975. Selected NBC News documentaries are held, but no NBC nightly news programs are held. The only example of "early" television news in M/B/RS is *Douglas Edwards With the News* (CBS) (40 issues, 26 Sep-11 Nov 1960), comprised primarily of coverage of the Kennedy-Nixon presidential election campaign, received as a gift from CBS.

NBC Television Collection. The two largest television special collections in the Library of Congress are the NBC Television Collection and the National Educational Television (NET) Collection. The NBC Television Collection was acquired by LC in July 1986. Neither of these collections are listed in *Three Decades of Television* and, for the near future, access to them is restricted. The NBC Television Collections is an historic collection of 18,000 television programs broadcast, preserved, and for the most part produced by NBC. With programs dating from the beginning of network television in the United States, 1948 through 1977, the NBC Television Collection includes not only performances by major actors and musical talents, but also numerous events featuring significant individuals in public affairs. This acquisition significantly increases M/B/RS's holdings of television programs from the late 1940s and early 1950s and incudes genres such as sports, game shows, children's programs, and daytime television. The NBC Television Collection does not include NBC's news archives nor any post-1977 material.

Kinescopes comprise most of the NBC Television Collection. The rest are programs produced on film prior to broadcast. M/B/RS holds mostly picture negatives with separate sound tracks. Viewing copies are presently available for only a few titles. In the spring of 1990 the NBC Television Collection was closed due to shortages of staff required to catalog and preserve the collection. It is hoped that this measure is temporary. Requests for purchase or reuse of material in the NBC Collection must be made directly to NBC Television Network Enterprises Department as NBC commercially licenses all rights to the material.

At present, access to this collection is gained by consulting a photocopy of NBC's packing list, arranged alphabetically by program or series title, primary performer, or other key identification word; researchers knowing series title and date of broadcast enjoy speedier access to material. M/B/RS more recently received copies of the NBC Program Analysis File — a microfiche of 1.25 million cards, somewhat comparable to the radio files described earlier. Cross-checking of inventories and even containers on LC shelves will still be necessary, however, to determine LC's actual holdings. Much organization of the collection is required before it can be easily used in research.

Documentary productions as well as about 2,000 entertainment programs have been retained by NBC while new masters are prepared for use by the network. These materials can be identified by using the packing lists, but the preparation of videotape viewing copies will take longer than for titles physically at the Library.

Despite the rudimentary finding aids for this collection, sample titles indicate the collection's wide scope. These include: *Kraft Television Theatre; Miss America Pageant; Colgate Comedy Hour; Wide, Wide World; Your Hit Parade; Your Show of Shows; Hallmark Hall of Fame; Kraft Music Hall; The Jack Paar Show; Today; Mrs. Roosevelt Meets the*

Public; Meet the Press (added to the Library's already extensive coverage); press conferences with Presidents Kennedy and Johnson; coverage of Martin Luther King, Jr.; and the astronaut John Glenn at Cape Canaveral.

NET Collection. NET (National Educational Television) programs held by LC total over 10,000 titles and date from 1955-69. NET metamorphosed into PBS (Public Broadcasting Service) in 1969, and a few PBS programs from the early 1970s are included in this group of NET programs. Little of the collection is cataloged and service copies have yet to be made from the negatives which make up most of the collection. However, it is clear that collectively they represent an invaluable record of early noncommercial American television.

The NET Collection is actually three separate collections. Cataloged and available to researchers are over 550 titles on 16mm prints, acquired from NET's general distribution center in Michigan (1965-67). Programs are instructional or educational, including the series *Touristen-Deutsch* (WTTW Chicago, 1957, 14 programs), teaching elementary conversational German; *The Nature of Communism* (Vanderbilt and Notre Dame Universities, 1964, 60 programs); and *Two Centuries of Symphony* (WGBH Bost, 1960, 20 programs) teaching music appreciation.

The second segment of the NET Collection comprises 1,019 titles, primarily instructional materials and all negatives. These came to the Library in 1982 from Indiana University, a distribution center for NET programs broadcast for public schools, colleges, and universities. Access is by title only using an inventory card file and list. Titles in this group include: *The Basic Issues of Man* (12 programs produced in the early 1960s by the Georgia Center for Continuing Education); *The Red Myth* (a series on the history of communism, produced ca. 1960 by San Francisco's KQED); and *Search for America* (a Washington University-produced series on American institutions and problems). There is likely to be an overlap between this collection and the first, resulting in both prints and negatives for some titles.

The third and largest group of NET titles at LC was acquired in 1984. Approximately 8,000 programs had been warehoused by PBS until their archives programs was cut back. A preliminary inventory list of unverified titles made by LC staff reveals that this collection includes many series of international scope, including *Casals Master Class; Civilization; Creative Person,* with such subjects as Nadia Boulanger, Georges Braque, Rudolf Bing and Satyajit Ray; and *Intertel,* as well as programs documenting the

73

social revolution of the 1950s and 1960s. Examples of the last category are: *Escape from the Cage* (on mental illness); *History of the Negro; Jazz Meets the Classics; NET Festival;* and *NET Journal.* An NET Inventory—a title list of the second and third segments combined—is available at the Motion Picture and Television Reading Room reference desk for consultation. Scholars needing access to programs in the latter two segments of the NET Collection should know that a *4-month* period for preparation and videotape transfer may be required for titles requested.

Print Copyright Deposits. Descriptive materials for copyrighted television programs often include shooting scripts or cutting continuities. All of these "copyright descriptions" have been retained by the Library. They are filed by copyright registration number and are available for study in the Motion Picture and Television Reading Room.

VII. Accessibility

The Library of Congress has recently published a guide to its film and television holdings relating to the Vietnam War. This and other published guides to radio and television collections at the Library are:

Johnson, Victoria. *Vietnam on Film and Television: Documentaries in the Library of Congress.* Washington, D.C.: Library of Congress, 1989. [Available from the Motion Picture, Broadcasting and Recorded Sound Division, Library of Congress.]

Scholars' Guide to Washington, D.C., for Audio Resources: Sound Recordings in the Arts, Humanities, and Social, Physical, and Life Sciences. James R. Heintze, Trudi W. Olivetti, Zdenoek V. David and Woodrow Wilson International Center for Scholars. *Scholars' Guide to Washington, D.C.* (no. 11). Washington, D.C.: Smithsonian Institution Press, 1985. [Published for the Woodrow Wilson International Center for Scholars.]

Smart, James R. *Radio Broadcasts in the Library of Congress 1928-1941.* Washington, D.C.: Library of Congress, 1982.

Special Collections in the Library of Congress: A Selective Guide. Library of Congress and Annette Melville. Washington, D.C.: Library of congress, 1980.

Footage 89: North American Film and Video Sources. Richard Prelinger and Celeste R. Hoffnar. New York: Prelinger Associates, 1989.

DISTRICT OF COLUMBIA

I. Organizational Information

The Library of Congress
Film and Television
Motion Picture Broadcasting
and Recorded Sound Division
Washington, D.C. 20540

Phone (202) 707-5840

II. General Formats

Film and Television

III. General Program Types

The film and television collections contain over 75,000 titles, with several thousand titles being added each year through copyright deposit, purchase, gift, or exchange. Items selected from copyright deposits include feature films and short works of all sorts, fiction and documentary, exemplifying the range of current film and video production and reflecting the diversity of American thought and experience. The collections also include some 300,000 stills.

IV. Subject Content Description

Historic Collections. The Library has an unusually large number of motion pictures produced before 1915, including 3,000 films restored in recent years from the paper print collection; the important Theodore Roosevelt Collection, comprising 380 titles especially revealing of the political and social history of the earliest days of this century; the Kleine Collection of 456 titles from the first decades of the film industry; the Mary Pickford Collection; the collections of Louise Ernst, John Allen, Gatewood Dunston, and others; and the more than 700 pre-1915 titles in the American Film Institute Collection. Copies of all films acquired by the AFI are deposited in the Library.

Major Studio Deposits. Films by all major American studios are represented in the collections. In some cases, studios have deposited historic pre-print materials: negatives, master positives, work prints. The American Film Institute, established in 1967, has been an important catalyst in stimulating studio deposits. The emphasis in the American Film Institute Collection has been on recovering American films produced between 1912 and 1942, the period during which the Library did not retain films. There is an active conservation and printing program in progress, making viewing copies of these films available for study; until copied, nitrate films and pre-print materials are not available for consultation.

Foreign Films Acquired During World War II. This collection includes several thousand feature films, documentaries, and newsreels produced in Germany during the Nazi period, 1933-1945: 1,400 similar films produced in Japan during the 1930s and early 1940s; and 500 films produced in Italy, 1930-1943. Viewing copies are available for many of the titles.

U.S. Government-Produced Films. The National Archives and Records Service in Washington, DC is the official repository for these films, as well as other federal records. The Library has a limited collection of reference prints of government-produced titles.

VI. Special Interests

From their beginnings, the film and television media have involved fragile materials. The preservation of its collections is therefore of prime concern to the Division.

VII. Accessibility

Services for Film and Television

The film and television research collections are not available for public projection, rental, or loan. The Division provides limited viewing facilities—35 mm and 16mm viewing machines and videotape players—for specialized individual research, without charge to the user. The facilities are not open to high school students; undergraduate college students must provide a supporting letter from a supervising professor.

The Division's reference staff answers written and telephone inquires about its holdings and makes appointments for the use of the viewing facilities.

Viewing times must be scheduled well in advance. Inquiries should be addressed to: Library of Congress, Motion Picture, Broadcasting and Recorded Sound Division, Washington, DC 20540. The facilities are open 8:30 a.m. to 4:30 p.m., Monday through Friday, and are located in the James Madison Memorial Building, Room 336, tel. (202) 287-1000.

Copies of works not restricted by copyright or by provisions of gift or transfer, and in sound physical condition, may be ordered through the Division. The requester is responsible for any necessary search—by mail or in person—of Copyright Office records to determine the copyright status of specific works. Inquiries may be addressed to: Library of Congress, Register of Copyrights, Washington, DC 20559.

Research Aids

The Motion Picture, Broadcasting and Recorded Sound Division maintains a reading room with extensive card catalogs of its film and television holdings. Primary access to the materials is by title.

The published catalog *Motion Pictures from the Library of Congress Paper Print Collection: 1894-1912*, by Kemp R. Niver, is available on the premises. Scheduled for early publication by the Library are three catalogs relating to specific collections: *The Theodore Roosevelt Memorial Association Catalog; The George Kleine Film Collection Catalog;* and *Television Programs in The Library of Congress: Programs Available for Research as of December 1979.*

Available in the reading room is a basic collection of reference books on cinema and television, along with distributors' catalogs, yearbooks, reviews, and trade periodicals. Fuller collections of published reference materials are included in the Library's general and periodical collections, and can be consulted in the larger reading rooms.

The Motion Picture, Broadcasting and Recorded Sound Division also has custody of descriptive materials (pressbooks, plot synopses, continuities) for motion pictures registered for copyright after 1912.

The Division's catalogers are experimenting with ways to computerize the cataloging information, so as eventually to replace the various card catalogs with a data base from which bibliographic information can be retrieved in a variety of ways.

Related Publications

The Library publishes catalogs of films and related materials, as it does for books. A book catalog, *Library of Congress Catalog—Audiovisual Material*, is issued quarterly and in annual cumulation, as volumes in the quinquennial cumulation of the Library's *National Union Catalog*, and as computer tapes produced monthly in a machine-readable cataloging (MARC) format. Printed catalog cards are available for individual titles. These items are for sale by the Library of Congress, Cataloging Distribution Service, Room 3004, Adams Building, Washington, DC 20541.

In addition, the Copyright Office prepares a semiannual *Catalog of Copyright Entries: Motion Pictures*, which lists all such materials registered for copyright in the United States, and five cumulative catalogs entitled *Motion Pictures*, which together cover registrations for films for the years 1894-1969. All are for sale by the Superintendent of Documents, U.S. Government Printing Office, Washington, DC 20402.

Publications—Radio Broadcast Collections

Heintze, James R. *Scholar's Guide to Washington, D.C. for Audio Resources* (pp. 49-56). Washington, DC: Smithsonian Institution Press, 1985.

Melville, Annette. *Special Collections in the Library of Congress: A Selective Guide.* Washington, DC: Library of Congress, 1980.

Publications—Television Broadcast Collections

Melville, Annette. *Special Collections in the Library of Congress: A Selective Guide.* Washington, DC: Library of Congress, 1980.

Prelinger, Richard and Hoffnar, Celeste R. *Footage 89: North American Film and Video Sources.* New York: Prelinger Associates, 1989.

Rowan, Bonnie. *Scholar's Guide to Washington, D.C. for Film and Video Resources.* Washington, DC: Smithsonian Institution Press, 1980. [Significant acquisitions have been made since publication of this book.]

Editor's Note: This is the most extensive collection in the nation. The staff is helpful, but you need to know what you are after. Utilize the suggested references here. If you still don't find what you're after, call—a continuing large portion of the collection remains in the process of organization.

DISTRICT OF COLUMBIA

I. Organizational Information

The Library of Congress
Sound Recordings
Motion Picture Broadcasting
and Recorded Sound Division
Washington, D.C. 20540

Phone   (202) 707-7833

II. General Formats

Sound recordings of all types, ranging from wax cylinders to compact audio discs.

III. General Program Types

Phonograph records (all types); field recordings of folklore and folk music; recorded radio programs; government recordings (including V-Discs made for American troops abroad, recorded broadcasts of the Office of War Information, the Armed Forces Radio Service, the Voice of America, and others); tape recordings. The Library's holdings have grown to more than one million recordings, with tens of thousands being added each year.

IV. Subject Content Description

The Collections

Until 1972, the Library's sound recordings were acquired by gift, exchange, or purchase. In that year, recordings were brought within the provisions of the copyright law, and many began to be deposited for copyright protection. While these were generally new releases, gifts continued to bring invaluable additions from the first decades of sound recording—the earliest, an 1890 wax cylinder recording of an Indian chant. The collection has thus come to reflect the entire spectrum of history of sound from wax cylinders to compact audio discs, and includes such diverse media as wire recordings, aluminum discs, zinc discs, acetate-covered glass disks, rubber compound discs, translucent plastic discs. The holdings also reflect a century of American life and culture and include a number of collections of unusual historic interest.

Berliner Collection. A selection of recordings representing the Berliner Gramophone Company, which invented and introduced the disc recording. The Library's earliest Berliner disc is dated 1892. The collection includes historic items contributed by the Berliner family.

Joel Berger Collection. Two hundred extremely rare operatic records from pre-Revolutionary Russia, dated from 1901 to about 1915. Many feature members of the Imperial Russian Opera.

John Secrist Collection. Comprises 2,800 commercial classical music releases from 1902 to 1925, including many rarities.

Raymond Swing Collection. Several hundred radio news commentaries of 1941-1946 by one of the most influential newsmen of the period.

OWI Collection. About 100,000 acetate discs representing the broadcasts of the Office of War Information in the global war of words, 1942-1945. Includes material in all languages of Western Europe and some of the Far East.

U.S. Marine Corps Combat Records. About 2,500 recordings of 1943-1945 from Guam, Okinawa, Saipan, Iwo Jima, and other locations in the Pacific. Interviews with men returning from combat, eyewitness descriptions of action.

Artists' Collections. Recording artists whose private collections have come to the Library include Sergei Rachmaninoff, Rosa Ponselle, Geraldine Farrar, Sigrid Onegin, Sigmund Romberg, Alma Gluck, Helen Traubel, Arnold Schoenberg, George Gershwin, and others.

House of Representatives Debates. In 1979 the House of Representatives began to record its proceedings on audiotapes, which are deposited in the Library of Congress, available to researchers.

Armed Forces Radio and Television Service Collection. Over 200,000 16" and 12" discs of radio programs broadcast to U.S. armed forces personnel from 1942 to the present. Programming represented in the collection includes both network commercial broadcasts and original AFRTS programs.

National Broadcasting Company Radio Collection. Over 175,000 instantaneous discs of NBC radio broadcasts between 1935 and 1970. Items in the collection are available to researchers only after they have been tape-recorded under the Library's preservation program. Over 8,000 hours of material is now available to researchers.

National Public Radio Collection. The Library of Congress is the repository for recordings of cultural programming broadcast by NPR. Tapes are transferred annually to the Library by NPR, approximately five years after their initial broadcast. NPR's news and public affairs programs are housed at the National Archives and Records Service.

Archive of Recorded Poetry and Literature. Several thousand recordings of authors reading their own works in the recording studios and Coolidge Auditorium of the Library of Congress are indexed in the publication, *Literary Recordings,* and in the uncataloged recording index in the Recorded Sound Reference Center.

VI. Special Interests

The making of sound recordings has involved various fragile and perishable materials. The preservation of its holdings is therefore of prime concern to the Division. A recording that would be injured by repeated playings is withheld from research use until the Division has had an opportunity to make an audiotape listening copy.

VII. Accessibility

Research Aids for Sound Recordings

Research in sound recordings or radio is conducted in the Recorded Sound Reference Center of the Performing Arts Reading Room, Library of Congress Madison Building, Room LM-113. The Recorded Sound Reference Center is open Monday through Friday, 8:30 a.m. to 5 p.m. The telephone number of the Recorded Sound Reference Center is (202) 707-7833.

Most of the sound recordings in the collections have not been fully cataloged. The Recorded Sound Reference Center houses the Library of Congress printed card catalog for sound recordings and a card index for many of the uncataloged recordings held by the Division. The Recorded Sound Reference Center also services, in conjunction with the Music Division in the Performing Arts Reading Room, manufacturers' published catalogs, trade catalogs, discographies, books and periodicals on sound recordings, finding aids, reference books, subject folders, and lists. Many materials on sound recordings are included in the Library's general and periodical collections and can be consulted in the general reading rooms.

The researcher may find the following reference tools helpful:

The Rigler and Deutsch Index. This is a union catalog, on 16mm microfilm, of the 78rpm discs held by five U.S. libraries, including the Library of Congress. Data in the catalog is unedited and is based on literal transcriptions from the sound recordings' labels, but provides the only available index to titles, performers, and composers on 78rpm discs.

Music, Books on Music, and Sound Recordings. This lists the recordings that have been fully cataloged and for which the Library's Special Materials Division has issued catalog cards for sale to libraries. These cards, available in the Recorded Sound Reference Center, are also reproduced in published volumes, which appear semiannually and may be purchased through the Library of Congress, Cataloging Distribution Service, Navy Yard Annex, Washington, DC 20541.

Radio Broadcasts in the Library of Congress, 1924-1941. This chronologically arranged index of the Library's holdings of radio broadcast recordings up to the end of 1941 was compiled by James R. Smart. Mr. Smart has also written *The Sousa Band: A Discography*.

The Library of Congress computerized catalog began including sound recordings in 1984. The computerized Copyright Office files, which include all copyright deposits made after January 1, 1978, index many sound recordings, though not all of the recordings deposited for copyright are in the Division's collections. Both the Library of Congress computerized catalog and the Copyright Office files are available on all public terminals at the Library.

Services for Sound Recordings

Listening facilities are available without charge, but are limited to those doing research of a specific nature, leading toward a publicly available work such as a publication, thesis or dissertation, or radio/television/film production. The research collections are not available for loan or rental. The Division's staff answers written and telephone inquiries about its holdings and makes appointments for use of its listening facilities. The listening facilities are open 8:30 a.m. to 5 p.m., Monday through Saturday. In order to use the listening facilities on Saturday, appointments must be made in the Recorded Sound Reference Center Monday through Friday.

The Division has its own magnetic recording laboratory, which performs many functions. In addition to making listening copies for research use, it records for the collections the Library's seasonal chamber music concerts and literary programs, scheduled in the Library's Coolidge Auditorium and elsewhere. The concerned recordings are broadcast over many radio stations on a subscription basis.

For purchase by researchers, the Division's laboratory is prepared to make taped copies of recordings in good physical condition, when not restricted by copyright, performance rights, or provisions of gift or transfer. The requester is responsible for any necessary search—by mail or in person—of Copyright Office records to determine the copyright status of specific recordings.

The Division also offers copies of some of its holdings for sale in disc form. These include a number of LP records of folk music, poetry, and other literature.

Inquiries concerning recordings available for sale and the making of tape copies should be addressed to the Public Service Coordinator, Motion Picture, Broadcasting and Recorded Sound Division, Library of Congress, Washington, DC 20540.

DISTRICT OF COLUMBIA

I. Organizational Information

National Archives and Records Administration
Motion Picture Sound and Video Branch (NNSM)
Washington, D.C. 20408

Individuals to Contact William T. Murphy, Chief
Leslie Waffen, Assistant Chief

Phone (202) 501-5402; (202) 501-5449

Profit/Nonprofit Nonprofit

II. General Formats

Disc (LP - 16" ETs or 78s): 109,000
Pressing: 8,000
Audiotape: 35,000
Videotape: 23,000
Tape & Format: All formats

III. General Program Types

Information talk (1,000); news/commentary (129,000); documentary (2,000); politics (15,000); speeches (5,000).

There are over 150,000 reels of film, 152,800 sound recordings, and a rapidly growing collection of several thousand videotapes (23,000).

IV. Subject Content Description

Most audiovisual documentation relates to the activities of the federal agencies. The Gift Collection contains numerous items such as newsreels and recordings of radio broadcasts that relate to many aspects of U.S. and world history since the turn of the century. Some of the larger government record groups and gift collections are:

U.S. Government. Agriculture Department, Air Force, Army Signal Corps, Foreign Records Seized, Marine Corps, National Aeronautical and Space Administration, Navy Department, Office of Economic Opportunity, Office of War Information, Peace Corps, Supreme Court, U.S. Information Agency.

Gift Collection. ABC Radio News, 1943-1972; Ford Film Collection, 1914-1956; Fox-Movietone News, 1957-1963; Harmon Foundation (films), 1930-1951; League of Nations (films), 1920-1946; March of Time Stock Film Library, 1935-1950s; Milo Ryan Phono Archive, 1938-1975; Mutual Radio News, 1935-1972; National Public Radio, 1971; News of the Day, 1963-1967; Paramount Newsreel, 1941-1957; Universal Newsreels, 1919-1967.

The Universal Newsreel Library

The Universal Newsreel Library, 1929-1967, consists of edited stories or volumes and related outtake footage. The donation contains finding aids such as theater flyers which describe each newsreel, production files, and an extensive card catalog. The flyers and the card catalog are also available on microfilm.

Volumes. Most edited stories, 1929-1967, are preserved, except for Volumes 14, 15, and 16 (1941-1943) in which only a few issues survive. Videocassette reference copies are available in the audiovisual research room. Film or video copies requested for purchase will be made from 16mm masters or negatives.

It should also be noted that the Library of Congress has many Universal newsreel issues from 1943 to 1967. Since they are copyright deposit prints, they may only be copied and sold with the written permission of MCA-Universal Pictures, Inc. For further information telephone the Library's motion picture section (202) 287-1000.

Outtakes. The nitrate motion picture fire of 1978 destroyed approximately 12.6 million feet of mainly outtakes from the 1930s and 1940s. A listing of nitrate-era outtakes that survived and were subsequently copied on to safety film is available in the research room. The safety-era outtakes, 1951-1967, were unaffected by the fire, but about 40% have been disposed of because they lacked sufficient research value. Videocassette copies of extant outtakes are available in the research room. Film or video copies requested for purchase will be made from 35mm; therefore reduction (optical) printing will be necessary to render 16mm copies for purchase.

Sound. In an economy measure, Universal unfortunately disposed of many separate music and narrative sound tracks before donating the library to the National Archives. Hence there is relatively little sound prior to 1957. The extant sound for the period 1929-1956 consists mostly of lip-synchronized speeches or interviews. Fortunately, the narrative tracks are complete for the last ten years, 1957-1967, and the script files that contain the written commentaries are also complete.

Restrictions. The donor, MCA-Universal Pictures, Inc., placed no restrictions on the use of the Universal Newsreel Library given to the National Archives. However, neither the donor nor the National Archives guarantees the public domain status of sound or pictorial elements in the Universal Newsreel Library, and it may therefore be necessary to obtain permission from owners of underlying rights before any commercial use or other use is made. (The National Football League, for example, has advised the National Archives of its rights to Universal's coverage of football games sponsored by the NFL.)

Universal Newsreels

One of the five major U.S. newsreels, Universal Newsreel was released in theaters from 1929 through 1967. Like the other newsreels, it appeared semi-weekly, averaging 10 minutes per issue initially, and 6 or 7 toward the later years. Universal was the last of the theatrical newsreels released in the United States, surviving Hearst Metrotone's "News of the Day" by 1 month.

The "Universal Newsreel" library is a gift to the National Archives donated in 1970 by MCA-Universal Pictures, Inc. In 1974, the owner deeded the library's rights and title to the people of the United States.

The Library consists of the edited versions released to theaters and the unedited footage not utilized in the final print. The disastrous nitrate fire on December 7, 1978, destroyed 73% of the outtakes from 1930 to 1950 and almost three volumes of releases: Volumes 14, 15, and 16 (1941-1943), as well as a few other issues. All remaining nitrate having archival value has been copied on to safety film. The original safety portion of the library, 1951-1967, was unaffected by the fire. The releases through Volume 27, release 576 are available for reference on videocassettes. From Volume 33 up, there are film reference prints. No prints are currently available for Volume 28 through Volume 32. Eventually, the entire Universal library will be available for research on videocassettes. Negatives and masters may not be viewed. Viewing copies are **not** available for any of the outtakes (unedited footage).

The library also includes a detailed catalog of over .5 million cards. These cards are arranged according to 13 major subject divisions: Foreign Locations, General, U.S. Locations, Conveyances, Education, Types of

86

People, Animals, Sports and Amusements, U.S. Government, Aviation, U.S. Army, U.S. Navy, and Personalities. The cards under U.S. Locations are the most inclusive because Universal routinely entered a card under each location or dateline. The cards from 1929 to 1943 are not as detailed as the later ones, but generally they contain subject descriptions, dates, cameramen or source, release and outtake numbers, footage counts, and designations whether sound or silent. There is also a chronological file of newsreel release sheets summarizing each issue stored in the research room, as well as cameramen's notes and production files stored in the stacks.

It should also be noted that the Library of Congress has many Universal newsreel issues from 1943 to 1967. Since they are copyright deposit prints, they may only be copied and sold with the written permission of MCA-Universal Pictures, Inc. For further information, telephone the Library's motion picture section (202) 287-5840.

Outtakes. Extant Universal outtakes, 1930-1967, are in a 35mm format. There are no viewing copies, but reproductions may still be purchased. Consult dope sheets for scene descriptions. Dope sheets for outtakes from a release are filed in the release folder; the remaining dope sheets are filed under the outtake number. A preliminary list of all nitrate era outtakes (#1 through 6,500) (1930-1951) still in existence is kept in the Universal catalog room. The safety-era outtakes, 1951-1967, like the later volumes, were unaffected by the fire, but about 40% have been disposed of because they lacked research value.

Restrictions. The donor, MCA-Universal Pictures, Inc., placed no restrictions on the use of the Universal Newsreel Library given to the National Archives. However, neither the donor nor the National Archives guarantees the public domain status of sound or pictorial elements in the Universal Newsreel Library, and it may therefore be necessary to obtain permission from owners of underlying rights before any commercial use or other use is made. (The National Football League, for example, has advised the National Archives of its rights to Universal's coverage of football games sponsored by the NFL.)

Army Air Forces Combat Subjects and Signal Corps Catalog

This catalog describes unedited and camera record footage covering military activity during World War II, the occupation of Germany and Japan, other post-war events, and the Korean War. Three different card formats (produced by the Air Force, the Army, and the National Archives) appear in the catalog, brought together in a unified system of subject headings. These headings, similar to those of the "**Main Catalog**" can be scanned in a two-volume list shelved near the catalog. Most fall under military subjects, such as ARMY and ARMY AIR FORCES, subdivided by units; AIRPLANES, MILITARY, subdivided by names or numbers; AIR BASES, MILITARY, subdivided by locations; and, of course, names of wars. In addition, many names of famous personalities, geographical locations and other subjects or events are entered directly.

The catalog begins with a numerical sequence, arranged by record group and item. Subject tracings on the reverse side of the cards can be helpful in locating related material. It is important to recognize that each card produced by the Army or Army Air Force (see attached diagrams) is indexed separately regardless of whether it is from a sequence of cards pertaining to a single item or reel. In contrast, entries produced by the National Archives (see diagram) are indexed by item, regardless of the number of continuation cards. For all entries, the body of the scene description consists of a summarized shotlist (LS = long shot; CU = close-up, etc.), and indicates breakdown by reel when necessary.

Richard M. Nixon Collection

Richard E. McNeill
Archives Specialist
Nixon Presidential Materials Staff
(703) 756-6725

The White House Photo Office Collection (1969-1974) consists of photographic coverage of President Nixon meeting with prominent social, political, and cultural personalities; Presidential domestic and foreign trips; social events involving the First Family; official portraits of the President, First Family, and high-ranking members of the Nixon administration; the 1969 and 1973 inaugurations; the 1972 Presidential campaign and other official activities of the Nixon Administration from January 20, 1969 until August 9, 1974. Finding aids for this collection of 435,000 images include 146 binders of contact sheets arranged in chronological order and a "master print file" arranged by subject content matter. There are no copyright restrictions for this collection. The pre-Presidential photo file, numbering approximately 1,200 prints, contains numerous photographs of Richard Nixon's activities taken at various times between 1950 and 1968. Much of this file is subject to copyright restriction. The cost for 8" x 10" photographs is $11.90 for color and $5.25 for black and white.

The Naval Photographic Center White House Film Unit Collection (1969-1974) consists of motion film coverage of selected official activities of President Nixon including diplomatic, ceremonial occasions, speeches, foreign and domestic trips, and activities of the First Lady. There are 517 separate titles totalling 1.2 million feet of 16mm motion film. Finding aids include a comprehensive index arranged by subject, name, date, and geographic location, a listing of production titles, and scene description "shot cards" for individual rolls of film. This footage is in the public domain and not subject to copyright restrictions or user fees. Reproductions are available either on motion film stock or broadcast quality video recordings. Duplication fees are minimal, limited to commercial lab costs plus a small administrative surcharge.

White House Communications Agency Video File (1968-1974) contains 4,082 broadcast quality 2" quadraplex videotapes comprising 3,900 hours of playing time. These productions are "off-the-air" recordings of televised programs. The file includes comprehensive coverage of President Nixon's appearances on national television, appearances by members of the Nixon administration, segments of national network news telecasts relating to the Nixon administration, special news reports, scheduled public affairs broadcasts, and coverage of all of the televised Ervin Select Committee hearings and the House Judiciary Committee impeachment hearings. The finding aid for this file is a program log describing title, date, producer, and running time for each program. This collection is subject to copyright restrictions. These recordings can be dubbed onto quadraplex tapes or transferred to broadcast quality 1" videotape or videocassette. Reproduction fees are determined by commercial lab costs.

White House Communications Agency Audio File (1969-1974) comprises 4,464 audiotapes that record the public utterances of President Nixon as well as selected speeches and remarks by Vice Presidents Spiro T. Agnew and Gerald R. Ford, members of the Nixon and Agnew families, Cabinet and Sub-Cabinet officers, and members of the White House staff. Also included are selected White House Press Briefings, entertainment at the White House, the 1971 China advance team telecommunications and the broadcasts of the Watergate hearings of the Senate Select Committee on Presidential Activities. All of these recordings are in the public domain and not subject to copyright restrictions or user fees. Reproduction costs per minute for these recordings are 95¢ for open reel and 65¢ for cassette.

Main Video File (1952-Present) consists of video programs documenting the career and times of Richard Nixon as a public figure. There are 175 titles totalling 132 hours of programming. These videotapes were withdrawn from White House Staff office files, received through gift donations, and recorded "off-air" by the White House and the National Archives and Records Administration. This is an ongoing program with newly recorded telecasts being routinely added to the file. The finding aid is a title listing with entries relating to subject matter, participants, date, geographic location, and applicable restrictions. Much of the material is copyrighted. Reproductions costs are printed in the NARA fee schedule. Broadcast quality duplication fees are determined by commercial lab costs.

Main Motion Film File (1953-1974) contains 512 titles featuring Nixon domestic and foreign trips, political spots for various Nixon campaigns, films produced by government agencies, educational films, Nixon speeches and press conferences, kinescopes of television broadcasts and newsreel footage. Motion films from the pre-Presidential era were deeded to the government by Richard Nixon. Presidential period films were deposited by organizations and individuals with the White House Theatre. The finding aid is a title listing with entries relating to subject matter, participants, date, geographic location, and applicable restrictions. Much of the materials is copyrighted. Duplication and transfer fees are determined by commercial lab costs.

These audiovisual materials may be examined in the research room at 845 South Pickett Street, Alexandria, Virgina from 8 a.m. to 4:30 p.m., Monday through Friday.

V. Related Manuscript Material

Production materials — Federal government information and public affairs programs often have production files including scripts, clearances.

VII. Accessibility

As a research service, the Motion Picture, Sound and Video Branch (NNSM) allows researchers to duplicate audiovisual reference copies on its premises free of charge provided that the records or gift materials are unrestricted or proper clearances have been secured in advance. Copies made from reference copies do not technically render the best reproductions, but they can satisfy some research purposes. Researchers must use their own equipment, tape, and connective cables, and must follow the procedures outlined later. Research Room hours are 8:45 a.m. to 5 p.m., Monday through Friday, except holidays. For appointments or information, call (202) 786-0041, 0042, or 0043.

Research Room Equipment. The Branch provides playback equipment for audio, video, motion picture, microfilm, or microfiche records. The equipment available includes: Sony VP-5000 3/4" and Panasonic 1/2" video players; Sony, Teac, and Califone audiocassette and reel-to-reel players; and 16mm and 35mm Steenbeck flatbed viewers and 16mm RTI upright viewers. Reference copies may only be played on branch equipment.

Researcher Duplicating Equipment. Researchers should bring the following equipment to make copies in the research room:

(1) Video duplication requires a video recording deck, blank tape, and a video cable with a BNC connector and an audio cable with a RCA phono plug. It is often useful to bring headphones and a portable monitor to view and listen to the recorded signal.

(2) Audio copying requires an open-reel recorder or cassette recorder with cables that have a mini-plug and/or cables with a RCA phono plug. Researchers should make sure their audio recorders have an "auxiliary-in" or "input" jack to receive a satisfactory recording signal.

(3) Copying from motion picture viewers requires a video camera and recorder in order to shoot an image directly from the screen, although the image is at a relatively low light level and may exhibit a flicker movement.

Please Note that the quality of the researcher copy, whether made from audio, video, or film, will necessarily vary depending on the equipment used and the quality of the reference copy provided. Reference copies are at least second generation copies and may not be of broadcast quality. However, copies made should be acceptable for study, display, classroom, preview, or home viewing. If a researcher requires broadcast quality copies, they can be provided form the archival copies for a fee. Please inquire.

Appointments. Researchers may make copies with or without an appointment. Appointments are strongly suggested, however, and may be made by calling the research room. Researchers with full-day appointments must arrive before 10 a.m., otherwise the appointment may be given to someone who is waiting. Researchers without appointments are welcome to arrive at any time during the day but delays may occur. An open-access videotape deck is available in 1-hour increments. Researchers without appointment should request the next available time slot upon their arrival. Researchers who wish to copy from motion picture viewers must not only have an appointment but must request the films in advance at least 1 day prior to the appointment.

Checking In. Upon entering the Pennsylvania Avenue lobby, researchers must show personal identification and register at the guard station. All bags and briefcases will be examined and equipment logged in. The guards will direct researchers to the second floor lobby to obtain a research card; or, if the researcher already has a card, he or she will be directed to Room G-13, Audiovisual Research Room, located on the entrance level behind the main elevators. Researchers must also register at the entrance to G-13. Pub bags, briefcases, large purses, parcels, and coats must be stored in lockers. Bring only pencils and paper into the research room along with recording equipment. Proceed to the reference desk to receive a coy of research room procedures and assignment of a viewing or listening station.

List of Items to be Recorded. Before connecting equipment, sign "A Warning Notice on Copying" and list on the reverse side the item numbers to be copied. Present this list to the reference desk attendant, who will review the list and initial it before any duplicating can begin. If during the course of research additional items are located for copying, add them to the list and obtain approval before copying. Items protected by copyright, agency, or donor restrictions will not be furnished for copying unless the copyright or proprietary owner submits written permission beforehand. The staff reserves the right to review any tapes made from reference copies.

Safety. To prevent accidents, keep all patch cords, connectors and power lines out of the aisles. Store excess equipment, carrying cases, etc., under the refile tables. Only two persons are allowed at each viewing station. Do not leave equipment or other belongings in the research room or lockers overnight.

Checking Out. After completion, rewind reference tapes and place on the refile table or cart. Take all equipment and researcher-made copies to the reference desk attendant for check out. Sign out on the research room ledger and at the guard station in the Pennsylvania Avenue lobby.

Editor's Note: The National Archive and The Library of Congress contain the most extensive collections of the nation.

DISTRICT OF COLUMBIA

I. Organizational Information

National Center for Film and Video Preservation
The American Film Institute
The John F. Kennedy Center
Washington, D.C. 20566

Individual to Contact   Susan Dalton
                                                                   Archivist

Phone   (202) 828-4070
                                             Telex: #910 240 9077 afi uq

II. General Formats

Film/Video Archive. Material available for research and reuse under certain restrictions. All types of film and video elements. Most of the films originally received on nitrate stock. Viewing copies are not always available.

III. General Program Types

The AFI Collection at the Library of Congress includes over 23,000 titles and consists primarily of theatrical features and shorts ranging from 1894 to the present, as well as substantial numbers of newsreels, documentaries and television programs.

IV. Subject Content Description

Major collections with the AFI Collection include:

- Hal Roach (approximately 700 films)
- Thomas Ince (55 features)
- Columbia Pictures (over 4,000 features and shorts from 1928-1952)
- Paramount (nearly 200 features from 1914-1937)
- RKO (740 features and 900 shorts from 1929-1956)
- Universal (600 features and shorts)

- United Artists Collection of Warner Bros. releases (approximately 1,175 features and 1,500 shorts dating from 1920-1950)
- Black Films Collection (over 100 films produced by or starring black Americans)

Additional films in the AFI Collection are held by over a dozen other archives, in particular UCLA, The Museum of Modern Art, and George Eastman House.

VI. Special Interests

The Center continues to locate, identify, acquire, and preserve a diverse range of films and television programs for inclusion in the growing body of more than 21,000 titles in the AFI Collection. Started in 1968, the collection is maintained at the Library of Congress and other archives throughout the country.

VII. Accessibility

The Center is not a custodial archive. While information about the AFI Collection may be obtained directly from the Center, information about access should be obtained from the Library of Congress and other appropriate archives. **Cataloging:** Cataloged by title only. **Rights:** Some material in public domain. Users must assume full responsibility for copyright search and/or securing any necessary clearances or authorizations required for use of the material. **Licensing:** Not applicable. **Viewing Facilities:** Contact appropriate archive. **Duplication Facilities:** Contact appropriate archive. **Publications:** *The AFI Catalog of Feature Films, 1911-1920, 1921-1930, 1961-1970.* The volume *1931-1940* will be available in 1991.

Editor's Note: The challenge of the AFI National Center for Film and Video Preservation is a large one. Contact here can lead the researcher to numerous referrals. While the emphasis is film, broadcasting is becoming increasingly important.

DISTRICT OF COLUMBIA

I. Organizational Information

National Geographic Television
National Geographic Society
Washington, D.C. 20036

Individual to Contact

Patricia Gang
Director, Film Library

Phone

(202) 857-7659

II. General Formats

Film and videotape. Preview cassettes are available for rental.

III. General Program Types

Premier collection of wildlife and nature footage, as well as a wide selection of exotic peoples and places, adventure, exploration, and scientific technology.

IV. Subject Content Description

The National Geographic Film Library has 10 million feet of 16mm film out-takes from their award winning TV specials, Explorer, TV Magazine Show, and Educational Films.

VII. Accessibility

Footage available for purchase.

Editor's Note: This is primarily a commercial film producer's stock footage library; however, the National Geographic programs (film and broadcast) are archived here. Special arrangements can be made for the advanced scholar on a one-on-one basis. Get such appointments in advance.

DISTRICT OF COLUMBIA

I. Organizational Information

NPR Program Library & Audio Archive
National Public Radio
2025 'M' Street N.W.
Washington, D.C. 20036

Individual to Contact   Margot McGann

Phone   (202) 822-2060

II. General Formats

30,000 audio, 7 1/2 ips; 10" reel; mono or stereo

III. General Program Types

Information Talk, 50%; Broadcast Music, 30%; Variety, 5%; Drama, 5%; News, 5%; Documentary, 5%.

IV. Subject Content Description

Contemporary NPR May 1971 - continuing.

VII. Accessibility

Computer: Yes. **On-site facilities:** Require permission to use. **Tape availabilities:** Copies are available at cost.

FLORIDA

I. Organizational Information

Louis Wolfson II Media History Center
Miami Dade-Public Library
101 W. Flagler
Miami, FL 33130

Individual to Contact   Steven Davidson, Director

Phone   (305) 375-4527

II. General Formats

16mm film, 3/4" video and VHS

III. General Program Types

Local news film collection.

IV. Subject Content Description

WTVJ Television local news film. The emphasis is on news/commentary, public affairs, politics, sports, and religion. Over 5 million feet of television newsfilm from 1949 to 1975. Over 2,000 hours of video from 1975 to the present. The collection gears to all of Florida as well as national and international events important to the region.

V. Related Manuscript Materials

Complete newscripts from 1959-1970, plus still photos, research files, etc.

VII. Accessibility

The collection is cataloged and accessible. On-site facilities exist and there is no restricted access. Tape availabilities, fees and exchange policies are treated individually and decisions are based on the type of use.

Editor's Note: There are a number of local news collections sprouting up throughout the country. This is one of the very important ones because of the geographical location of Miami and the part it has played throughout the cold war and the Cuban crisis. Many events of national significance are documented here.

GEORGIA

I. Organizational Information

The George Foster Peabody Collection
College of Journalism and Mass Communication
The University of Georgia
Athens, GA 30602

Individuals to Contact

Dr. Worth McDougald
Director, Peabody Awards

Dr. Barry Sherman
Associate Director (Archives)

Dr. Don Davis
Assistant Director (Awards)

Ms. Kay Weeks
Administrative Assistant

Phone

(404) 542-3787

Profit/Nonprofit

Nonprofit

II. General Formats

Estimated 3,000 LP-16" ETs or 78s; 6,000 audiotapes; 21,000 videotapes. Virtually all audio and video formats.

III. General Program Types

1,000 broadcast music; 5,000 variety; 5,000 drama; 2,000 news/commentary; 10,000 documentary; 2,000 politics; 1,000 comedy; 4,000 other.

VII. Accessibility

Listings: Peabody Office and UGA Libraries have complete lists of all entries. **Index:** Very limited, a few by subject matter for a few years. **Computer access:** Only for Peabody Award Winners. **Other:** OCLC has limited listings of some early years.

Use Conditions: On-site use only; access limited to approved research; no sales of material, no loans of materials, no materials removed from library. **Hours:** 8 a.m. to 5 p.m., Monday through Saturday. No published catalog. A winner's list will be available in April, price undetermined.

GEORGIA

I. Organizational Information

WSB Television NewsFilm Archive
Instructional Resources Center
University of Georgia
Athens, GA 30602

Individual to Contact

John R. Stephens, Jr.
Director

Phone

(404) 542-1582

II. General Formats

VHS access/16mm orig.

IV. Subject Content Description

During 1984, 1985, and 1986, the Instructional Resources Center of the University of Georgia received from WSB-TV, Atlanta, the complete news film collection which had been acquired during the past 30 years of broadcast news operations.

VII. Accessibility

The collection has been indexed and that index is being entered into a computer database to allow ease in searching for specific subject areas.

The database search will allow search by a person's name, a descriptor, date, or a location. Additional searches may be made upon special request. *The New York Times Thesaurus* in conjunction with a locally generated thesaurus for local names and items of interest, will indicate the proper spelling and format (i.e., "Dwight D. Eisenhower" not "Ike").

Film or video materials will not be available for political use. The definition of political use will rest solely with the Director, IRC; University of Georgia.

Academic and research interest is encouraged. As the collection is developed and additional indexing continues, access for these purposes will be easier to accommodate. It should be noted that these are not complete news programs, but only the film segments that were inserted into news programs.

Editor's Note: There are access fees, so call ahead.

GEORGIA

I. Organizational Information

CNN Library
Cable News Network
Box 105366, One CNN Center
Atlanta, GA 30348

Individual to Contact

Ainie Hastings
Library Tape Sales Coordinator

Phone

(404) 827-1378

Profit/Nonprofit

Profit

II. General Formats

Videotapes, 1" and 3/4"

III. General Program Types

News/information.

VI. Special Interests

Worldwide news coverage.

VII. Accessibility

Computer access; on-site facilities; access not open to public — available for duplication and licensing through library personnel — research fees charged, licensing fees charged.

No published catalog.

Editor's Note: Internal archives only. The "CNN World Report Archive" is being organized by Dr. John E. Fryman, School of Mass Communication, Texas Tech University, Lubbock, TX 79409, (806) 742-3385.

GEORGIA

I. Organizational Information

Georgia State University
Special Collections Department
Library, 100 Decatur Street SE
Atlanta, GA 30303-3081

Individual to Contact	Christopher Ann Paton
Phone	(404) 651-2477
Profit/Nonprofit	Nonprofit

II. General Format

300+ broadcast recordings total.

III. General Program Types

Material relating to radio broadcasting in Atlanta.

IV. Subject Content Description

The WSB Radio Collection contains correspondence, memos, news clippings, publicity materials, program log books, photographs, artifacts and sound recordings dating from 1922 through approximately 1984.

V. Related Manuscript Materials

The manuscript materials are processed and available for use at the present time. Broadcast recordings in the collection include nearly 300 transcription discs dating from 1942 through approximately 1956 and a number of audiotapes dating primarily from the 1970s and early 1980s. The recordings include political speeches, news programs, music, and drama; use of the recordings is restricted until preservation copying is complete.

VI. Special Interests

Primary focus is American popular music.

VII. Accessibility

Written finding aids are available for the manuscript collections. In-house indexes are available for some sound recordings.

GEORGIA

I. Organizational Information

The Martin Luther King, Jr.
Center for Nonviolent Social Change
449 Auburn Avenue, NE
Atlanta, GA 30312

Individual to Contact

Althea Sumpter
Director, Media Services

Phone

(404) 524-1956

II. General Formats

Cassette tapes.

III. General Program Types

The library includes cassettes of speeches and sermons.

IV. Subject Content Description

The King Center's Library and Archive is the home of the world's largest collection of primary source material on the civil rights movement. Comprehensive collection of personal papers with some broadcast materials.

VII. Accessibility

The King Center is open daily from 9 a.m. to 5:30 p.m.

HAWAII

I. Organizational Information

The University of Hawaii
Honolulu, HI 96822

Wong Audiovisual Center
Sinclair Library
(808) 956-8009

Pacific Collection
Hamilton Library
(808) 956-8473

II. General Formats

Videotapes, 16mm film, phonodisc, audiocassettes.

III. General Program Types

Documentary, local television, some feature film.

IV. Subject Content Description

Special effort is being made to create a comprehensive collection of materials on Hawaii and the Pacific. Unique materials include the "Video Encyclopedia of the Twentieth Century."

The Wong Center is primarily an on-campus support collection. The Pacific Collection is the primary research repository.

V. Related Manuscript Materials

Broadcast materials included among other primary materials.

ILLINOIS

I. Organizational Information

Robert Fitzner
1942 East Avenue
Berwyn, IL 60402

Phone

(708) 484-3587

II. General Formats

2500 recordings, LPs, 78s, CDs. Mostly commercial issues. Some audio-
and videotapes.

IV. Subject Content Description

99% music.

VI. Special Interests

The "Big Band" themes. Many music magazines (e.g., *Downbeat, Metro-
nome*) and similar, dating back to 1930s.

VII. Accessibility

On-site facilities. Call for appointment.

One-page listing available.

ILLINOIS

I. Organizational Information

Chicago Historical Society
Prints and Photographs Collection
Clark Street at North Avenue
Chicago, IL 60614-6099

Individual to Contact

Clare Cass

Phone

(312) 642-4600

Profit/Nonprofit

Nonprofit

II. General Formats

16mm film, small amount of videotape.

IV. Subject Content Description

News/information; WGN newsfilm library.

VII. Accessibility

Card catalog, subject/name; on-site facilities. Possible to have film transferred to tape. Inquire about fees. **Hours:** 9:30 a.m. to 4:30 p.m. Tuesday through Saturday.

ILLINOIS

I. Organizational Information

Museum of Broadcast Communications
800 S. Wells
Chicago, IL 60607

Individuals to Contact

Michael Mertz
Director, Archives and Programming

Laura Levitt
Television and Research Archivist

Mark Vail
Radio and News Archivist

Phone

(312) 987-1500

II. General Formats

Audiotape: 45,000 reel-to-reel, 982 cassettes
Videotape: 4,868 (SP speed, VHS format)

III. General Program Types

Television: Children's, comedy, commercials, cooking, dance, doctor/lawyer, documentary, dramatic, entertainment, entertainment special, musical, musical comedy, musical variety, newscast, police/mystery/spy, seminars, sports, talk/interview, western.

Radio: Adventure, adventure/serial, biography, children's, comedy, comedy panel, comedy/drama, comedy/dramatic, comedy/variety, detective, documantary, drama, dramatic, entertainment special, music/comedy, musical, musical comedy, musical variety, musical/drama, mystery, news, news special, newscast, oral history, police/mystery/spy, promotional, public affairs, quiz/panel, science fiction, situation comedy, soap opera, sports, talent contest, talk, talk/interview, top 40 music, variety, western.

IV. Subject Content Description

The Museum of Broadcast Communications Archives is a growing collection of radio programs, television programs and commercials, cataloged and made available to the public for on-site listening and viewing.

Over 5,000 programs and commercials are accessible for research as well as for entertainment. Major categories included in the collection are:

- Dramatic television program ("Kraft Television Theatre," "Robert Montgomery Presents," "Armstrong Circle Theatre")
- The Chuck Schaden Radio Collection (vintage radio programs)
- Chicago television newscasts (local newscasts taped nightly on a rotating basis since January of 1987)
- Television and radio commercials
- Radio and television sports programs ("The Wide World of Sport," "The Sportswriters on Television")
- Children's television programs ("Kukla, Fran and Ollie," American Children's Television Festival award winners)
- Talk-information television program (Tom Snyder's "Tomorrow Show," Steve Allen's "Meeting of the Minds")
- Musical programs ("Kraft Music Hall," "SoundStage")
- Documentary television programs ("Between the Wars," "The Fabulous Sixties")
- Television westerns ("Gunsmoke," "Bonanza")
- Television programs about the Vietnam War ("Agent Orange," "Vietnam: The 10,000-Day War")
- Television programs about civil rights ("Eyes on the Prize," Peabody Award winners)
- Popular television comedy programs, 1950s-1980s ("I Love Lucy," "The Dick Van Dyke Show," "The Honeymooners")

V. Related Manuscript Materials

33 oral histories on audiotape.

VI. Special Interests

The Museum's collections are wide-ranging. Special interests are sparked by the Museum's exhibitions, such as westerns, politics on television, the

Civil Rights Movement, the Vietnam War, etc. The current exhibition, Rock and Roll on Television, has brought programs to the Museum that have not been aired since their original air date. One area of interest is Chicago programming, especially the Chicago School of Broadcasting made famous in the 1950s.

VII. Accessibility

Computer access: DTI DataTrek that allows the researcher to search by networks, topic/name, series title, type of show, and keyword search by series title and type of show. **Published catalog:** None.

"Use" Conditions:

1. All facilities are on-site. This includes the Nielsen Research Center (10 study carrels with audio and video equipment), the computer system, the Kraft Television Theatre (100-seat large screening room), and warehouse.

2. The radio collection (45,000 programs) is on reel-to-reel tape and is not readily accessible. Only the 982 radio cassettes are immediately available to the public and are accessible by computer. The rest of the collection can be inquired about by appointment, letter, or telephone. The collection is Chuck Schaden's, a local radio collector and broadcaster in Chicago who has been collecting programs for 20 years.

3. The Museum holds two large collections that are all on film and 2" tape. These collections are not available for screening but we would be happy to talk with anyone who would be interested in them. The first collection is our David Susskind Collection, 3,000 of his talk shows and dramatic productions. The second collection is our "Tomorrow Show" with Tom Snyder Collection. This collection numbers 800 programs from 1973 to the program's demise in 1981. Both of these collections are stored on-site at a warehouse facility adjacent to the Museum. Very little of either collection has been transferred to 1/2" tape (47 "Tomorrow" programs and 20 Susskind dramatic programs are the current totals) and the Museum does not have the budget to transfer these for research requests although we have had some transferred for production purposes. None of the warehoused programs are available via computer searching so we usually need a week or so to search them out manually.

4. The Archives are open to the public during the regular Museum hours of Wednesday through Sunday, 12 p.m. — 5 p.m., and 10 a.m. — 5 p.m. on Saturdays. The archives' staff is available Monday—Friday and we will open the archives to any serious researcher on Monday and Tuesday if they make an appointment first. We advise this as the Museum can be quite crowded and there is often a waiting list for study carrels.

5. The Museum is not a stock footage house and we generally discourage requests for duplicates of our collections. We must do this in order to honor our donor's agreements. However, there are certain situations that we will duplicate programs and that can only be done with the donor's permission in writing and it is up to the interested party to get this permission. Our staff is too small to do the leg work needed to obtain permissions. In some cases this can involve a myriad of attorneys, producers, and other rights holders so it can be tricky to obtain permission.

6. We do not actively exchange our tapes as we get back to the whole problem of permission.

A staff Archivist is available for research assistance. To use this service, it is best to call (312) 987-1500 in advance of your visit, and ask for a staff Archivist. During your visit, the staff person at the Research Center should be able to assist with most of your questions.

ILLINOIS

I. Organizational Information

Wayne W. Kupferer (Private Collection)
1535 W. Highland
Chicago, IL 60660

Individual to Contact   Wayne Kupferer

Phone   (312) 274-5139

II. General Formats

There are well over 5,000 audio recordings, motion pictures, and video-tapes. Formats range from cylinders, wire, 78RPM, 16RPM, 16" transcriptions, 10/12" LPs through 16mm films, and BETA/VHS/3/4" videotapes.

III. General Program Types

Broadcast music, variety, drama, human interest, documentary, commercial messages.

IV. Subject Content Description

Radio Transcriptions: Front Page Drama; Comic Weekly; No Trumpets; Heart of Show Business; One-Minute Appeals; American Cancer Society; Tribute to Peter DeRose; Here's to Veterans; Panama Hattie-MGM Reporter; Man Against the Crippler (infantile paralysis); Dramatic Show-NBC Thesaurus; Hollywood Open House; NBC Thesaurus; What America Means to Me; Guest Star; Treasury Star Parade; The Waiting People; Who Am I?; Homeward Passage; Miracle of the Stage Door Canteen; Spirit of the Vikings; Norway Fights; Let's Go to Town; Spectrum Use; USO 1968 Campaign; Navy Chronicle; Great Leader! Great Ship; Guard in Session; Brammy Treasure Chest; Christmas Greetings; Fight Arthritis; Join Up—Join In; Mutual Radio Theater; Our Changing World.

Television Programs: "Rocky Jones"; "Space Ranger"; "You Are There: The Chicago Fire"; "Arthur Godfrey and His Friends"; "This is Your Music"; "The Star and the Story"; "Mamma"; "Gloria Swanson Showcase"; "The Life of Riley"; "The Jack Benny Show"; "Ford Theatre"; "My Little Margie"; "Goldie"; "You Asked For It"; "Duffy's Tavern"; "Biography: Clarence Darrow" (flawed); "Biography: Helen Keller"; "Amos and Andy"; "Dr. Hudson's Secret Journal"; "Barbara Stanwick Playhouse"; "Our Miss

Brooks"; "George Burns and Gracie Allen Show"; "The Abbott and Costello Show"; "The Fay Emerson Show"; "The Big Story"; "Liberace"; "Stu Irwin Show"; "Talent Scouts" (very bad condition).

Television Commercials (1960 - 1971): "Alcoholism"; "Youth Fitness"; Metropolitan Life Insurance Co.; "Safe Use of Pesticides"; Boys Clubs; U.S. Savings Bonds; National Guard; "Hell Fighters"; "Benedict Lift"; "Steward"; "Walking Man"; "Earl of Bisco"; "Blo-Ball"; "Dune Buggy"; "Sailor"; "Kid Drawing"; "Tang Orange Drink"; "Cool Whip"; "Maxwell House Coffee"; "Versa-Tuna-Tility"; "Sandwiches"; "Shake and Bake"; Birds Eye Frozen Foods; "Bavarian"; CARE; Gaines Prime Dog Food; Gaines Meal Dog Food; Gaines Burgers Dog Food; "Camero Camera Car"; Chevrolet; "Power Disc Brakes"; "Cowboy."

Television Commercials (Winter, 1975-1976): Fashions by Lilyands; "Meat Locker"; "Jobs"; Hidden Camera; "Good News"; "Vacation"; "Chocolate Mint Pie"; "Adoption"; "Firemans Picnic"; "Lady Sewing"; "Woman with Plants"; "Something Special"; "Modern Woman"; "Little Girl"; "School Bus"; "Split Screen"; "Over Done by the Sun"; "The Time It Takes"; "Revolving Door"; "Rows and Frows"; "Sunshine"; "Fresh and Lovely"; "Two Girls"; "Riddle Brush"; "Plane Drop"; "Buffalo."

VI. Special Interests

TV/radio is a small portion of the collection which is primarily 19th and 20th century for culture. There is a general cutoff of 1970 (approximate).

VII. Accessibility

Listings: Cataloged by forms and decade. **Computer access:** In development. **Published Catalog:** None yet, but would copy any sections desired—at cost. The entire collection is over 5,000.

Since this is a personal library, the formalities of extensive cataloging and ready accessing by the public would be difficult. A computerized catalog is in the early stages. As for accessibility: Open to inquiries and welcome the opportunity to make copies, provided clearances are obtainable or the material. Audio copies on audiocassette or 1/4" at 15, 7.5 or 3 3/4 IPS on full, four or half-track.

Editor's Note: The collection is small, programs listed are single.

111

ILLINOIS

I. Organizational Information

WBBM—TV News Library
630 N. McClurg Court
Chicago, IL 60611

Individual to Contact

Monroe Anderson

Phone

(312) 944-6000

II. General Formats

3/4" and Beta tapes; audiotapes, from 1977 to present.

III. General Program Types

TV news; WBBM-TV news film and related scripts.

VII. Accessibility

Computerized listing; access by approval only; fees.

ILLINOIS

I. Organizational Information

WPA Film Library
12233 S. Pulaski Rd., 2nd Fl.
Evanston, IL 60658

Individuals to Contact

Matthew White
Archivist and CEO

Sharon Sandusky
Research Chief

Phone

(708) 385-8535

Profit/Nonprofit

Profit

II. General Formats

Two million feet of 16mm film, most of it camera originals. Also 150,000 feet of 35mm (all camera originals). Some 500 "programs" or cut-films from a variety of sources — much of it corporate, ephemeral.

III. General Program Types

In 1953, Lem Bailey founded The Color Stock Library—one of the first commercial stock footage houses in the country, and a consistently reliable resource for the world's creative community. In 1987, we negotiated to purchase the library and in 1988 we gave the film a new home and the library a new name. Lem Bailey's Color Stock Library of Hollywood, California is now The White Janssen Film Library of Evanston, Illinois.

IV. Subject Content Description

The Library contains millions of feet of original film materials on thousands of individual subjects ranging from accidents to zoos. The following is a random sampling:

American (1945-1965); Baby Doc's Haiti (1982); Beauty Contests (1940s-1960s); Cars of the 40s & 50s; Dance Around the World; Fashions of the

Fifties; The Industrial Films of F.K. Rockett; Israel (1948-1975); Lyndon Baines Johnson; Missionary Films (1950s to 1978); Native Americans (1975-1981); Petroleum; Rose Parade (1957-1964); San Francisco (1940s); Tobacco; Vietnam.

V. Related Manuscript Materials

All scripts for travelog television series "This Island Earth."

VI. Special Interests

Early television commercials (some over 20 minutes long) from Academy Production, Chicago, Il. Corporate materials from Chrysler 1950s. Much automotive film materials. Rose Parade 1954-1962; American Indian Reservations 1970s; American Home Life 1950s; History of Suburban Living.

VII. Accessibility

Materials being listed on MacIntosh Hypercard. Free brochure. On-site facility; no restricted access; research fees charged; standard business hours.

Research: On-site research by the client is available by appointment, and is preferred. If you are unable to come to our facilities, our staff will do the research for you. The research involves locating the footage within the library, screening the footage, selecting appropriate footage, transferring the footage to a screening (preview) cassette. The cassette will be of nonbroadcast quality, and is for selection purposes only. The charge is $25/hour ($100 minimum) for research. Additional charges will be made for licensing, laboratory, and production.

Editor's Note: Primarily stock film footage. Programs primarily corporate, some broadcasts. Write for brochure.

ILLINOIS

I. Organizational Information

The Radio Closet
1427 W. American
Freeport, IL 61032-4778

Individual to Contact

H.K. Kinkley

Phone

(815) 235-3753

Profit/Nonprofit

Profit/Private Collection

II. General Formats

Disc: One 16" ET
Audiotape: 686 reels, 3 3/4ips (7")

III. General Program Types

Variety (1,500 programs); drama (2,500 programs); comedy (4,000 programs).

IV. Subject Content Description

See **Program Index**. Individual programs are listed with page numbers directing user to collection.

VI. Special Interests

All Fibber McGee & Molly; Science fiction.

VII. Accessibility

General catalog available. **"Use" Conditions:** On-site in private home; restricted access — Call for appointment.

ILLINOIS

I. Organizational Information

Ronald Colman (1891-1958)
341 Iris Lane
Highland Park, Il 60035

Individual to Contact   George E. Schatz

Phone   (708) 432-8556

Profit/Nonprofit   Nonprofit

NOTE: All materials are on Ronald Colman only.

II. General Formats

Discs: 12 (78 and 33RPM), one 16RPM. Audiotapes: 143 reel-to-reel, 45 cassettes. Videotapes: 25 (from silent and sound films), VHS.

III. General Program Types

Variety (12); drama (110); information talk (8); comedy (20).

IV. Subject Content Description

Drama (1920s): film, radio, phonograph and TV, audiotapes.
World War II: Ronald Colman on radio for Armed Forces Radio, "Everything for the Boys" series; war bond programs, Red Cross, etc., messages; "Command Performance," etc.

V. Related Manuscript Materials

Oral histories (making "Lost Horizon," 1937, with crew members).

VI. Special Interests

Ronald Colman (1891-1958), winner of 1947 Academy Award as "Best Actor"; nominated as "Best Actor" in 1929 and again in 1942; selected as "Motion Picture Actor Most Effective on Radio" in 1950; many other awards; known especially for his exceptional quality of speech.

VII. Accessibility

Listings: List of appearances in motion pictures (silent and sound), radio, phonograph, and television by year, usually in ongoing update. Copy of listing available for duplicating costs only. **"Use" Conditions:** Private home; trade information, tapes, etc. Call for appointment.

ILLINOIS

I. Organizational Information

University Archives
University of Illinois
1408 W. Gregory
Urbana, IL 61801

Individuals to Charge Maynard Brichford
Staff William Maher, Robert Chapel

Phone (217) 333-0798

Profit/Nonprofit Nonprofit

II. General Formats

3,114 discs; 2,381 audiotapes; 103 videotapes.

III. General Program Types

News, information (information more than hard news).

IV. Subject Content Description

Slides, photographs, microfilm, manuscripts, textscripts. Transcripts of tapes (audio); personal papers of faculty/alumni.

VI. Special Interests

University-related material — national importance (i.e., Nobel Prize winners).

VII. Accessibility

5 x 8 control card listing for smaller collections; folder-by-folder index of larger collections. Catalog can be purchased — on microfiche — flyers available. Information to guides on request. **"Use" Conditions:** On-site facilities; access restricted on collection-by-collection basis, some totally restrict, some by permission. Tape availabilities depends on collection — tape or broadcast access more limited than manuscripts. **Hours:** 8 a.m. to 5 p.m. during academic year.

ILLINOIS

I. Organizational Information　　　Archives of the Billy Graham Center
Wheaton College
Wheaton, IL 60198

Individuals to Contact　　　Robert D. Shuster
Director

Paul A. Ericksen
Associate Director

Janyce H. Nasgowitz
Reference Archivist

Phone　　　(708) 260-5910

Profit/Nonprofit　　　Nonprofit

II. General Formats

Disc: 200 (mostly 78s)
Audiotapes: 8,850 (reels & cassettes combined)
Videotapes: 950 (8mm & 16mm combined)

III. General Program Types

Diaries, correspondence, business records, posters, films, slides, scrapbooks, audiotapes, videotapes, phonograph records, maps, photographs, microforms. The archives of the Billy Graham Center tells the dramatic story of Protestant nondenominational missions and evangelism.

IV. Subject Content Description

Religion. Most of the collection falls within this category (contemporary programming), but the collections also contains some earlier materials.

V. Related Manuscript Materials

A few scripts scattered throughout the materials; a few items of production materials scattered throughout. Personal papers and organizational records make up the bulk of the Archive's holdings. Of the 8,850 audiotapes, approximately 650 are oral histories.

VI. Special Interests

North American Protestant nondenominational missions and evangelism.

VII. Accessibility

Subject listing on microfiche; computer access by staff person only.

Catalog: *Researching Modern Evangelicalism: A Guide to the Holdings of the Billy Graham Center*, published July 1990; *Semiannual Checklist: From the Archives of the Billy Graham Center*, published Spring and Autumn, $3/year. **"Use" Conditions:** On-site facilities: Materials must be used in Archival Reading Room or through Interlibrary Loan. There are some restrictions on some collections. Write for lists of materials available through Interlibrary Loan.

The archives reading room is on the third floor of the Billy Graham Center on the Wheaton College Campus, Wheaton, Il. A member of our staff is always available there to help you. A limited number of collections have restrictions on their use. Photocopying of nonrestricted materials is available. Located in the same building is the Graham Center library with its collection of books, periodicals, and microforms about missions and evangelism.

Hours: Monday through Friday, 10 a.m. to 6 p.m.; Saturday, 10 a.m. to 2 p.m.

INDIANA

I. Organizational Information

Gordon Kelley (Private Collection)
8600 University Blvd.
Evansville, IN 47712

Individual to Contact

Gordon Kelley

Phone

(812) 464-1702

II. General Formats

Very few discs; audiotapes.

III. General Program Types

Broadcast music (25); variety (200); drama (10,000); human interest (50); information talk (200); news/commentary (50); documentary (25); sports (25); comedy (5,000); western (500); detective (500); science fiction (500).

IV. Subject Content Description

1920s (10); the Depression (100); radio's golden age (15,000); World War II (40).

V. Related Manuscript Materials

One Lone Ranger script, no date, about 1952.

VI. Special Interests

Golden Age of Radio, especially suspense (Inner Sanctum). Major interest in all Sherlock Holmes and all varieties of science fiction. Secondary area of interest is radio drama since 1960.

VII. Accessibility

Listings of programs in collection not yet available.

On-site facilities: Private collection, phone for appointment. **Tape availability:** Willing to exchange tapes.

INDIANA

I. Organizational Information

Indiana Historical Society
WRTV Film Archives
315 W. Ohio St.
Indianapolis, IN 46202

Individual to Contact
Stephen Fletcher

Phone
(317) 232-1879

IV. Subject Content Description

4DD + titles. Primarily WRTV newsfilm.

VI. Special Interests

Documentaries, commercials, corporate films from the WRBM Production Division from early 1960s to mid-1970s.

VII. Accessibility

In-house inventory list only; still in process of being cataloged; highly restricted.

INDIANA

I. Organizational Information

Indiana State Library
140 North Senate Avenue
Indianapolis, IN 46204

Individual to Contact

Charles Ray Ewick
Director

Phone

(317) 232-3675

IV. Subject Content Description

The Will Hays Collection. His career as President of the Motion Picture Producers and Distributors of America, Inc., may be of interest to those in the broadcasting field.

VI. Special Interests

Indiana materials only; Civil War, community organizations, business records, Indiana history.

VII. Accessibility

Listings: Some inventories for specific collections. **Card Catalog:** Subject, personal name, corporate name. **Published Catalog:** *A Guide to Manuscript Collections of the Indiana Historical Society and Indiana State Library,* by Eric Pumroy. Indianapolis: Indiana Historical Society, 1986, 513 pp. **"Use" Conditions:** On-site facilities: reading room; some collections have restrictions; photocopy charge of 25¢ per page and postage charge if mailed. **Hours:** 8 a.m. to 4:30 p.m., Monday through Friday.

INDIANA

I. Organizational Information

Public Affairs Video Archives
Purdue University
Stewart Center, G-39
West Lafayette, IN 47907

Individual to Contact

Robert X. Browning

Phone

(317) 494-9630

Profit/Nonprofit

Nonprofit

II. General Formats

10-11,000 programs on videotape.

III. General Program Types

News/information; C-Span and C-Span 2 programs.

VII. Accessibility

Computer access, database; on-site facilities except for close-up foundation programs—"viewed" but not distributed; distribute tapes to educators by mail or calling; fees are $35 for 2 hours VHS, $50 for compiled tapes. **Hours:** 8 a.m. to 5 p.m., weekdays.

IOWA

I. Organizational Information

Iowa State University Library
Archives of the Factual Film
Ames, IA 50011-2140

Individual to Contact   Stanley Yates

Phone   (515) 294-6672

Profit/Nonprofit   Nonprofit

II. General Formats

Four videotapes/16mm films; about 200 tapes and upwards of 12,000 films.

III. General Program Types

The AAFF contains films of TV programs (mostly documentaries and special programs). Specific subject areas not identified; however, lists can be furnished of films by sponsors (e.g., CBS, NBC).

V. Related Manuscript Materials

The AAFF does have manuscript collections including the files and records of the American Science Film Association and the University Film and Video Association.

VI. Special Interests

Particular strengths of the AAFF would include agriculture; World War II; social concerns/problems in post-World War II period; substantial holdings of films from National Film Board of Canada, EBEC, Exxon, and U.S. NASA.

VII. Accessibility

Two moviolas on-site; no restrictions; tapes can be purchased with written permission of copyright holder. **Hours:** 8 to 11:50 a.m. and 1 to 5 p.m., Monday through Friday. **Published Catalog:** AAFF Film Index, $35.

IOWA

I. Organizational Information   Sioux City Public Museum
2901 Jackson Street
Sioux City, IA 51104

Individual to Contact   Bill Diamond

Phone   (712) 279-6174

Profit/Nonprofit   Nonprofit

III. General Program Types

News/information, general local history, station: KCAV-TV channel 9, newsfilm.

VI. Special Interests

Local history and photographs of Sioux City.

VII. Accessibility

Computer access in progress. Catalog that is "a little dated" available at no charge. On-site facilities with some restricted access; photo use fee. **Hours:** Monday through Friday, 9 a.m. to 5 p.m.

IOWA

I. Organizational Information

Herbert Hoover Pres. Library
Parkside Drive
P.O. Box 488
West Branch, IA 52358

Individual to Contact

J. Patrick Wildenbell
Audio/Visual Archivist

Phone

(319) 643-5301

II. General Formats

500 reel-to-reel, audiotape.

VI. Special Interests

Herbert Hoover speeches, radio interviews from 1924 to present, and related reading scripts.

VII. Accessibility

Listings arranged by date; on-site facilities; free access, reproduction fees. **Hours:** Monday through Friday, 9 a.m. to 5 p.m.

KANSAS

I. Organizational Information

The Dwight D. Eisenhower Library
Abilene, KS 67410

Phone

(913) 263-4751

II. General Formats

All formats

III. General Program Types

The Eisenhower years.

IV. Subject Content Description

The Eisenhower audiovisual collection consists of over 585,000 feet of motion picture film and videotape, and 2,298 hours of audio recordings.

The largest portion of the motion picture film holdings cover the presidential years and was given to the President by CBS. The Library also has a number of documentary films relating to World War II, including the film version of General Eisenhower's book, *Crusade in Europe*.

Audiotapes and discs cover 1944 to the late 1960s. A series of discs made by the White House Army Signal Corps comprises the largest portion of the audio collection and pertain primarily to President Eisenhower's roles in ceremonial occasions, national addresses, and press conferences.

V. Related Manuscript Materials

As with all presidential libraries, related manuscript material is significant.

VI. Special Interests

Dwight D. Eisenhower

VII. Accessibility

Many of the audiovisual materials are subject to copyright or other restrictions. Researchers wishing to use the materials or to obtain information about these restrictions are asked to submit an application form stating the nature and purpose of the research to the Director of the Eisenhower Library.

KANSAS

I. Organizational Information	Thomas Gorton Music Library
	Archive of Recorded Sound
	University of Kansas
	Lawrence, KS 66045
Individual to Contact	Susan Hitchens
Phone	(913) 864-3496
Profit/Nonprofit	Nonprofit

II. General Formats

72,753 discs (LP-16"ETs or 78s); 5,625 audiotapes; 3 videotapes (VHS).

III. General Program Types

Broadcast music: 5,000 (contemporary).

VI. Special Interests

Opera; jazz (collection consists of reel-to-reel tapes of local radio shows on these subjects).

VII. Accessibility

Listings are made at time of acquisition; in-house database of jazz sound discs; discopies. Materials do not circulate, use by appointment only; closed stacks, staff-only access; user must bring blank tape(s); $5/hour recording charge. Hours are by appointment only.

KENTUCKY

I. Organizational Information

University of Kentucky Libraries
Audiovisual Archives
111 King Library North
Lexington, KY 40506-0039

Individual to Contact   Tom House

Phone   (606) 257-8611

Profit/Nonprofit   Nonprofit

II. General Formats

All formats.

III. General Program Types

Music, entertainment, mostly news/information. Scripts, oral histories
(history of broadcasting in Kentucky). Broadcasting archives; early 1930s
radio material through last year. Work prints/outtakes—Harlem County
USA—(1975) Koppel's "best" documentary.

VII. Accessibility

Computer access; on-site facilities; no restrictions for use on-site; to
reproduce, go to station, Archives has no rights. **Hours:** 8 a.m. to 4:30
p.m., Monday — Friday (until 7:30 p.m., Wednesday); 8 a.m. to 12 p.m.,
Saturday; 2 p.m. to 5 p.m., Sunday (need to make arrangements for
Wednesday evening and weekends).

LOUISIANA

I. Organizational Information

New Orleans Public Library: Louisiana Division
WVUE-TV Collection
219 Loyola Avenue
New Orleans, LA 70140

Individual to Contact   Patricia Green

Phone   (504) 529-7323

Profit/Nonprofit   Nonprofit

II. General Formats

SOF, 6,000 reels.

III. General Program Types

News, scripts, WVUE-TV news footage, 1969-1979. Station has copyright to film but is very receptive to let researchers use the footage.

VII. Accessibility

Card catalog (3x5 cards); no published catalog; on-site facilities; station has copyright to film; fees charged on a case-by-case basis. **Hours:** 10 a.m. to 6 p.m., Monday through Thursday; 10 a.m. to 5 p.m., Friday and Saturday (by appointment).

LOUISIANA

I. Organizational Information

Louisiana State University
Archives Department
1 University Place
Shreveport, LA 71115

Individual to Contact — Laura Street

Phone — (318) 797-5226

Profit/Nonprofit — Nonprofit

II. General Format

A few LP-16" ETs or 78s; a few Hank Williams audiotapes; microfilm (cable vision).

III. General Program Types

Music, entertainment, mostly information. Scripts, production materials, personal papers, oral histories. Northwest Louisiana documentation with emphasis on Shreveport.

VI. Accessibility

Listings, card catalogs, indexes, computer access ("Louisiana" Collection only); restricted to on-site use—or Xerox. **Published Catalog:** Call for inquiries. **Hours:** Monday through Friday, 8 a.m. to 4:30 p.m.

MAINE

I. Organizational Information

Northeast Historic Film
Bangor Historical Society
Route 175
Blue Hill Falls, ME 04615

Individuals to Contact

David S. Weiss
Executive Director

Stephani Boyd
Archives Manager

Phone

(207) 374-5462

Profit/Nonprofit

Nonprofit

II. General Formats

200 2", 3/4" VHS videotapes; 800,000 ft 16mm film, plus reference copies of 16mm film. TV only, no radio. WABI, WGAN, WCSH: Local TV news film collections.

III. General Program Types

Human interest 57%; news/commentary 70%; documentary 5%; politics 5%; commercial messages 10%; sports 5%. Tapes contain segments from local programs, interviews, news stories, sports, and commercials. It includes such notables as Senator Edmund Muskie, President Eisenhower receiving the first Penobscot River salmon of the 1953 season, and Richard Nixon campaigning in Maine. Commercials for Life Pack survival rations for the family bomb shelter, the Kelvinator Food-a-Rama and the Gadget Master salesman recorded live in the WABI-TV studio in 1955 will beguile you.

IV. Subject Content Description

The following are new collections, not yet quantified. **Cold War Television:** News/commentary, public affairs, politics, commercial messages, sports. **Television's Golden Age:** News/commentary, public affairs, politics, commercial messages, sports. **Korean War Era:** Human interest, news/commentary, public affairs, politics, commercial messages, sports. **Vietnam War Era:** Human interest, news/commentary, public affairs, politics, commercial messages, sports. **Contemporary Programming:** Human interest, news/commentary, public affairs, politics, commercial messages, sports.

V. Related Manuscript Materials

Some scripts.

VI. Special Interests

Northeast Historic Film is a regional moving image archives collecting in all areas, including amateur, industrial, educational, dramatic. TV is one aspect of collection: three collections from two markets: Bangor (the country's smallest market with ABC, NBC, CBS + PBS); and Portland.

VII. Accessibility

Index, computer access (cataloging in progress). **Published Catalog:** Call for database information. **"Use" Conditions:** On-site facilities; reference copies available; call or write for fees. **Hours:** 8:30 a.m. to 5 p.m. Eastern time. **Published Research:** "Moving Image Review" (semiannual newsletter of Northeast Historic Film); compilation videotapes,including *Maine's TV Time Machine* from WABI Collection (30-minute VHS).

MARYLAND

I. Organizational Information   Golden Radio Buffs of Maryland, Inc.
Gr. B. Tape Library
301 Jeanwood Court
Baltimore, MD 21222

Individuals to Contact   Gene Leitner, Co-Founder
Jerry Michael, Librarian

Phone   (301) 477-2550

Profit/Nonprofit   Nonprofit

II. General Formats

All types.

III. General Program Types

Hundreds of broadcast music, variety, drama, news/commentary, comedy recordings/programs. A few human interest, talk entertainment, information talk, politics, commercial messages recordings/programs.

IV. Subject Content Description

1920s: Music (50); **Depression:** Music (25), variety (few), drama, comedy, talk entertainment, news/commentary (few), public affairs, commercial messages (few); **Radio's Golden Age:** Music (100), variety (100s), drama, comedy, news/commentary (quite a few), politics (few); **World War II:** Music (50), variety, drama, comedy, news/commentary (50), politics (few); **Television's Golden Age:** very few programs/recordings.

V. Related Manuscript Materials

Scripts (old time radio programs); production materials (our road show).

VI. Special Interests

Nostalgia maintaining our old time radio museum exhibit.

VII. Accessibility

Listings; on-site facilities and by mail; must be a member to use (exceptions determined by librarian and board members). Members receive tape library catalog upon joining. It is updated in each bimonthly newsletter.

MARYLAND

I. Organizational Information

University of Baltimore Library
WMAR-TV News Archives
Langsdale Library, Special Collections
1420 Maryland Ave.
Baltimore, MD 21201-5779

Individual to Contact

Gerry Yeager

Phone

(301) 625-3135

Profit/Nonprofit

Nonprofit

II. General Formats

7 million feet 16mm film (2", 3/4", 1/2"); 400 videotapes.

III. General Program Types

News/commentary, whole collection 1948-1989; 100 documentary recordings/programs. WMAR-TV news, local.

IV. Subject Content Description

Collection includes news/commentary programs/recordings from The Cold War Television, Television's Golden Age, Korean War Era, Vietnam War Era, and Contemporary Programming.

VII. Accessibility

Listings by date; log sheets by reel, partial subject index (about 30% of the collection); on-site facilities; copyright held by station WMAR; fees charged on a case-by-case basis, tape copies produced by request. **Hours:** 8:30 a.m. to 4 p.m., Monday through Friday (by appointment).

MARYLAND

I. Organizational Information

National Library of Medicine
Historical Audiovisual Collection
History of Medicine Division
8600 Rockville Pike, Bldg. 38
Bethesda, MD 20894

Individual to Contact   Sarah Richards

Phone   (301) 496-8949

Profit/Nonprofit   Nonprofit

II. General Formats

Many different categories. Almost all of the collection is available for loan through the interlibrary loan system. Duplication and reuse is available subject to clearance and restrictions. Formats include: 35mm and 16mm film, videotape (1", 3/4", and 1/2"), slides, audiotapes, and filmstrips.

III. General Program Types

Approximately 4,000 audiovisuals ranging in date from 1917 to 1980 in the historical collection. There are approximately 221 titles which were created for broadcast. Most of these appear to be PBS or BBC Productions.

V. Related Manuscript Materials

Scripts, production materials, and personal papers.

VI. Special Interests

Medical films.

VII. Accessibility

Computer access; on-site facilities and interlibrary loan. **Published Catalog:** On-line catalog $29.95 for software, per minute (database called AVLINE). Fee charged as well. Printed copy available as well.

MARYLAND

I. Organizational Information

David L. Easter
Time Machine
1900 Angleside Rd.
Fallston, MD 21047

Individual to Contact

David L. Easter

Phone

(301) 877-2949

Profit/Nonprofit

Nonprofit (Personal Collection)

II. General Formats

30-40 LPs - 16" ETs or 78s; greater than 20,000 hours audiotape, 3-3/4 and 1-7/8 IPS.

VI. Special Interests

Although owner has a special interest in science fiction, the vast bulk of the collection is general in nature.

VII. Accessibility

Current listings; computer access (personal home computer); trade with collectors. **Published Catalog:** *Time Machine* (free in exchange for requestor's catalog).

MASSACHUSETTS

I. Organizational Information

Audio Visual Archives
John F. Kennedy Library
Columbia Point
Boston, MA 02125

Individual to Contact

Allan B. Goodrich

Phone

(617) 929-4530

Profit/Nonprofit

Institutionally sponsored

II. General Formats

800 discs, 7,000 tapes; audio 1-7/8, video 15ips; 1/4", 3/4", 1", and 2" videotapes.

III. General Program Types

Broadcast music 10%; news 20%; documentaries 20%; politics and government 50%.

IV. Subject Content Description

Radio's Golden Age: Music 5%, politics 5%; **World War II:** Politics 5%; **Cold War:** News 5%, politics 10%; **TV's Golden Age:** News/politics 45%; **Korean War Era:** News/politics, 5%; **Vietnam Era:** News/politics, 15%; **Contemporary:** 5%.

VII. Accessibility

Card Catalog: Chronological card catalog available for processed film collection, speeches of President Kennedy and Senator Robert Kennedy (audio). **Index:** Indices for speeches of President Kennedy; name index for speeches of other public personalities; title index available for speeches, documentaries, etc. **Catalog:** General Library Catalog. **On-site Facilities:** Yes, for use by qualified researchers. **Restrictions:** Certain donations closed, others still being processed. **Tape Availabilities:** No rentals or loans. Reproductions available if unrestricted by donor or copyright. Exchanges are possible, but rare.

MASSACHUSETTS

I. Organizational Information

Christian Science Monitor Broadcast Service
Archives (Videotape)
175 Huntington Avenue
Boston, MA 02116

Individual to Contact	Allysen Palmer
Phone	(617) 450-2271
Profit/Nonprofit	Nonprofit

II. General Formats

20,000-30,000 videotapes.

III. General Program Types

News/information. Limited number of scripts. Strong international focus.

VII. Accessibility

Database; on-site facilities; case-by-case restrictions; fees charged on case-by-case basis. No published catalog at this time. **Hours:** 10:30 a.m. to 8 p.m., Monday through Friday.

MASSACHUSETTS

I. Organizational Information   WGBH Educational Foundation
                              The WGBH Educational Foundation Archives
                                                118 Western Avenue
                                                 Boston, MA 02134

   Individual to Contact   Carl Piermarine
                                           Program Materials Supervisor

                                                  Cheryl Andonian
                                                        Assistant

   Phone   (617) 492-2777 x4206

   Profit/Nonprofit   Nonprofit

II. General Formats

20,000 1/4" audiotapes, 1,000 2" audiotapes; 10,000 1" videotapes, 7,000 2" videotapes, 5,000 V-matic cassettes.

III. General Program Types

The **WGBH Educational Foundation Archives** were organized in 1979 to permanently store and preserve all of the program materials produced by WGBH, the award-winner PBS affiliate in Boston. Since its inception, the WGBH archives, instituted on the foundation's tradition of producing excellent quality television, has grown to become one of the largest collections of public television programming in the country.

The WGBH name represents a standard of excellence and innovation for broadcast production. It is frequently seen on public television and heard on public radio. WGBH supplies one-third of all prime time programming offered nationwide by PBS. The WGBH Archives protects and preserves this legacy.

The WGBH Archives Collection contains over thirty years of television and radio production and with it, many technological advances in programming materials. Our holdings currently include 15,000 reels of 16mm motion picture film, 7,000 programs on 2" quad videotape, 9,000 programs on 1" videotape, 3,000 programs on 3/4" videocassette, 1,000 titles on 2" audiotape, and over 20,000 listings on 1/4" audiotape. This material is cataloged by a full-time staff archivist and assistant using a Digital Vax mainframe, linking the archives with the WGBH Film, Traffic,

Broadcasting, and Production Service departments. This system is augmented by a Macintosh SE computer which is used for cross indexing, bar code labeling and other library services. Access to this collection is limited to the WGBH Educational Foundation, its commercial marketing division and the stations of the Public Broadcasting Service. Public access to these materials is restricted.

The WGBH Archives is a state-of-the-art storage facility utilizing the latest techniques of film and videotape preservation. Environmentally sensitive program materials are stored in a 1,900 sq.ft. climate controlled, thermally sealed vault where they are stabilized at the optimum temperature and humidity. The vault is protected by a specially designed Halon gas fire prevention system and access into the vault is through a single fire resistant steel security door.

Inside the vault, 15 custom made high density mobile shelving units, holding more than 50,000 reels of tape, can be moved along depressed steel tracks to create access aisles only where they are needed thereby turning unused aisle space into storage space. The entire vault, walls and ceiling, together with the shelving units and mobile carriers are all completely modular which facilitate very simple expansion in the future.

IV. Subject Content Description

Contemporary Programming: Music, 7,000 programs/recordings; drama, 14,000; comedy, 2,000; human interest, 3,000; news/commentary, 7,000; public affairs, 4,000; sports, 1,500.

V. Related Manuscript Materials

Scripts and production materials.

VI. Special Interests

Preservation of all program materials produced by WGBH, the award-winning PBS affiliate in Boston; grown to become one of the largest collections of public programming in the country.

VII. Accessibility

All listings, index systems, and computer access are restricted to specific divisions or departments within the WGBH Educational Foundation and other public broadcasting service stations.

MASSACHUSETTS

I. Organizational Information

Lou Dumont
History of Radio in Sound
P.O. Box 596
Harwich, MA 02645

Phone

(508) 896-9322

Profit/Nonprofit

Private Collection

II. General Formats

Magnetic tape, discs, wire recordings.

III. General Program Types

Broadcast music (75%); variety (25%); The Depression Era (Al Jolson); The Golden Age of Radio (Nora Bayes); Vaudeville (Jack Norworth).

VII. Accessibility

Tape availability: Exchange possibilities.

MASSACHUSETTS

I. Organizational Information

Archives of the Airwaves
P.O. Box 4
Needham, MA 02192

Individual to Contact

Roger C. Paulson

Phone

Unlisted

Profit/Nonprofit

Nonprofit (until publication of
Archives of the Airwaves)

III. General Program Types

All types. 20,000 audiotapes.

IV. Subject Content Descriptions

A few tapes covering the 1920s, Depression, some radio recordings for the Korean War Era; all types of programs/recordings for Radio's Golden Age and World War II.

V. Related Manuscript Materials

Many radio scripts; many filing cabinets of NYT radio SKED 1920s-1950s; obituaries; radio magazines; pictures; hundreds of books on radio program history.

VII. Accessibility

Specific research aids information supplied by mail; catalog no longer available; specific requests honored. **Published Research:** Forthcoming encyclopedia *Archives of the Airwaves* (10 years in preparation), expected publication in 1992.

I. Organizational Information

The Rutenberg and Everett Yiddish
Film Library and Others
The National Center for Jewish Film
Lown Building 102
Brandeis University
Waltham, MA 02254

Individuals to Contact

Sharon Pucker Rivo
Executive Director

Miriam Saul Krant
Associate Director

Staff

Sylvia Fuks Fried
Translator

Arlenee Miller
Administrative Assistant

Phone

(617) 899-7044

Profit/Nonprofit

Nonprofit

II. General Formats

Films and 200+ videotapes (film transferred to videotape); 3/4" and 1"
VHS; 3,000+ (ca. 2/3 = 16mm) 16mm and 35mm films. Many only for
lease or in-house use. Those for sale are listed in catalog.

III. General Program Types

The Center's library contains over 3,000 films. The original nucleus, *The
Rutenberg and Everett Yiddish Film Library*, has grown to include 55
features, the largest extant collection in the world. A worldwide search has
uncovered missing titles and reels. Thirteen feature length films, made in
the 1930s and 1940s in Europe and the United States have been restored
with complete English subtitles and are available for public exhibition. The
collection includes classics such as *Tevye, Uncle Moses, The Dybbuk*, and
Green Fields.

144

A rare collection of early American silent shorts and features depicting Jewish subjects has been ingathered providing a unique resource for educators and film buffs. The collection begins with Cohen's *Advertising Scheme* (1904), *Old Isaacs The Pawnbroker* (1980), *Romance of a Jewess* (1908), and includes *His People* (1925) and *Surrender* (1929).

Together with these fiction films, the Center has amassed a most significant collection of documentary and factual films depicting Jewish life in the multitude of places they have lived. The collections focus on European Jewry, Nazi antisemitic propaganda, The Holocaust, Israel, American and Soviet Jewry, newsreels, together with the archival collections of ORT, JNF, JDC, UJA, and other organizations.

IV. Subject Content Description

The 1920s and **The Depression**: 100+ programs/recordings; **World War II**: Drama (50+), news/commentary (100+), public affairs (100+), religion (100+).

V. Related Manuscript Materials

The collection especially has a lot of items in manuscript-related materials that relate to Yiddish-language films. Materials include scripts, production materials, personal papers, oral histories, photographs, and production stills.

VI. Special Interests

Films with Jewish content and Yiddish-language films; films produced by the American Jewish Joint Distribution Committee; films from the 1940s-1960s aimed at raising funds for the state of Israel; early American silent films; Israeli features; Post-war German cinema dealing with Jewish life; film materials on European Jewry and The Holocaust. An archive and study center, the National Center for Jewish Film also rents films, sells videotapes, and leases stock footage.

VII. Accessibility

Research Aids: Listings, card catalog, and files. **"Use" Conditions:** On-site facilities; access by appointment only; fees charged for screening. **Hours:** By appointment. **Published Catalog:** Available, includes film and video lists.

Editor's Note: This is a film archive. The importance of the subject matter is self-evident.

MASSACHUSETTS

I. Organizational Information

James R. Belpedio
P.O. Box 906
Worcester, MA 01613

Personal Collection

II. General Formats

75 records (250 programs); 200 videotapes (1,200 separate programs).

III. General Program Types

Broadcast music (10); variety (50); drama (400); human interest (20); talk entertainment (20); news/commentary (20); documentary (10); politics (15); sports (10); comedy (700); other types in collection (195).

IV. Subject Content Description

Radio's Golden Age: Music (10); variety (50); drama (400); comedy (700); talk entertainment (20); human interest (20); news/commentary (20); public affairs (15); commercial messages (10).

VI. Special Interests

Personal collection of radio programs from the 1930s to the 1950s, mostly adventure, comedy and drama, on tape and record.

VII. Accessibility

Personal listing available upon request.

MICHIGAN

I. Organizational Information

Gerald R. Ford Library
1000 Beal Avenue
Ann Arbor, MI 48109

Individual to Contact

Dr. Frank Mackaman

Phone

(313) 668-2218

II. General Formats

2,000 hours audiotape; 750 hours videotapes, 3/4", 2" VHS.

IV. Subject Content Description

The Gerald R. Ford Library has approximately 700,000 feet of reversal 16mm film with a synchronous 16mm magnetic sound track. The film covered President Ford's 2 1/2 years in the White House.

The Library also has about 700 hours of videotape. The tape was recorded by the White House Communications Agency for the White House Press Office. The programs were taken off the air so they are all network footage.

VII. Accessibility

A 70-page film title list can be copied and sent to requestor for 35¢ per page, or $24.50 for the entire list. Reproduction fees vary but a color corrected film-to-tape transfer would cost approximately $225 per hour.

The 55-page videotape list can be copied for $19.25. The minimum tape-to-tape transfer fee is about $45 per hour plus the cost of the tape.

The reproduction fee for audiocassettes is 50¢ per minute.

For information about most of President Ford's audiotapes, the Gerald R. Ford Library suggests that researchers look at the *Public Papers of the Presidents: Gerald R. Ford.* These five volumes contain all of his public speeches made during his presidency. Your local library may have copies of these books.

Hours: The Library is open for research from 8:45 a.m. to 4:45 p.m., Monday through Friday, except for federal holidays. The Library strongly encourages advance inquiry and notice of a visit.

MICHIGAN

I. Organizational Information Archives of Labor and Urban Affairs
Wayne State University
Walter Reuther Library
Detroit, MI 48202

Individuals to Contact Thomas Featherstone

Margery Long

Phone (313) 577-4024

Profit/Nonprofit Nonprofit

II. General Formats

16mm film, color, 2,000 reels (SOF).

III. General Program Types

News; scripts, limited (50%); daily news footage, 1973-1978; local NBC
affiliate WDIV stock footage.

VII. Accessibility

Inventory list; on-site facilities; copyright restrictions only; tape availabilities, fees, policies on a case-by-case basis. **Hours:** 9 a.m. to 5 p.m.,
Monday through Friday (call for appointments for information).

MICHIGAN

I. Organizational Information

Arnold's Archives
Arnold Jacobsen
1106 Eastwood, S.E.
East Grand Rapids, MI 49506

Phone

(616) 949-1398

Private Collection

II. General Formats

78s and audiotape.

III. General Program Types

Extensive music collection, includes broadcast holdings. 200,000 recordings in the collection.

IV. Subject Content Description

Dance bands, old time radio songs, country-western and folk, comedy, popular vocalists from 1929+, blues and jazz.

"The Spoken Word" portion of the collection includes speaking voices of famous personalities — over 1,200 listed.

"Presidential Voices" includes 139 recordings of various presidents.

VII. Accessibility

Everything has been cataloged and cross-indexed by title and artist. Lists of "Spoken Word" and "Presidential Voices" Collection available.

Editor's Note: The emphasis of the collection is music. Call and inquire as to your specific interest in broadcasting.

MICHIGAN

I. Organizational Information

The G. Robert Vincent Voice Library
Michigan State University
East Lansing, MI 48824-1048

Individual to Contact

Dr. Maurice A. Crane, Director

John Shaw, Audiovisual Head

Rick Peiffer, Technician

Phone

(517) 355-5122

Profit/Nonprofit

Nonprofit

II. General Formats

Audiotapes: 4,800 7" reels, 2,000 cassettes.

III. General Program Types

The National Voice Library was established at Michigan State University in the Spring of 1962 when Dr. Richard E. Chapin, Director of Libraries, offered a home to G. Robert Vincent's Collection of recordings of 8,000 famous voices, far and away the most extensive collection of its kind in the world. The Library, to help its users—major networks and museums as well as students and faculty—recreate a lively sense of the past, has created a storage and retrieval system, cataloged so that any item in the collection can be found and put on a playback machine within 5 minutes. This standard has remained through the years of collection building to five times the original nucleus. With 40,000 utterances, covering the entire range of human experience, cataloged by speaker and subject, all items can still be retrieved within minutes.

IV. Subject Content Description

Strong areas particularly useful to researchers are:

American Political Figures. Recordings of heads of state and governors of states are easier to come by than black leaders in small towns, but these smaller social forces, along with Black, White, and Grey Panthers, Nazis, Klansmen, Weathermen, gays, theosophists, food faddists, and their

150

enemies are also preserved, in statements both passionate and tranquil, on the Libraries' shelves.

The Voice Library has a formidable and famous collection of speeches by Teddy Roosevelt, both in and out of office, and contains large samplings of every president since TR, as well as speeches by unsuccessful candidates for nomination and election. Presidential press conferences, with lists of topics covered, fill the catalog, as do less formal moments in the lives of the first families. The Voice Library has produced an album on the presidency ("Voices of Liberty") and one on the Franklin Roosevelt Administration ("History Speaks").

Foreign Political Figures. Many speeches by heads of foreign states appear in English or with interpolated translations, but frequently dignitaries speak in their native languages, so that scholars conversant with European, Asian, and African tongues can catch the personal styles of a Lenin, a Mussolini, and Eva Peron, a Nasser, a Ho Chi Minh, Chou en Lai, Bao Dai, Franco, Tojo, or Attaturk. As an example, the French radio debates between Valerie Giscard d'Estaing and Francois Mitterand (donated by Michigan State University Professor Emeritus George Joyaux) pit two successive French Presidents of opposing philosophies in spirited debate.

Labor Leaders. Individuals in the MSU School of Labor and Industrial Relations contribute regularly to the large collection of addresses dealing with labor garnered from the unions themselves: convention proceedings, strike votes, labor-oriented radio spots, news broadcasts, and election campaigns: "UMW and Mine Safety," "The Taft-Hartley Act," "Right to Work Legislation," "Early 20th Century Rights of Workers," "The AFL/CIO Merger," "Expulsion of Teamsters," "Political Action," "Foreign Policy," "Civil Rights," "Organizing Farmworkers," "The War Effort," "Industrial Conflict," "Labor and Communism."

Catalog cards commenting on labor issues from outside the union movement, from William Jennings Bryan's classic "Cross of Gold" speech to Communist Party chief William Z. Foster's radio debate with Senator Karl Mundt, also carry a "labor" notation. Changes in policy and strategy often result from internecine warfare on convention floors, debates which are best preserved along with the audience reaction in unedited form in a voice library.

Show Business People. In broadcasts ranging from informal interviews by Alec Wilder, Oscar Brand, Studs Terkel, Eugenia Zuckerman, Beverly Sills, and Billy Taylor, through the more formal Dick Cavett and William Buckley conversations, to the audience-involved Dinah Shore, Merv Griffin, Mike Douglas, Phil Donahue, and Oprah Winfrey shows, popular performers crowd the air with shoptalk and opinions; even notably publicity-shy performers like Marlon Brando and George C. Scott. The tradition goes back to the earliest days of sound recording, to the likes of Eva Tanguay, Sarah Bernhardt, Edwin Booth, Joseph Jefferson, William Gillette, and George M. Cohan. From Phineas T. Barnum to the current rock stars, the heroes of popular culture often display themselves as name droppers, praising and criticizing the "greats" with whom they work.

The Media Past and Present. The late George Garabedian, president of Mark 56 Records, which preserves classic radio on discs, donated his entire canon of 180 recordings to the Voice Library. Radio entrepreneurs Jack Carney of KMOX St. Louis and John Salisbury of KXL Portland, Oregon, have contributed nostalgic collections of their own creation, welcome additions to the various Golden Age Collections purchased in earlier years. In September 1981 the Voice Library received form private collector Anthony Janak 5,000 boxed and indexed tapes covering news and public interest broadcasts made during 15-year period over six television networks and six radio stations in greater Manhattan. Mike Whorf, formerly of Detroit radio station WJR, contributed to the Voice Library the masters of most of his famous "Kaleidoscope" radio series, which was broadcast in the Midwest for many years.

Academic Lectures and Demonstrations. The Voice Library has the raw data "notes" from which edited copy is created, like the interviews which grew into former Michigan State University Professor Milton Rokeach's book, *Three Christs At Ypsilanti*, and the tapes of Michigan governors, legislators, and educators which became a dissertation on the funding of higher education in Michigan.

The Canadian Broadcasting Company donated academic lectures by Galbraith, Steiner, Ward, Dubos, Heyerdahl, Myrdal, and Zuckerman, among others; the Jeffery Norton Company's largesse includes lectures by Highet, Edel, Spender, Van Doren, Oppenheimer, Krutch, Reik, Montagu, in a gift of more than two hundred talks. The "Wingspread" tapes, covering more than a thousand conferences, come as a gift from the Johnson Foundation, and the "Common Ground" broadcasts are a gift from the Stanley Foundation. National Public Radio and Television and their local affiliates have been both benefactors to and beneficiaries of the Voice Library.

Sports. Grandslam homeruns, touchdowns, knockouts, and great moments from racing stand ready for reliving in the Library, along with more placid interviews with the likes of Cobb, Matthewson, Gehrig, Ruth, Rockne, Namath, Grange, and Lombardi. The Voice Library owns 185 *Sports*

Illustrated interviews with past and present athletes. The Voice Library monitors daily sports broadcasts and keeps a running file of the exultant and philosophical statements of winners and losers alike.

Campus and Local History. The Voice Library has become a repository for Michigan State University and local community history. The Library has a complete set of the oral history of East Lansing collected as a bicentennial project and has itself produced a Michigan sesquicentennial program from its own holdings. Hundreds of interviews of local service-men, recorded on the battlefields of Europe in the closing days of World War II, were donated to the Library in 1974 by Jack Parker, a long-time Lansing resident. The discs were converted to modern open-reel magnetic tape for easy retrieval and each interview is cataloged by the name of the interviewee. A decade later, Robert Ripps, a Bethlehem, PA collector, donated his home recordings of news broadcasts made daily during the World War II years.

Jazz and Popular Song. The Institute for Popular Culture Studies at Northeastern Illinois University has donated hundreds of examples of ethnic popular music, songs of the KKK, of sexist stereotype, of the trade union movement, from World Wars I and II, Korea and Vietnam, of protest and counterculture, categorized for maximum use to social historians. G. Robert Vincent, for many years, recorded ASCAP banquets and other functions at which legendary figures like Berlin, Rodgers, Lerner, and others performed their own works. These are now part of the Voice Library Collection.

Literary Figures. From George Bernard Shaw to Tom Wolfe, writers have been performers, playing themselves at parties, making prose and verse exciting by dint of personality and dining out, like Brendan Behan and Dylan Thomas, on pixie charm. In 1985 the Library of Michigan gave its entire collection of authors reading their own works to the Voice Library. The Voice Library itself records the likes of Nelson Algren, James T. Farrell, and Meyer Levin when they appear on campus; more frequently it dubs readings and interviews from educational and commercial radio and TV. Authors like A.J. Budrys and Harlan Ellison have been interviewed in their quarters on campus and the tapes added to the Science Fiction Oral History Association's Collection, housed at the Voice Library.

VII. Accessibility

Card catalog, computer access (not yet completed). **Published Catalog:** *A Dictionary Catalog of the G. Robert Vincent Voice Library at Michigan State University* (G.K. Hall & Co., 1975).

MICHIGAN

I. Organizational Information

Merle G. Perry Archives
Alfred P. Sloan Museum
1221 East Kearsley Street
Flint, MI 48503

Individuals to Contact

David White

Carol deKalands

Profit/Nonprofit

Nonprofit

II. General Formats

400 reels, mainly 16mm film; some videotapes.

III. General Program Types

News.

V. Related Manuscript Materials

Scripts for TV footage.

VI. Special Interests

Film, local doctors, 1920s; scenes of early history, cars, hospital; Chicago World's Fair; WWII efforts; RAH RAH; Buick and Buick promotionals; 1950s — 400 reels — footage — local television — Ch 12.

VII. Accessibility

Database computer access; on-site facilities case-by-case; restricted access case-by-case; fee charges on case-by-case basis. **Hours:** 9 a.m. to 5 p.m., Monday through Friday (best to call for appointment).

MICHIGAN

I. Organizational Information

Gene Bradford
19706 Elizabeth
St. Clair Shores, MI 48080

Individual to Contact

Gene Bradford
(Private Collection)

II. General Formats

Audiotapes (10,000 more or less).

IV. Subject Content Description

Radio's Golden Age; scripts, production materials, personal papers.

VI. Special Interests

Children (kid) shows; westerns; soaps and serials (cereals).

VII. Accessibility

Incomplete listing, hunt-and-peck. No access—no sales; trade only. Owner's comment: "This is a hobby that got away from me — there is more material than I can listen to in a lifetime!"

MINNESOTA

I. Organizational Information

Minnesota Historical Society
Sound and Visual Collections
Audio Visual Library
690 Cedar Street
St. Paul, MN 55101

Individual to Contact

Bonnie Wilson

Phone

(612) 296-1275

Profit/Nonprofit

Nonprofit

II. General Formats

Reel-to-reel, cassette, 16mm film. Videotape: all different formats.

III. General Program Types

News/political.

V. Related Manuscript Materials

Scripts and personal papers.

VI. Special Interests

Hubert Humphrey, most documentation speeches, television appearances, news releases for candidates. Political figures, 107 cubic feet of film/video (leaders). 151 cubic feet of sound recordings on political leaders.

VII. Accessibility

Inventories by collection; on-site facilities (some satellite storage--entire collection will be housed together in 1992); restrictions and fees on a case-by-case basis. **Hours:** Monday, 8:30 a.m. to 8:30 p.m.; Tuesday through Saturday, 8:30 a.m. to 5 p.m.

MINNESOTA

I. Organizational Information

Old Radio Shows & Memorabilia
424 E. 1st St.
Waconia, MN 55387

Individual to Contact

Dale L. Hilk
(Private Collection)

Phone

(612) 442-2926

II. General Formats

LPs and cassette tapes.

III. General Program Types

Variety, 200 recordings/programs; drama, 100; news/commentary, 10; documentary, 100; commercial messages, 3; comedy, 300; other types, 100.

IV. Subject Content Description

Radio's Golden Age: 700 programs; **World War II:** 100.

V. Related Manuscript Materials

Fibber McGee and Molly scripts.

VI. Special Interests

Playing original radio shows through my original 1930s model Philco radio.

VII. Accessibility

This is a personal collection and has no research aids.

MISSISSIPPI

I. Organizational Information
News Film Collection
Mississippi Dept. of Archives and History
P.O. Box 571
Jackson, MS 39205-0571

Individual to Contact
Dan Den-Bleyker

Phone
(601) 359-6874

Profit/Nonprofit
Nonprofit

III. General Program Types

Information/news, mostly 16mm film, some videotapes.

VI. Special Interests

Black/white and color material related to Mississippi; news footage; local television; civil rights movement; politically oriented footage.

VII. Accessibility

Index to newsfilm; on-site facilities; no fee for viewing (copying/research fees). **Hours:** Call for appointment. **Published Catalog:** *NewsFilm Index: A guide to the Newsfilm Collection, 1954-1971.* Call for information.

Film Usage Policy:
1. Because of the time necessary to fill film viewing requests, users wishing to view film are requested to make an appointment to view material three days in advance.

2. Users are responsible for costs, as listed later, incurred in reference service, film duplication, videocassette duplication, or transfer of film to video.

Reference
One hour of the Curator's time is allotted without charge for answering each reference request. The patron will be charged $15 per hour, flat rate, for each hour in excess of this first hour. (Retrieval of requested reels, film editor operation for viewing, and reshelving of requested reels is not considered a reference service and, therefore, not chargeable.)

Duplication

    A. Charges will be levied for mileage, equivalent to authorized state government mileage charges (currently 20¢ per mile), and for meals and lodging costs incurred in duplication.

    B. For duplication services performed in-house (currently only reference copy videocassettes can be produced), a charge of $15 per hour, flat rate, and materials costs will be levied.

    C. Vendor costs will be billed directly to the patron. However, no vendor duplication work will be authorized by the Department until the patron supplies the vendor with a purchase order number or other vendor-acceptable work authorization.

3. Before reference copies are supplied for pre-production or any of the Department's film used in production, an agreement will be signed between the Department and the user stating each party's rights and obligations.

4. Each user of material from the Department's film collections will agree to indemnify the Department for any liabilities incurred by the Department as a result of misuses by the user of the Department's film or videotape material.

5. The Department will select the vendor to provide duplication services. The Department is not responsible for the quality of duplication work performed by the vendor.

6. Film or video credit will be given as "Audio-Visual Records, Mississippi Department of Archives and History" for film or video material used in a production.

7. If the Department's material is used in a production, the Department will be supplied with a complimentary copy of the final product, to include all episodes of multi-episode productions. The format of the copy will be determined by the Department.

8. Any film or video duplicates received by a patron and subsequent authorized reproductions that are not used in the production will be returned to the Department upon completion of the production.

9. After a license is issued, if additional rights are requested, the original license fee will not be deducted form the costs of additional rights.

10. The Mississippi Department of Archives and History reserves the right to discount for quantity use.

I. Organizational Information
Harry S. Truman Library
Audiovisual
24 Highway and Delaware
Independence, MO 64050

Individuals to Contact
Ray Geselbracht
Pauline Testerman

Phone
(816) 833-1400

Profit/Nonprofit
Nonprofit

II. General Formats

268 hours 53 minutes LP-16" or 78s discs; 274 hours 41 minutes audiotape; 81 hours videotape (3/4", audio 7-1/2, 3-3/4).

III. General Program Types

Broadcast music, variety, drama, news/commentary, documentary, politics, comedy, and speeches of President Truman and others.

IV. Subject Content Description

The Depression: Music, politics.
World War II: Music, news/commentary, public affairs, politics.
Cold War Radio: Music, variety, drama, news/commentary, politics.
Cold War Television: News/commentary, politics.
Korean War Era: Variety, comedy, talk entertainment, news/commentary, politics.
Vietnam War Era: Music.

VI. Special Interests

Speeches, documentaries, newsreels relating to President Truman and persons and events from his administration.

VII. Accessibility

List of speeches of President Truman; subject and chronology files. On-site facilities; reproductions available for purchase.

MISSOURI

I. Organizational Information

Oral History of Broadcasting in Kansas City
Rockhurst College
1100 Rockhurst Road
Kansas City, MO 64110

Individual to Contact   William J. Ryan
Personal Collection

Phone   (816) 926-4000 X4042

Profit/Nonprofit   Nonprofit

II. General Formats

85 audiotape and history cassettes.

IV. Subject Content Description

All oral histories are taped interviews with individuals who have worked in any part of the broadcasting field in Kansas City and the broadcast region of Kansas City since 1922. Includes radio and TV. Individuals include pioneer engineers and announcers, early and contemporary radio and television news announcers, management, artists, stage hands, and continuity writers. Includes one interview with an engineer who worked with mechanical "flying spot" television. Some tapes have been transcribed.

V. Related Manuscript Materials

A few typed transcripts are available.

VII. Accessibility

Currently, this collection is not available to the general public. It is a private collection owned by the interviewee and is being used for his own research. However, individual research requests will be considered.

A list of names in the collection is available; transcripts of some tapes have been typed; access is restricted at this time. **On-site facilities:** audiotape player. **Restrictions:** Individual requests in writing, not open to public. No exchanges, no mailings. **Hours:** Not open except by individual appointment; all tapes restricted to researchers at this time.

MISSOURI

I. Organizational Information
University of Missouri-Kansas City
Marr Sound Archives/Miller Nichols Library
5100 Rockhill Road
Kansas City, MO 64110-2499

Individual to Contact Chuck Haddix

Phone (816) 235-2798

Profit/Nonprofit Nonprofit

II. General Formats

2,633 LP-16" ETs or 78s discs; 1,048 12" pressings; 6,759 audiotapes; and 7 1/2 and 3 3/4ips audiotapes.

V. Related Manuscript Materials

700 NBC radio scripts.

VI. Special Interests

Popular music, jazz, radio programs, and newscasts — The American Experience as reflected in recorded sound.

VII. Accessibility

Listing of approximately 1/3 of the collection; presently working on an index of the collection. **On-site Facilities:** Listening and recording facilities; **Restrictions:** Up to discretion of sound recording specialist; **Tape availabilities, fees, etc.:** Tapes made within "fair use" clause of copyright laws. **Hours:** 1-4 p.m. Monday through Friday.

MISSOURI

I. Organizational Information

KSDK-TV/Multi-Media, Inc.
Archives Five/KSDK-TV
1000 Market St.
St. Louis, MO 63101

Individual to Contact Bob Garger

Phone (314) 444-5110

Profit/Nonprofit Profit

II. General Formats

520 LP-16" ETS or 78s discs; 120 audiotapes; 9,517 videotape cassettes, 3/4" and Beta Cam.

III. General Program Types

Broadcast music (600 recordings); variety (300 recordings); drama (135 feature films); information talk (300 programs); news-commentary (22,800 hrs. news footage); documentary (1,800 series reports); politics (100 commercials); commercial messages (4,000 commercials); sports (1,315 hrs. sports footage); comedy (400 cartoon films).

IV. Subject Content Description

Archives Five is the only intact news film collection in St. Louis dating back to the early 1950s with a few clips going back to 1929. The Collection includes numerous NBC Network, INS film reports on national and international stories of the past 43 years—since KSDK-TV went on the air.

V. Related Manuscript Materials

Nearly 40,000 news program scripts dating back to 1961.

VII. Accessibility

Thousands of news cards dating to 1980; computer printouts of 1975-1979 news stories, and computer access to stories from September 1986. On-site facilities limited to newsroom viewing on a limited basis. **Restrictions:** Management is agreeable to the sale of generic footage or spot footage for restricted educational or commercial uses, but management reserves the copyright for all materials. Price generally is $100 per minute of footage provided, depending on the subsequent use of the footage.

NEW JERSEY

   I. Organizational Information　　　　　　　　　　Richard J. Biunno
　　　　　　　　　　　　　　　　　　　　　　　　　　　　5 Potter Place
　　　　　　　　　　　　　　　　　　　　　　　　　　Milltown, NJ 08850

      Individual to Contact　　　　　　　　　　　　Richard J. Biunno

      Phone　　　　　　　　　　　　　　　　　　(201) 846-2225

  II. General Formats

     2,000 discs; 4,000 audiotapes; 1,300 1 7/8 VHS videotapes.

  III. General Program Types

     Broadcast music (2,500 recordings/programs); news/commentary (500); politics (500); sports (3,500).

  VI. Special Interests

     Play-by-play of sporting events from actual broadcasts.

  VII. Accessibility

     Index. Restricted access.

NEW JERSEY

I. Organizational Information

NFL Films
330 Fellowship Road
Mt. Laurel, NJ 08054

For complete description, see Culver City, CA, Fox Hills Video.

I. Organizational Information
John E. Allen, Inc.
116 North Avenue
Park Ridge, NJ 07656

Individual to Contact
John E. Allen

Phone
(201) 391-3299

Profit/Nonprofit
Profit

II. General Formats

Hundreds of videotapes, 1", U-Matic, Ed Beta; thousands of 16mm and 35mm films.

III. General Program Types

John E. Allen, Inc. is a motion picture stock footage library and laboratory, providing archival quality restoration services.

IV. Subject Content Description

The John E. Allen, Inc. Motion Picture Collection dates from 1896 to 1955. In excess of twenty five million feet of 35mm and 16mm materials are available. The archive is located 50 minutes from Manhattan by public transportation. Film-to-film and film-to-tape transfers are handled by our own technicians.

Other Categories of Special Interest

Kinograms, 1915-1931. Original negatives, prints, trims, and outs of a major newsreel which had camera crews covering news in the U.S. and abroad.

Telenews, 1947-1953. Original negatives, prints, trims, and outs. A syndicated film service for television news programs, patterned after theatrical newsreels. Covered news from all over the world.

World War I. Approximately 250,000 feet of 35mm newsreels and documentaries of the time, covering various aspects and views of the war.

U.S. and European titles include "The German Side of the War," "On the Italian Battlefront," and "France in Arms."

World War II. Approximately 100,000 feet of 35mm film materials. Miscellaneous newsreels include some Wochenschau and Soviet films.

Conflicts. Spanish-American War, Mexican Revolution, Russian Revolution, Hungarian Revolution (1919-1920), Sino-Japanese War, Spanish Civil War, French-Indochina War, and Korean War.

Industry, 1910-1950s. 350,000 feet of 35mm materials covering a broad range of businesses in the U.S. and abroad.

Transportation, 1900-1950s. 150,000 feet of 35mm materials related to all types of transportation, autos, aviation, ships, and railroads.

Educational/Ethnographic/Travel/Nature, 1910-1940s. Approximately 800,000 feet of 35mm film, almost exclusively black and white. Materials from almost every country in the world include such subjects as Native Americans—North and South America; early polar exploration; early everyday life in Europe, China, Japan, Brazil, etc.

Features, 1905-1950s. Shorts and feature-length comedies, westerns, animation, and other genres, particularly strong in the silent era.

V. Related Manuscript Materials

Dramatic motion picture production scripts; production materials from motion picture production, stills, lobby cards, pressbooks, posters, books; some personal papers which are motion picture production-related.

VII. Accessibility

Listings, card catalog, index, computer access, and other means of accessibility to the collection. On-site facilities include viewing equipment for film and tape. **Restrictions:** Window coded videotapes available. **Tape availability, fees, etc.:** Footage charges are based on a production market. Research charges for drawing together material and pre-selection of footage are based on the complexity of the request; the average research fee is $150 which includes viewing time. Appointments for viewing should be made in advance. **Hours:** Five days a week by appointment.

NEW JERSEY

I. Organizational Information

Yesteryear Museum
20 Harriet Drive
Whippany, NJ 07981

Individual to Contact

Lee Munsick
Director

Phone

Profit/Nonprofit

Nonprofit (chartered in NJ)

II. General Formats

Discs (180,000); 3,000 audiotapes; 1,000 videotapes, mostly 1/2" VHS.

III. General Program Types

All types with exception of sports.

VII. Accessibility

Limited, by previous arrangement.

NEW MEXICO

I. Organizational Information

Historical Film Collection
New Mexico State Records Center and Archive
404 Montezuma
Santa Fe, NM 87503

Individuals to Contact   Richard Salazar
                                                   Ron Montoya

Phone   (505) 827-7332

Profit/Nonprofit   Nonprofit

II. General Formats

16mm film, some videotapes (3/4, 1/2).

III. General Program Types

Information/news, KGGM-TV and KOAT-TV newsfilm.

VI. Special Interests

Donated news footage (CBS—KGGM-TV, ABC—KOAT-TV); films related
to tourism, history of New Mexico; also film footage related to Mary
Pickford, Tom Mix, and Native Americans.

VII. Accessibility

Listings include inventory of historical films. On-site facilities; fees and
availabilities on a case-by-case basis. **Hours:** 8 a.m. to 5 p.m., Monday
through Friday. Call for appointment.

NEW YORK

I. Organizational Information

Celia Nachatovitz Memorial Library
of Classic Television Commercials
Brooklyn College of
The City University of New York
Brooklyn, NY 11210

Individual to Contact   Phil Messina

Phone   (718) 780-5585

Profit/Nonprofit   Nonprofit

II. General Formats

Videotapes (1", 3/4", or 1/2").

III. General Program Types

Commercial messages. Celia Nachatovitz Diamant Memorial Library of Classic Television Commercials' Collection consists of 69 classic television commercials (almost 2 hours worth of material) that were done both live and on film during the decade prior to 1958.

IV. Subject Content Description

Sponsors: Lucky Strike, Old Gold, Muriel Cigars, Kool Cigarettes, Marlboro, Robert Burns Cigars, Winston, Chesterfield Cigarette, Ajax, SOS, Raid, Kleenex, Mr. Clean, Tide, Bufferin, Alka-Selzer, Band-Aid, Gillette, Remington, Mum Deodorant, Pepsodent, Clairol, Crest, Lipton Chicken Soup, Ritz Crackers, Heinz Worstershire, Skippy Peanut Butter, E-Z Pop Popcorn, Jello, Kroger Eggs, Pet Evaporated Milk, Wesson Oil, Nestle's Quick, Maypo, Anderson Pea Soup, Chinese Jello, Maxwell House, Lipton Tea, Wilkens Coffee, Hamms Beer, Carling Beer, Piels Beer, Schwepps Tonic Water, Rheingold, Budweiser, Ballantine Beer, Gallo Wine, Bardal, Delco, Speedway 79 Power Fuel, Esso, Chevron, Bank of America, Yellow Pages, Robert Hall, Keds, Chemstrand Co., RCA, Bulova Watches, Westinghouse, Dodge, Chevrolet, Renault Dophine.

VII. Accessibility

The facility is able to make this collection available to qualified researchers and nonprofit organizations and schools for a moderate duplication charge provided that an adequate supply of videotape and payment accompany the order.

Material will be duplicated on the following formats for the following fees:

1" Type C	$200
3/4" U-Matic Cassette, 1/2" VHS	$100
1/2" Reel-to-Reel	$ 75

Please mail all tapes and payment to the attention of Robert C. Williams, Chairman. Make checks payable to the Department of Television and Radio. Tapes will be returned to you via mail. Should you need additional information, please feel free to contact Phil Messina at (718) 780-5585.

Editor's Note: Small but unique collection of TV commercials.

NEW YORK

I. Organizational Information

Harris W. Davis
301 Baltic Street
Brooklyn, NY 11201

Individual to Contact

Harris W. Davis

Phone

(718) 625-3885

Profit/Nonprofit

Nonprofit

II. General Formats

145 disks (LP-16" ETs or 78s); 114 audiotapes; 74 (+41) videotape, LP, VHS.

III. General Program Types

Broadcast music (66 recordings/programs); variety (21); drama (32); human interest (6); talk entertainment (1); information talk (20); news/commentary (49); documentary (19); politics (12); sports (2); comedy (15); public affairs (95).

IV. Subject Content Description

The 1920s: News/commentary (5 programs/recordings); public affairs (2); politics (3); sports (3); religion (2).

The Depression: Music (13 programs/recordings); variety (2); comedy (1); talk information (1); human interest (1); news/commentary (3); public affairs (34).

Radio's Golden Age: Music (20 programs/recordings); variety (14); drama (12); comedy (13); talk information (2); human interest (1); news/ commentary (1) public affairs (1) politics (1); sports (2).

172

World War II: Variety (4 programs/recordings); drama (2); comedy (1); talk information (1); news/commentary (31); public affairs (40); politics (4).

The Cold War Radio: Music (7 programs/recordings); drama (1); news/commentary (4); public affairs (6).

Television's Golden Age: Music (3 programs/recordings); variety (1); drama (4); talk entertainment (1); talk information (4); news/commentary (1); public affairs (3).

Korean War Era: Music (2 programs/recordings); public affairs (3); sports (1).

Vietnam War Era: Music (1 program/recording); talk information (2); public affairs (5); politics (4).

Contemporary Programming: Music (22 programs/recordings); drama (13); talk information (10); human interest (4); news/commentary (4); public affairs (10); politics (3); documentaries (10).

VI. Special Interests

The main thrust of this collection is the speeches and life of President Franklin Delano Roosevelt; also any information regarding World Wars I and II.

VII. Accessibility

Card catalog; on-site facilities include VCR, cassette players, 78rpm phono; will loan to responsible people; no charge for loan. **Hours:** Evenings best, 6 to 10 p.m. Call for appointment.

NEW YORK

I. Organizational Information

Ray Stanich
173 Columbia Heights
Brooklyn, NY 11201

Sponsor

Private

II. General Formats

Disc (LP- 16" ETs or 78s): 400 (music). Audiotape: 4,000 radio programs, 7.5/3.75 ips. Videotape: VHS-SP-LP-EP.

III. General Program Types

Music, 30%; variety, 30%; drama, 30%; comedy, 10%.

IV. Subject Content Description

See **Program Index**. Individual programs are listed with page numbers directing user to collection.

V. Related Manuscript Materials

Scripts.

VI. Special Interests

The collections specialize in serious music programs (over 1,000 operas) such as Railroad Hour, Nelson Eddy, John Charles Thomas, Family Hour, Mario Lanza; dramas by Ray Bradbury, Arch Oboler, Ellery Queen, Sherlock Holmes; personalities such as country-western stars, opera stars, Snooks, Bickersons, Vera Lynn, Orson Welles, Vaughn Monroe, Andrews Sisters, Mills Brothers, Ink Spots, Stan Freberg, Fred Allen, etc. Collection spans 1932 to present.

VII. Accessibility

Has assisted in several research projects. Willing to furnish copies to serious researchers on a trade basis (hour-for-hour) or will provide copies for cost of tape and time. Have produced over 100 radio logs (list/cost available).

NEW YORK

I. Organizational Information   David S. Siegel Radio Archives
P.O. Box 610
Croton-on-Hudson, NY 10520

Individual to Contact   David S. Siegel

Phone   (914) 962-3680

Profit/Nonprofit   Nonprofit

II. General Formats

Audiotapes, approximately 65,000 hours.

III. General Program Types

All types.

IV. Subject Content Description

Very few programs dated in the 1920s; a fair number of Depression or 1930s programs; a large number of 1940s and 1950s programs; a fair number of contemporary broadcasts. Catalog is probably the best source for breakdown.

V. Related Manuscript Materials

1,000+ scripts; 1,000 *Radio Magazines* (1920s, 1930s, 1940s, 1950s, etc.). Collection of books dealing with radio numbers over 700. Also has radio interviews on tape.

VII. Accessibility

Catalog: Approximately 100 pages and lists approximately 65,000 hours. It is available for the cost of printing and mailing ($5). Catalog is always "in process of revision" with thousands of programs in the collection not yet listed.

"Use" Conditions: On-site facilities; no restricted access. **Tape Availabilities, Fees, etc.:** Trade. **Hours:** To be arranged.

NEW YORK

I. Organizational Information

Rod Serling Archives
The School of Communications
Ithaca College
Ithaca, NY 14850

Individual to Contact   Dr. T.W. Bohn

Phone   (607) 274-3895

Profit/Nonprofit   Nonprofit

II. General Formats

Disc (LP - 16" ETs or 78s): 35+ transcription recordings.
Audiotape: 14 reel-to-reel.
Videotape: 120+ 3/4", VHS, 2", 1" video.

III. General Program Types

Drama, 170+.

IV. Subject Content Description

Due in large part to his family, friends and colleagues, the Rod Serling Archives have continued to grow. Today the Archives represent the most complete collection of Rod Serling's work in private hands. Holdings include 116, 16mm "Twilight Zone" films with the remaining 40 on videotape, duplicate videotapes of all "Twilight Zone" episodes, and 140 "Twilight Zone" scripts (many with Rod's handwritten notations in them). Additionally, the Archives is a major source of negatives and stills for such publications as the *Twilight Zone Companion* and the *Twilight Zone Magazine*. Several *Night Gallery* episodes are available on both film and videotape as are Rod's early and later works in television, including *Requiem for a Heavyweight* and *The Time Element*. The Archives also has recordings of radio dramas created and acquired by Rod in the late 1940s and 1950s and many books from his private library.

V. Related Manuscript Materials

Scripts: Over 200 original and xeroxed scripts from "The Twilight Zone," "Night Gallery," "The Loner," "Playhouse 90," et al.; many with Serling's personal notations.

Production Materials: Production call sheets, correspondence, advertising from "The Twilight Zone."

Personal Papers: Congratulatory letters and responses, personal notes, dictaphone belts.

Oral Histories: Miscellaneous biographical information available.

VI. Special Interests

For several years until his death in 1975, Rod Serling taught advanced screenwriting in the School of Communications at Ithaca College. After his death, his wife Carol Serling donated his personal collection of films, scripts, and related materials to Ithaca College. The Rod Serling Archives represent the work of an artist who has given television some of its most insightful, creative, and meaningful moments. It is a wealth of material for historians, scholars, and anyone who has an interest in Rod Serling and the early days of television.

VII. Accessibility

An index is forthcoming as is a catalog (price to be announced). On-site facilities.

A complete detailed listing of all the Archives' holdings is available at a cost of $2.50.

Call for hours and additional information.

NEW YORK

I. Organizational Information

ABC News Library Information Department
ABC News
47 W. 66th St.
New York, NY 10023

Individual to Contact   Sara Meyerson

Phone   (212) 887-4377

Profit/Nonprofit   Profit

II. General Formats

Videotapes (3/4 Beta Cam) and film (16mm).

III. General Program Types

Some materials on human interest, information talk, and commercial messages. The entire collection — 350,000 videotapes — includes programs, outtakes, stock shots; 50 million feet of film.

IV. Subject Content Description

World War II: National Archive material incorporated into the collection on human interest, news/commentary, public affairs.

Cold War Television: Material 1963-1976; 80,000 stories on film of human interest, news/commentary, and public affairs.

Vietnam War Era: 50,000 videotapes, 40 million feet of film on news/commentary, public affairs, and politics.

Contemporary Programming: 250 videotapes, 10 million feet of film on news/commentary and public affairs.

V. Related Manuscript Materials

Scripts from evening news from 1970 to the present.

VII. Accessibility

Computer access. Scripts are sold by subscription or individually. Material can be screened at the Sherman Greenberg Libraries, 630 North Ave., New York, NY 10022. For a fee, material is licensed for use.

NEW YORK

I. Organizational Information

CLIO Awards
Film Department
30 E. 59th Street
New York, NY 10022

Phone

(212) 593-1900

II. General Formats

Audiotapes, 16mm reels.

III. General Program Types

Commercials.

IV. Subject Content Description

Radio, TV prints, and slides. Winners roughly 1960 to present.

VI. Special Interests

Yearly CLIO journal.

VII. Accessibility

No on-site facilities; rentals for schools and Ad club, $70 per week per reel. **Hours:** 9:30 a.m. to 5 p.m. in the winter; 9:30 a.m. to 4:30 p.m. in the summer.

I. Organizational Information

Columbia University, School of Journalism
Alfred I. Dupont Center for Broadcast Journalism
701 Journalism Building
New York, NY 10027

Individual to Contact	Lesley Kuchek
Phone	(212) 854-5047
Profit/Nonprofit	Nonprofit

II. General Formats

Audiotape, videotape (1,000 3/4" tapes), cassettes reel-to-reel.

III. General Program Types

News, public affairs, and related scripts.

VI. Special Interests

Public affairs — reflect former Dupont Award winners — once a year — dozen given — general excellence awards — given to network television, cable, and radio, all markets of television (writing, production, reporting) — program judged on overall content, etc.

VII. Accessibility

Card catalog by subject/date. **Computer Access:** Archive. On-site facilities; must be viewed in archive; fees charged on a case-to-case basis. **Hours:** Monday through Friday, 9 a.m. to 5 p.m., by appointment only.

NEW YORK

I. Organizational Information

Museum of Television & Radio
23 West 52nd Street
New York, NY 10019

Phone

(212) 752-7684 (Museum offices—recorded)
(212) 752-4690 (recorded announcements)

Sponsor

Institution

II. General Formats

Audio- and videotape.

III. General Program Types

All types represented. 25,000 television (network, cable, and local); 10,000 commercials; 15,000 radio.

IV. Subject Content Description

Television, 1939 to present; Radio, 1920 to present (complete D-Day, VE-Day and VJ-Day coverage, Kennedy assassination); NBC radio programs from 1927-1937; music and entertainment programs. Collection covers the genre of television and radio.

VII. Accessibility

Open to the public. Members of the Museum have priority in reserving playback areas. Serious researchers should make special arrangements with museum personnel. **Card Catalog:** Cross reference by title, subject, production credits, date, network genre, and cast. **Hours:** Closed Monday; Tuesday, Wednesday, Friday, and weekends: 11 a.m. to 6 p.m.; Thursday, 11 a.m. to 8 p.m. Theatre screening series and exhibitions open Friday until 9 p.m.

NEW YORK

I. Organizational Information

NBC News Archival Services
30 Rockefeller Plaza, Rm 922
New York, NY 10112

Individual to Contact

Yuian Chin

Phone

(212) 664-3797

Sponsor

Commercial

II. General Formats

News and documentary, 1940 to present.

VII. Accessibility

Scholarly access to NBC material is provided through the Library of Congress and Museum of Broadcasting ... see their listing.

The purpose of the NBC Archive is to serve the News division. Research and sale footage must be approved by NBC. Outside researchers must request use of the facility by mail, including references and the purpose of the study.

NEW YORK

I. Organizational Information   New York City Municipal Archives
                                                        Division of the
                                                        31 Chambers Street
                                                        New York, NY 10007

Individual to Contact   Kenneth Kobb

Phone   (212) 566-5292

Profit/Nonprofit   Nonprofit

II. General Formats

Two million black/white color images; lots of glass plate images, turn of century, one of the "largest photo collections in New York." Lacquered disc sound recordings, 5,000 cans of 16mm film, some 35mm film. Various formats of audio- and videotape.

III. General Program Types

Music, and news/information, WNYC-TV.

V. Related Manuscript Materials

Scripts, production materials, and personal papers. Good music selection in audiotapes; lacquered transcription of some rare sessions.

VI. Special Interests

WNYC, Municipal broadcast station, supplied most of the holdings. Press conferences, etc. Collection deals heavily with history of city of New York.

VII. Accessibility

Card catalog; computer access (working on database to sound recordings and film); on-site facilities; very minimal access; fees on a case-by-case basis. **Hours:** Call for appointment.

NEW YORK

I. Organizational Information

Sherman Grinberg Film Libraries, Inc.
630 Ninth Avenue
New York, NY 10036

Phone

(212) 765-5170
Fax: (212) 262-1532

Note: For complete description, see Hollywood, CA, Sherman Grinberg Film Libraries, Inc.

NEW YORK

I. Organizational Information

Worldwide Television News
WTN, UPITN, British Pathé News
1995 Broadway
New York, NY 10023

Individuals to Contact

Vincent O'Reilly, Library Manager

Harold Phillips, Chief Librarian

Phone

(212) 362-4440

Profit/Nonprofit

Profit

II. General Formats

Audiotape: 120,000 stories.
Videotape: 100,000, 3/4" video and recently Betacam.
16mm film.

III. General Program Types

Human interest, news/commentary, documentary, politics, sports, comedy (limited). Anything newsworthy, including feature materials.

IV. Subject Content Description

Worldwide Television News (WTN) is a full-service stock footage library, based in New York and London, handling the film and videotape collections of United Press International (UPI) News Film (1963-67), UPITN (WTN) 1967-present) and British Pathé News (1896-1966). WTN, a functioning news-gathering service with principal bureaus in every continent, feeds 24 hours a day to over 1,000 broadcasters, affiliates, and cable network operators around the world, and adds material to its library on a daily basis. WTN is owned by ABC in America, ITN (Independent Television News) in Britain and the Nine Network in Australia.

WTN began as an association between UPI and Fox Movietone News in 1951. Between 1951 and September 30, 1963, UPI-Movietonews provided a daily newsclip service for local television stations in the United States. (This 16mm black and white newsfilm is now held by Twentieth Century-Fox Movietonews, Inc. [q.v.].) In October 1963, Movietonews ceased production of its daily service and UPI assumed responsibility for operation of the news gathering operation, picking up most of the staff.

In 1967, UPI joined forces with ITN in the United Kingdom, founding UPITN, and began servicing networks and stations overseas. The name was changed to Worldwide Television News in 1980.

WTN holds or represents various collections, including:

British Pathé News. Representative for stock footage sales in North America. A limited amount of material is held on videotape in the New York office, but the collection is physically located at Elstree Studios near London, England. British Pathé features weekly newsreel coverage of major events and features (1896-1966). Coverage is strongest for British and British Commonwealth news and features, but there is some coverage of United States events. A microfiche catalog is available for research in the New York office. The Pathé Collection was the footage source for a series of yearly wrapups called the *Time to Remember* series. These are also available for stock footage sale. (Note: There is no connection between the different "Pathé" newsreel companies.)

UPI News Film and UPITN Collection (1963 through mid-1980s). The UPITN Collection covers U.S. and foreign news events and personalities until approximately 1975-1977, when U.S. coverage was phased out. From 1977, coverage is restricted to foreign events. Holds in-depth coverage of events in the United States until the mid-1970s; for example, the file on Selma, Alabama is 5" thick. The Vietnam war at home and abroad is also well covered, with several drawers of index cards describing footage of pro- and antiwar demonstrations in the United States and in foreign countries and battle coverage.

As a rule, stories originating in North or South America were covered by the U.S. bureau, and stories elsewhere by the British bureau. However, in the case of Vietnam, coverage was coordinated out of New York. The New York office, therefore, retains camera original and all the outtakes. The collection is also strong on coverage of the Middle East, Iran, South Africa and Israel. South African and Middle East coverage is strong in the early 1960s, when the situation there received far less attention from other news gathering services. During the days of the Iranian hostage crisis, as well, the UPITN cameras were among the last Western eyes to remain in the country.

As a general rule, the film in the UPITN Collection resides in New York if shot in the United States. If shot elsewhere, the original will be at ITN in London. If the material was used by WTN, a copy will also be in the New York library.

VII. Accessibility

Open to the public. Available for licensing and reuse, subject to restrictions. Research fees charged.

Research requests accepted by mail, telephone, and in person (by appointment only). It is advisable to make an initial call to one of the librarians to determine how the library can best serve the client's needs. If a large amount of material is being sought, generally a follow-up letter and search list would be the next step. The card catalog is available for use by clients (by appointment). Fees are not charged for client access to the card catalog; fees apply for librarian services and screening.

Researchers and clients should allow sufficient time for film and videotapes to be brought in from the WTN storage facility in Fort Lee, New Jersey.

Rights: Full rights held to all material. **Licensing:** Available for licensing and reuse, subject to restrictions. License fees charged (fee schedule available). **Restrictions:** Restrictions apply in some cases, depending on intended use. Additional clearances and permissions may be required for commercial use of material. **Viewing Facilities:** Film (16mm); videotape (3/4"). **Duplication Facilities:** Videotape. Film-to-videotape transfers are made out-of-house. **Cataloging:** Material from the UPI News Film and UPITN Collection can be accessed through a card catalog. The catalog is a "small entry" system with most subjects filed under their own alphabetical listings.

WTN and ITN material (1980-present) is indexed on a computer located in London and can be accessed in New York. A printed catalog is available to access the *Roving Report* Collection, containing a general index and special indexes covering countries and personalities.

A microfiche catalog of the British Pathé News Collection is available in the New York office.

I. Organizational Information

Eastman Audio Archives
Eastman School of Music
University of Rochester
26 Gibbs Street
Rochester, NY 14604

Individuals to Contact

Suzanne Stover
Archivist

Phone

(716) 274-3180

Profit/Nonprofit

Nonprofit

II. General Formats

6,700 instantaneous disks (12" and 16"); 20,000 audiotape reels (only 5% are broadcast).

III. General Program Types

Broadcast music and information talk about music (very few).

VI. Special Interests

Five percent of the collection is broadcast material, all music or talks about music. Emphasis on 20th-century American composition, Eastman School performances; Annual Festivals of American Music; broadcasts over NBC or CBS; milestones in the History of Music; milestones in American music; NBC University of the Air; orchestras of the nation's broadcasts, 1933-present, with emphasis on 1930s-1940s. Ninety-nine percent broadcasts from the Eastman School of Music.

VII. Accessibility

Card catalog; computer access only to recordings preserved by transfer. Playback services by appointment.

NEW YORK

I. Organizational Information

International Museum of Photography
at George Eastman House
Film Department
900 East Avenue
Rochester, NY 14607

Individuals to Contact

Jan-Christopher Horak
Curator of Film

Paolo Cherchi Usai
Assistant Curator, Film Study Center

Edward E. Stratmann
Assistant Curator, Preservation

Ruth C. Kanner
Cataloging Officer

Kay McRae
Administrative Assistant

Robin B. Bolger
Curatorial Assistant
Photo and Paper Collections

Phone

(716) 271-3361
FAX (716) 271-3970

II. General Formats

Film — all formats and some television kinescopes.

III. General Program Types

The Film Collection: The archive's collection of approximately 13,500 titles comprises of feature films, shorts, documentaries, newsreels, amateur films, and television programs, produced between 1894 and the present.

The silent film collection at George Eastman House is unsurpassed in the world. It includes early British, French, and American cinema (pre-1914), the films of Cecil B. DeMille and Thomas H. Ince, westerns with William S. Hart, Maurice Tourneur, all of Greta Garbo's surviving films, and films with Louise Brooks. The collection is also rich in Weimar cinema, classic Hollywood silents from Metro-Goldwyn-Mayer and other independent studios as well as early American avantgarde filmmakers like James Sibley Watson and Theodore Huff.

The studio era after the coming of sound is represented by MGM, including the studio's Technicolor negatives, Reliable Studios, Nazi film productions, and many French films from the 1930s and 1940s. In the post WWII era, Italian, Swedish, and American films are strongest.

The Department also has many classical documentaries, including the Lothar Wolff Collection, the Third World Newsreel Archives, the films of Emile deAntonio, and many younger documentaries.

Television is represented by a collection of kinescopes from the 1950s and 1960s, as well as a growing collection of video.

VII. Accessibility

Once preservation needs have been accommodated, it is a fundamental aim of the archive to promote the study and availability of its films. To this end, the Film Study Center exists to encourage and provide private viewings for *bona fide* researchers. A small fee is charged.

The archive's viewing facilities consist of individual rooms with flatbed viewing machines, videotape monitors, a small projection room, as well as the Dryden Theatre and the Peck Curtis Theatre. A microfilm reader is also available.

Applicants are required to send a written request at least 3 weeks in advance to the Assistant Curator, Film Study Center, providing a list of titles for films or other related materials, and indicating a suggested time period for visiting the Center. Film viewing fees are free for students from the University of Rochester, the Rochester Institute of Technology, the Visual Studies Workshop, S.U.N.Y. Brockport. As with external screenings, copyright clearance must be obtained before material can be supplied for publication.

Research in the paper collections is free of charge.

NEW YORK

I. **Organizational Information**

Balfer Audio Archives
Syracuse University
222 Waverly Ave.
Syracuse, NY 13244-2010

Individual to Contact

Susan Stinson
Collection Manager

Phone

(315) 443-3477

II. General Formats

Discs (LP - 16" ETs or 78s) 175,000 commercially released; pressings; audiotapes (approximately 50,000 noncommercial).

III. General Program Types

All types from mid 1930s — early 1960s. Scripts and printed material in library.

VI. Special Interests

Soundtrack from TV shows, radio shows; test pressing from Columbia — from mid-1930s - 1963.

VII. Accessibility

In process of being cataloged. Advance requests necessary for use at library facility. **Hours:** 8:30 a.m. to 5 p.m., Monday through Friday.

NORTH CAROLINA

I. Organizational Information

Jim Blythe Library
941 Redding Rd.
Asheboro, NC 27203

Individual to Contact

Jim Blythe

Phone

(919) 629-4039

Profit/Nonprofit

Nonprofit

II. General Formats

Disc (LP - 16" ETs or 78s): Approximately 150:16"/150:78s.
Videotape: 9,000 hours 3 3/4ips, 1/4 T.

III. General Program Types

Broadcast music (est. 1,000 hrs. recordings/programs); variety (est. 1,000 hrs.); drama (est. 4,000 hrs.); comedy (est. 3,000 hrs.).

IV. Subject Content Description

See **Program Index**. Individual programs are listed with page numbers directing user to collection.

VII. Accessibility

Catalog listing. In process of printing "Highlights of Collection" catalog, which will be free.

All materials available at "nominal" fee, hour-for-hour — exchange (trade).

NORTH DAKOTA

I. Organizational Information

State Historical Society Archives of North Dakota
North Dakota Heritage Center
612 East Blvd.
Bismark, ND 58505-0179

Individual to Contact	Gerald Newborg
Phone	(701) 224-2668
Profit/Nonprofit	Nonprofit

II. General Formats

Audiotape: Oral interviews (less than 300); 2 1/2 million ft of 16mm film.
Videotape: 250-300 videotapes, 3/4"/1/2".

III. General Program Type

Mostly news/information.

V. Related Manuscript Materials

Scripts of newsbroadcasts — one of the stations.

VI. Special Interests

General news with public affairs from few local stations; some material on local personalities or first broadcasts; small amount of material on news personalities; videotapes, public broadcasting.

VII. Accessibility

Very few finding aids — in process of developing. On-site facilities; access restrictions, tape availabilities, and fees on a case-by-case basis. **Hours:** 8 a.m. to 5 p.m., Monday through Friday.

OHIO

I. Organizational Information

Music Library and Sound Recordings Archives
Bowling Green State University
Bowling Green, OH 43403-0179

Phone   (419) 372-2307

II. General Formats

More than 230,000 LP albums; 190,000 45-rpm singles; 80,000 78-rpm singles; 800 cylinder recordings.

III. General Program Types

The Music Library contains over 25,000 books and scores related to all aspects of the study of music. Included in the book collection are studies ranging from biography to general histories of music, from theoretical treatises to generic studies of such diverse aspects as country music, opera, and band music. The score collection includes solos, orchestral studies, exercise books, and chamber music with ensembles from two to ten parts. The recordings collection, which does not circulate except to university faculty and music teaching assistants, contains over 15,000 recordings of music from all periods of music history as well as ethnic music, musical theater, and jazz. Recitals from the College of Musical Arts dating from 1963 are housed in this library. Also located in the collection are all masters' theses and documents written by graduate students in the College of Musical Arts.

The Music Library houses two special collections: The Sound Recordings Archives and the New Music Festival Archives. The **Sound Recordings Archives**, considered the nation's premier collection of popular music sound recordings, contains 500,000 recordings representing all styles of popular music and all recorded formats. Established in 1967 for the serious study of popular music, the Sound Recordings Archives serves not only campus patrons but researchers from the United States, Canada, and Europe. Discographies and periodicals related to popular music and the recording industry are also included in this collection. Established in 1987, the **New Music Festival Archives** contains music both submitted to and performed at the College of Musical Arts' New Music Festival. At present, the collection contains over 600 scores of contemporary music, many in manuscript.

V. Related Manuscript Materials

Some radio programs and television scripts.

VII. Accessibility

The **Listening Center** has 40 stations including 28 stations equipped with cassette players, turntables, compact disc players or open-reel tape decks. The facility is available during the hours the Music Library is open and can be used for class/private lesson listening, as well as recreational listening. Patrons using the Listening Center must present their own current university I.D. card or library courtesy card. Courtesy cards are available from the Jerome Library circulation desk. Out-of-state researchers should make arrangements for access in advance of their visit.

Although taping from the Listening Center equipment is not permitted, taping for class use, research, or specific needs may be requested at the Listening Center window. Taping must be requested 48 hours in advance (excluding weekends) and is restricted by the Copyright Laws of the United States (Title 17).

Locating Materials: Music Library materials are accessed through the University Libraries' LS/2 public access catalog. In addition, the Music Library also maintains card catalogs on the third floor for recordings, for scores, and for reference books. A copy of the University Libraries' periodicals printout is also available for use in the reference area on the third floor.

Hours: During academic semesters, the hours of the Music Library are: Monday through Thursday, 8 a.m. to 10 p.m.; Friday, 8 a.m. to 5 p.m.; Saturday, 10 a.m. to 5 p.m.; Sunday, 1 p.m. to 10 p.m.

Intersession and holiday hours vary. Please call the University Libraries' hours tape (419) 372-2885, or the Music Library (419) 372-2307, to obtain hours during these times.

Editor's Note: While the collection is primarily music, there are radio and television tie-ins to material, some radio programs and television scripts.

OHIO

I. Organizational Information

Popular Culture Library
Bowling Green State University
Bowling Green, OH 43403-0600

Phone

(419) 372-2450

II. General Formats

Primarily research materials on 19th- and 20th-century American popular culture.

III. General Program Types

In addition to many rare hardcover and vintage paperback books and magazines, the Popular Culture Library also houses archival and special collections, such as literary manuscripts, movie and television scripts, and visual and graphic materials. Such non-traditional library resources as dime and other serial novels, pulp magazines, fanzines and other amateur publications, cartoon and comic books, and graphic materials (such as posters, postcards, greeting cards, and advertisements) are located in the Popular Culture Library.

IV. Subject Content Description

Major strengths of the Popular Culture Library are the performing arts and the entertainment industry (including popular drama, dance, radio, television, film, and the mass communications industry), graphic arts, recreation and leisure, social history, and popular science and religion. Nearly 80,000 volumes of cataloged books are housed in the Popular Culture Library. Popular fiction predominates, particularly novels in the mystery/detective, science fiction/fantasy, western, romance, movie and TV tie-in, and historical fiction genres. The Library also contains extensive collections of late 19th- and 20th-century juvenile/young adult series fiction (Horatio Alger, Tom Swift, the Bobbsey Twins, and Nancy Drew, for example). Nonfiction holdings include books on the occult and supernatural, parapsychology, manners and customs, etiquette and advice, arts and crafts, hobbies, games and amusements, sports, foodways and specialized cookery, domestic arts, costume and dress, and humor. Popular reference and informational materials (self-help and how-to books, for example) are also in the Library's holdings.

Other collections include: The Ray and Pat Browne Popular Culture Research Collections; Robert S. Bravard Collection of comic books; the E.T. (Ned) Guymon Collection of detective books, literary manuscripts, and correspondence; the Leo S. Rosencrans Collection of Chatauqua, radio, and motion picture research material; and the Jeffrey J. Gailiun Vintage Paperback Collection.

V. Related Manuscript Materials

Literary manuscripts, movie and television scripts, and visual and graphic materials.

VI. Special Interests

The Popular Culture Library is the largest most comprehensive research facility in the United States dedicated exclusively to the acquisition and preservation of primary research materials on 19th- and 20th-century American popular culture.

VII. Accessibility

Locating Materials: Magazines may be located by means of the Jerome Library's computer-generated Periodicals List. The majority of the book holdings of the Popular Culture Library may be accessed through the LS/2 online catalog terminals that are located throughout the Jerome Library. The Popular Culture Library also maintains author/title and subject card catalogs on the fourth floor. Users should write down the call numbers (**all** the letters and numbers found on the top left corner of the catalog card or indicated on the terminal screen) of the items they need to use at the Popular Culture Library.

Other specialized reference aids to Popular Culture Library include manuscript inventories and registers, and specialized indexes to non-traditional holdings, such as theater arts playbills and programs, movie advertisements, movie pressbooks, movie posters, comic books, pulp magazines, and fanzines. A supporting collection of reference books is also housed on the fourth floor at the Popular Culture Library.

Hours: Monday through Thursday, 8 a.m. to 10 p.m.; Friday, 8 a.m. to 5 p.m.; Saturday, 10 a.m. to 5 p.m.; Sunday, 1 p.m. to 10 p.m. Operating hours vary during semester breaks, holidays, and summer semesters. The hours may be verified by calling the Popular Culture Library (419) 372-2450, or the Jerome Library recorded message at (419) 372-2885.

OHIO

I. Organizational Information The Cincinnati Historical Society
1301 Wester Avenue
Cincinnati, OH 45203

Individual to Contact Linda Bailey

Phone (513) 287-7030

Profit/Nonprofit Nonprofit

II. General Formats

Discs (LP - 16" ETs or 78s) dating back to turn of century; audio- and videotapes; 16mm film. (New collection in process of organization.)

III. General Program Types

Music, entertainment, and information talk.

V. Related Manuscript Materials

All memorabilia.

VI. Special Interests

Major focus is on history of broadcasting (TV and radio) in Cincinnati. This is a new and large collection just opening. Focus is on locally produced radio program, 1930s, 1940s, 1950s; late 1940s to present, locally produced television programming. 1994: Exhibit in museum of a recreated radio studio from the 1940s and an early TV studio from the 1950s.

VII. Accessibility

Card catalog; on-site facilities; access, availability, and fees on a case-by-case basis. **Hours:** 9 a.m. to 4:30 p.m., Tuesday through Saturday.

OHIO

I. Organizational Information

Frederic W. Ziv Archive
College Conservatory of Music
Division of Broadcasting
University of Cincinnati
Cincinnati, OH 45221

Individual to Contact   Morleen Getz Rouse

Phone   (513) 556-9489

Profit/Nonprofit   Nonprofit

II. General Formats

20,000 ETs.

III. General Program Types

40 different series. Broadcast music, variety, drama, human interest, talk entertainment, news/commentary, sports, comedy.

IV. Subject Content Description

Bold Venture, Cisco Kid, Easy Aces, Eddie Cantor Show, Favorite Story, The Guy Lombardo Show, Korn Kobblers, Mr. District Attorney, World's Greatest Mysteries.

V. Related Manuscript Materials

Scripts (Cisco Kid, Boston Blackie, Favorite Story, Mr. D.A.); production materials; personal papers (including some contracts); oral histories (cassette tape interview with F.W. Ziv and others in preparation of documentary on Ziv by Morleen Getz Rouse).

VII. Accessibility

Research Aids: Listings, card catalog, index.

Information provided through mail when possible. On-site use allowed, however, the ETs have never been transferred to tape/cassette.

OHIO

I. Organizational Information

University Archives
The Ohio State University
209 Converse Hall
2121 Tuttle Park Place
Columbus, OH 43210

Individual to Contact

Raimund Goerler, University Archivist

Ken Grossi, Assistant Archivist

Phone

(614) 292-2409

Profit/Nonprofit

Nonprofit

II. General Formats

Sound recordings (33s and 78s); audiotape from sound recordings (disc); OSU commencement (31 videotapes), Spring 1979 to Summer 1989.

III. General Program Types

Sound recordings include a variety of topics (i.e., education, government).

V. Related Manuscript Materials

Collection has some oral histories.

VI. Special Interests

Sound recordings are being transferred to tape on request. Recordings date from the 1940s. A project to transfer some of the recordings to tape has been completed. This project, "The Historical Recording Project-Education," was completed in 1988. The Archives has a list of tapes and their contents for this period.

VII. Accessibility

Some inventory listings; index available for use. On-site facilities for sound recording transfer to tape (78s and 33s); restrictions depend upon type of material. **Hours:** Monday through Friday, 8 a.m. to 12 p.m., 1-5 p.m.

OHIO

I. Organizational Information	North American Radio Archives Cassette Lending Library 2055 Elmwood Avenue Lakewood, OH 44107
Individual to Contact	Thomas H. Monroe Cassette Lending Librarian
Phone	(216) 226-8189
Profit/Nonprofit	Nonprofit

II. General Format

4,585 audiocassettes of radio shows.

III. General Program Types

Entire collection is radio programming.

Broadcast music (111); variety (152); drama (7,302); talk entertainment (1); information talk (69); news/commentary (66); documentary (79); politics (6); commercial messages (3); sports (7); comedy (1,374).

Please note that each cassette has two sides so that would indicate two programs.

IV. Subject Content Description

See **Program Index**. Individual programs are listed with page numbers directing user to collection.

The 1920s: Comedy (3 tapes); **The Early 1930s:** Music (1); variety (12); drama (3); comedy (12); news (3); **1938 thru 1941:** Music (10); variety (8); drama (733); comedy (157); news (5), sports (1); **World War II:** Music (13); variety (28); drama (359); comedy (241); news (64); politics (6); sports (2); **Sept. 1945 thru 1949:** Music (37), variety (39), drama (935), comedy (499), news (5), politics (1), sports (1); **The 1950s:** Music

(25), variety (46), drama (1,187), comedy (206), news (2), politics (1), sports (1); **The 1960s:** Music (4), drama (58), comedy (5), news (9); **The 1970s:** Drama (491), comedy (1), news (20), politics (2); **The 1980s:** Drama (343), comedy (70), news (6).

VII. Accessibility

Research Aids: Catalog listing, index to the catalog, computer discs or printout available by your sort requirements on special request.

Printed Catalog: Available; a $7 donation would be appreciated but not required.

"Use" Conditions: Appreciate your joining NARA (membership is $15 per year) but it is not an absolute requirement. Cassettes are available for rental at a nominal fee of 60¢ per cassette plus shipping. An order blank is supplied with the catalog.

Editor's Note: The NARA is an important network for locating privately held materials. See Preface for contact information.

OHIO

I. Organizational Information

Old Time Radio Show Collectors'
Association of England
Cassette Lending Library
2055 Elmwood Avenue
Lakewood, OH 44107

Individual to Contact

Thomas H. Monroe
Director, North American Operation

Phone

(216) 226-8189

Profit/Nonprofit

Nonprofit

III. General Program Types

Drama (358 cassettes), information talk (6).

IV. Subject Content Description

Contemporary Programming: Drama, 358 cassettes, talk information, 6.

VI. Special Interests

This cassette library contains only material that was initially broadcast in English outside the North American continent. Most of it is British and is being supplied by our parent group located in Leeds, England. That group is saving material and providing us with copies. We will be getting older material from England as we make available to them tape for transcribing the programming for us.

VII. Accessibility

Research Aids: A catalog that is periodically updated; reviews of the cassettes describing content in greater depth is periodically updated. **Published Catalog:** Catalog and reviews are available free but a small donation would be appreciated. **"Use" Conditions:** All cassettes are available for borrowing by members of ORCA (membership is $15 per year). Cassettes rent for 60¢ each plus shipping.

Editor's Note: English programming. A very important association for those interested in British radio.

OHIO

I. Organizational Information

WMUB Record Collection
Williams Hall
Miami University
Oxford, OH 45056

Individual to Contact

Jim Haskins

Phone

(513) 529-5885

II. General Formats

4,000 78s; 8,000 33 1/3.

III. General Program Types

CBS news documentaries (mid-1945 to 1960) on record. Big band music and classical recordings (1940 to present).

VII. Accessibility

Card index for classical. On-site facilities. **Hours:** Monday through Friday, 8 a.m. to 5 p.m.

OHIO

I. Organizational Information
John Carroll Broadcast Archives
John Carroll University
University Hights, OH 44118

Individual to Contact
Alan Stephenson

Phone
(216) 397-4679

II. General Formats

65,000 rolls news film; 30,000 video clips from **News Channel 5** (1949 to 1985); 7,000 news actualities from **WGAR** radio from 1930 —

III. General Program Types

All newscast-type materials, 1940-1985.

IV. Subject Content Description

WEWS-TV gave John Carroll University all of its 16mm news film shot since its activation in December 1947. This is estimated at 50,000 rolls ranging from 30 seconds to 1 hour (in the case of documentaries).

WEWS has been giving John Carroll University the "Save Tapes" news items shot since 1979 on 3/4". These are mostly 60-minute 3/4" cassettes with 20 or more segments per cassette. At this point, about 2/3 of the collection has been checked. (If the label is wrong, it may be years before we know it.) Now in the process of putting all this in a database on the University's main frame.

With the aforementioned gifts as a trigger, one of the local radio stations has given the University about 100 16" transcriptions which go back into the 1930s and all their news actualities since 1973. Numerous other smaller gifts have expanded the collection further.

V. Related Manuscript Materials

On file are scripts, production materials, and personal papers.

VI. Special Interests

Local and national news events and personalities over the last 40 years, including interviews with the likes of JFK, Nixon, etc.

While all the collection has a Northeastern Ohio orientation, many national events and national figures are included. Unfortunately, no good index to the collection existed. Staff are in the process of inventorying it on the basis of the label on each roll.

VII. Accessibility

On-site facilities, dubbing capabilities for 1/" and 3/4"; access by appointment. **Hours:** 9 a.m. to 5 p.m., Monday through Friday.

OKLAHOMA

I. Organizational Information

Political Commercial Archive
Political Communication Center
Department of Communication
University of Oklahoma
Norman, OK 73019

Individual to Contact

Lunda Lee Kaid, Project Director

Julian Kanter, Project Archivist

Phone

(405) 325-3114

Profit/Nonprofit

Nonprofit

II. General Formats

6,000 audiotapes, 7 1/2, 15-audio; 32,000 videotapes, 3/4", 2", 1/2" VHS.

III. General Program Types

News/commentary, documentary, politics, commercial messages. The collection has over 40,000 radio and television commercials from political campaigns at all office levels from 1936 to present.

VI. Special Interests

The collection specializes in political radio and television commercials from political campaigns and also contains commercials from public issue campaigns and referenda. Commercials come from national, state, and local races and some foreign countries. Radio spots date back to mid-1930s and television from 1950. Materials are on film, video and audio formats.

VII. Accessibility

Inventory records; computerized database partially complete (access via OCLC by 1991). On-site audio and video viewing facilities; a few donor restrictions; on-site use, occasional off-site rental. **Hours:** Monday through Friday, 8 a.m. to 5 p.m. Closed holidays and university breaks.

Published Catalog: Available in 1991.

OKLAHOMA

I. Organizational Information

Broadcast Collection
Archives and Manuscripts Division
1900 N. Lincoln Blvd.
Oklahoma City, OK 73105

Individual to Contact

William Welge

Phone

(405) 521-2491

Sponsor

Institution

II. General Formats

3,000 audiotapes; 10 audio discs; 300 videotapes (oral interviews and historic events); 50,000 ft movie film (newsreel), oil, ranching, political figures, etc.

III. General Program Types

Most programs of an oral history nature, dealing principally with Oklahoma subject matter.

VII. Accessibility

On-site facilities; no restrictions. **Hours:** Monday through Friday, 8 a.m. to 5 p.m.

OREGON

I. Organizational Information Golden Age of Radio
P.O. Box 25215
Portland, OR 97225

Individual to Contact Rex E. Bills

Sponsor Private

II. General Formats

Audio, reel, and cassettes.

III. General Program Types

All categories with an emphasis on radio comedy and drama. Radio's Golden Age and World War II.

VII. Accessibility

Catalog for reels, $5; catalog for cassettes, $1. Free mini-catalog.

OREGON

I. Organizational Information

Oregon Historical Society
Film Archives
1230 SW Park Avenue
Portland, OR 97205

Individuals to Contact

Michele Kribs

Mikki Tint

Phone

(503) 222-1741

Profit/Nonprofit

Nonprofit

II. General Formats

16mm film; 3/4 videotape.

VI. Special Interests

News/information. Focus on historical area of Pacific Northwest: Alaska, Washington, British Columbia, California, Oregon.

VII. Accessibility

In-house catalog. On-site facilities; restrictions, availabilities, and fees on a case-by-case basis (commercial, nonprofit rates). **Hours:** Monday through Saturday, 10 a.m. to 4:45 p.m.

PENNSYLVANIA

I. Organizational Information

Annenberg Television Script Archive
The Annenberg School for Communication
3620 Walnut Street
University of Pennsylvania
Philadelphia, PA 19104

Individuals to Contact   Sharon Black, Archive Librarian

Elizabeth Moersh, Bibliographic Specialist

Susan Williamson, Director of Annenberg Library

Phone   (215) 898-7020

Profit/Nonprofit   Nonprofit

II. General Formats

Scripts

III. General Program Types

TV Guide Collection (20,000 scripts and growing); Agnes Nixon Collection
(9,000 scripts by Agnes Nixon); and the new ABC Soap Opera Collection
(a few hundred scripts from "All My Children").

IV. Scripts Listing

See **Program Index**. Individual programs are listed with page numbers
directing user to collection.

V. Related Manuscript Material

Over 29,000 television scripts.

VI. Special Interests

The ASC Television Script Archive currently houses over 29,000 scripts.
It has three components. The *TV Guide* Collection comprises virtually
every script of a prime time series from 1976 to the present (over 20,000
and growing), the Agnes Nixon Collection (made up of 9,000 scripts by

Agnes Nixon that span from 1954 to 1984), and the new ABC Soap Opera Collection (a few hundred contemporary scripts from the ABC-TV soap opera "All My Children" that have been sent to ASC since 1986 on a weekly basis).

VII. Accessibility

Computer Access: TSAR (Television Script ARchive) database. The Archive's in-house database to the collection containing over 8,500 records representing fully cataloged and indexed scripts from more than 200 prime time series, mostly from 1976-1982.

Published Catalog: Available from the Annenberg School for $10: *The Annenberg Television Script Archive Catalog of Holdings*. Available from Oryx Press: *Thesaurus of Subject Headings for Television: A Vocabulary for Indexing Script Collections* ($39.50) and *Index to the Annenberg Television Script Archive: Volume 1, 1976-1977* ($115).

"Use" Conditions: TSAR database, photocopying prohibited. Open to researchers by application and appointment only. **Hours:** Monday through Friday, 10 a.m. to 4 p.m.

Published Research: Joseph Turow, *Playing Doctor* (New York: Oxford University Press, 1989).

User Fees: The collection is available free of charge to members of the University of Pennsylvania community--students, faculty, and staff. Outside users will be assessed in the following manner.

Nonprofit researchers	$25
Corporate-affiliated researchers	75

An educational discount of $10 applies to researchers who are degree candidates at other institutions.

Access fees include full reference assistance from the staff, use of the database, and printouts of computer searches.

Non-Penn. researchers needing access to the Archive in excess of six hours will be assessed $5 for each subsequent session of use (a "session" may range from 1 to 6 hours).

Additional Services/Sales: The Annenberg Script Archive Holdings Guide (ASC): $10. Remote requests for TSAR database searches: 75¢/page plus handling.

Editor's Note: Excellent television script archive.

212

PENNSYLVANIA

I. Organizational Information

Archives of Industrial Society
363 Hillman Library
University of Pittsburgh
Pittsburgh, PA 15260

Individual to Contact Frank Zabrosky

Phone (412) 648-8197

Profit/Nonprofit Nonprofit

II. General Formats

16mm film, videotape.

III. General Program Types

Information, news. Scripts: KOKA for one series.

VI. Special Interests

Footage provided by local TV station. KDKA-TV and WQED-TV (educational TV) news shows/general local news.

VII. Accessibility

Chronological subject index file; in-house tools. WQED available on site; KDKA very restricted; fees determined on a case-by-case basis. **Hours:** Monday through Friday, 8:30 a.m. to 5 p.m.

PENNSYLVANIA

I. Organizational Information

The National Cable Television Center and Museum
Mitchell Building
The Pennsylvania State University
University Park, PA 16802
(814) 865-6535 and (814) 865-1875

Oral History Project:

Level B, Sparks Building
University Park, PA 16802
(814) 865-3668

Library Project:

Level B, Sparks Building
University Park, PA 16802
(814) 865-3133

Development:

Level B, Sparks Building
University Park, PA 16802
(814) 865-2397

IV. Subject Content Description

To establish a comprehensive national archive of the history and development of the cable television industry in order to preserve the recollections and contributions of industry pioneers, contemporary leaders in cable television, and persons in government, by means of oral histories to be recorded, transcribed, and deposited at the archive.

To provide a repository for historical and current papers and documents, and programming and technical artifacts among other things, for study by students, scholars, and researchers interested in the history, growth, and development of the industry; and to otherwise provide facilities and resources for research and scholarly activity in the field of cable television.

VII. Accessibility

Call for information.

RHODE ISLAND

I. Organizational Information

Presidential Campaign TV Ads
Department of Speech Communication
University of Rhode Island
Kingston, RI 02881

Individual to Contact   L. Patrick Devlin

Phone   (401) 792-1000 or
(401) 792-2552

Profit/Nonprofit   Profit

II. General Formats

Hundreds of videotapes, 1/2" VHS with some 3/4" VHS.

III. General Program Types

Politics: Primary and general elections ads.

IV. Subject Content Description

Television's Golden Age: Hundreds of ads from 1952 to 1988.
Contemporary Programming: All current presidential campaign ads.

V. Related Manuscript Materials

Written analyses of campaigns of 1972, 1976, 1980, 1984, and 1988, by
L. Patrick Devlin (previously published in academic journals).

VI. Special Interests

Negative ads; primary campaign ads; longer ads and speeches; full
collections of ads used in 1972, 1976, 1980, 1984, and 1988.

VII. Accessibility

Research Aids: Listing of ads from 1952 to 1988 available on request.

"Use" Conditions: Any scholar can come to view portions of collection at no charge; a charge will be made if ads need to be copied.

Availability and Fees: Six ad tape selections for classroom use, 45 minutes each:

1. 1988 ads	$200
2. 1984 ads	$150
3. 1980 ads	$100
4. Negative ads, 1952-1984	$200
5. Historic short ads, 1952-1980	$150
6. Historic longer and short ads, 1960-1988	$150

Published Research: List available.

SOUTH CAROLINA

I. Organizational Information

Broadcasting Archives
McKissick Museum
University of South Carolina
Columbia, SC 29208

Individuals to Contact

John Heiting
University Archivist

Lee Gardner
Assistant Archivist
Broadcasting Archives

Phone

(803) 777-7251

Profit/Nonprofit

Nonprofit

II. General Formats

Disc (LP - 16" Ets or 78s): 1,850 recordings.
Pressing: 65.
Audiotape: 1,000.
Videotape: 250.

III. General Program Types

Broadcast music (1,300 recordings/programs); variety (50); drama (40); human interest (300); information talk (150); news/commentary (30); commercial messages (25); comedy (30).

IV. Subject Content Description

The 1920s: Music (300 programs/recordings).
The Depression: Music (175); variety (25).
Radio's Golden Age: Music (500); variety (20); drama (40); comedy (20).
World War II: Music (400); variety (175); drama (40); comedy (20); news/commentary (50); commercial messages (25).
The Cold War Radio: Music (75); politics (80).

Korean War Era: Music (150); politics (45).

Vietnam War Era: Music (50); talk information (150); politics (250).

Contemporary Programming: Music (200); talk information (45); human interest (100); politics (100).

V. Related Manuscript Materials

Scripts from local stations featuring local radio personalities in South Carolina; production materials including advertising rates, rating charges, schedules, channel applications — all in state material; personal papers include papers of Claude Casey, Jack Cook, G. Richard Shafto, and other prominent South Carolina broadcasters; oral histories focus on black broadcasters in the state, local celebrities, and musicians.

VI. Special Interests

Collection limited to broadcasting in South Carolina. Larger collections include "Whitaker's Waxworks," a collection of early 20th-century music, "Old Time Radio Shows," "Kaltenborn Edits the News." Topics of special interest are black broadcasters in South Carolina and women in broadcasting.

VII. Accessibility

Research Aids: Listings, by box; card catalog, partial for frequently used collections; index; and inventory guide. Computer database in planning stage.

"Use" Conditions: On-site facilities only; availabilities, fees, etc., on a case-by-case basis. **Hours:** Monday through Friday, 9 a.m. to 4 p.m. — prefer to call for appointment.

Published Catalog: In planning stage.

SOUTH CAROLINA

I. Organizational Information

Newsfilm Library
Instructional Services Center
University of South Carolina
Columbia, SC 29208

Individual to Contact

Andrew Murdock

Phone

(803) 777-6841

II. General Formats

16mm and 35mm, BW motion picture film.

III. General Program Types

Broadcast music, talk entertainment, information talk, and news.

IV. Subject Content Description

WIS-TV News Collection; footage from 20th Century Fox-Movietone News.

VII. Accessibility

Card catalog and computer access database; some restricted access; no charge for research. Call for an appointment.

TENNESSEE

I. Organizational Information

The Library Channel, TV-9
Memphis Shelby County Public Library
and Information Center
1850 Peabody Avenue
Memphis, TN 38104

Phone

(901) 725-8895

II. General Formats

VHS Videotapes.

III. General Program Types

News/commentary with 1,210 recordings/programs.

IV. Subject Content Description

Contemporary programming.

VI. Special Interests

Archive of WMC-TV's 5 p.m. weekday newscast. This archive of local news dates back to June 1985.

VII. Accessibility

The public may view the collection by appointment.

Research Aids: Computer access with D-Base III; printed abstract available. On-site facilities. **Hours:** Monday through Friday, 9 a.m. to 5 p.m.

TENNESSEE

I. Organizational Information

Radio Program History Collection
Department of Theatre & CMU Arts
Memphis State University
Memphis, TN 38152

Individual to Contact   Marvin R. Bensman

Phone   (901) 678-2565

Sponsor   Institution

II. General Formats

All audiotape. 7" reels recorded 3 3/4 dual track and audiocassette.

III. General Program Types

All types. The object of the collection is to obtain at least one example for every program on radio so as to make available representative sampling for use by teachers and researchers.

IV. Subject Content Description

Primarily Radio's Golden Years. Some contemporary programs and interview material relating to programming and personalities.

VII. Accessibility

Catalog: Computer catalog, free upon request.

TENNESSEE

I. Organizational Information

Huell Howser Collection
School of Mass Communication
P.O. Box 58
Middle Tennessee State University
Murfreesboro, TN 37132

Individual to Contact

William D. Jackson
Associate Professor

Phone

(615) 898-2382

III. General Program Types

All formats.

IV. Subject Content Description

Huel Howser is a well-known broadcaster in Tennessee. Materials within the collection come from his personal collection acquired between 1970 and 1976 when he was a producer for a daily "Happy Features" package on the Nashville TV station.

V. Related Manuscript Materials

Various framed and unframed items of realia, including photos, awards, certificates, and file folders of newspaper clippings, correspondence, and memos.

VII. Accessibility

The collection is in the organizational process.

TENNESSEE

I. Organizational Information

Vanderbilt Television News Archive
110 21st Ave.
S. Baker Bldg., Suite 704
Vanderbilt University
Nashville, TN 37203-0007

Individual to Contact   Dorothy Hamilton

Phone   (615) 322-2927

Profit/Nonprofit   Nonprofit

II. General Formats

Audio- and videotapes from August 8, 1969 on.

III. General Program Types

Information news.

VI. Special Interests

ABC/NBC/CBS news network tapes — all the newscasts; some CNN beginning 1989; Nightline. Tape various specials — Democratic/Republican conventions, 1968 to present.

VII. Accessibility

Listing of index and abstracts of network newscasts; can order duplications; fees charged for processing (3/4" or 1/2") with minimum pay of half-hour tape. **Hours:** Monday through Friday, 8 a.m. to 4:30 p.m.

TEXAS

I. Organizational Information

Lyndon Baines Johnson Library
2313 Red River Street
Austin, TX 78705

Individual to Contact

E. Philip Scott
Audiovisual Archivist

Phone

(512) 482-5279 or
(512) 482-5137

II. General Formats

All formats.

IV. Subject Content Description

Sound Recordings: President John F. Kennedy speeches, 245 tapes; Lyndon B. Johnson speeches and remarks, 1,443 tapes; Mrs. Lyndon B. Johnson speeches, 156 tapes; press conferences, 101 tapes; congressional briefings, 101 tapes; government agency tapes, 1,564 tapes; Democratic National Committee, 1,698 tapes.

Videotape Recordings: White House Communications Agency off-the-air or White House feeds, 3,163 tapes; LBJ Library Series, 529 tapes; Walt W. Rostow lectures, 124 tapes.

Motion Pictures: White House Naval Photographic Unit, 611 reels; government agencies, selected titles; films from television networks, 173 titles; films from columnist Drew Pearson, 82 titles (not open to research).

VII. Accessibility

Audiovisual Archives is open from 9 a.m. to 4:30 p.m. weekdays except federal holidays.

TEXAS

I. Organizational Information

University Archives
The University of Texas at Austin
SRH2.109
Austin, TX 78713-7330

Individual to Contact

Don E. Carleton
Director
Archives of American History

Phone

(512) 471-3434 or
(512) 471-1741

II. General Formats

Audio- and videotapes.

III. General Program Types

News and information.

IV. Subject Content Description

The University Archives is the repository for the Walter Cronkite Collection including personal papers, scripts, notes, correspondence, research files, photographs, audiotape recordings, videotape recordings, and miscellaneous publications and documents relating to Cronkite's career. In addition, the University houses a collection of the records of the CBS News Division during Cronkite's tenure as managing editor. Access to the CBS material is controlled by CBS, Inc.

VII. Accessibility

The collection is still in the process of being transferred and organized. It is closed at present.

TEXAS

I. **Organizational Information**
Southwest Film/Video Archives
BGLO Newsfilm Collection
P.O. Box 4194
Southern Methodist University
Dallas, TX 75275

Individuals to Contact
G. William Jones, Director

Walid Khaldi, Archivist

Marica Chaconz, Assistant to Director

Phone
(214) 373-3665 or 3666

Profit/Nonprofit
Nonprofit

II. **General Formats**

16mm b/w and color reversed field footage, 2 million + feet.

III. **General Program Types**

News/commentary, documentary, politics: Over 2 million feet of unedited footage representing each day 1960-1975.

IV. **Subject Content Description**

Vietnam War Era: News/commentary, public affairs, politics: Over 2 million feet representing every day, 1960-1975, locally, regionally, nationally, as well as some internationally.

VI. **Special Interests**

The most important collections focus on World War II, animation, documentary, black audience films, "formula" westerns, independent features, comedy, and both silent and sound classics of the foreign film.

VII. **Accessibility**

Applications now in for grant to catalog and preserve collection - NHPRC, etc. Present catalog and recall minimal. The facility has copyright for all historical/educational use.

TEXAS

I. Organizational Information

National Museum of Communications
Four Dallas Communications Complex
6305 N. O'Connor, Ste 123, LB 55
Irving, TX 75039-3510

Individual to Contact

Bill Bragg
Executive Curator/Founder

Phone

(214) 556-1234

Profit/Nonprofit

Nonprofit

II. General Formats

All types.

III. General Program Types

News/commentary: WFAA-TV newsfilm, 1964-1974.
Commercial messages: Assorted 1950s commercials.

The National Museum of Communication is the world's largest permanent museum of communications artifacts. It is a nonprofit, tax-exempt (501(c)3), historical, educational, and community-oriented organization established in 1979.

IV. Subject Content Description

See **Program Index**. Individual programs are listed with page numbers directing user to collection.

VII. Accessibility

The library contains thousands of phonograph records, audio- and video-tapes of news and entertainment material, operating equipment and service manuals, communications trade and hobbyist magazines, and electronics reference books. This area is open to those wishing to research the history of communications. In addition, any obsolete audio- or videotape format can be transferred onto modern media. Call for direct accessibility and fees. **Hours:** 10 a.m.—4 p.m. Tuesday—Sunday. **Tickets:** Adults $2; Seniors $1; children 12-18 $1, under 12 free; groups of 20 or more half price.

TEXAS

I. Organizational Information

Southwest Collection
P.O. Box 4090
Texas Tech University
Lubbock, TX 79409

Individuals to Contact

David Murrah
Director

Jim Matthews
Multimedia Collections

Phone

(806) 742-3749

Profit/Nonprofit

Nonprofit

II. General Formats

Disc (LP - 16" ETs or 78s): 4,900 recordings; audiotape: 4,550; videotape: 380; short play; 3/4"-120, 1/2" VHS-260.

III. General Program Types

Broadcast music (3,000 recordings/programs); talk entertainment (30); information talk (40); news/commentary (2,000); documentary (650); politics (30); commercial messages (5); sports (15); comedy (10); oral history (3,000).

IV. Subject Content Description

The 1920s: Music (175 programs/recordings).
The Depression: Music (175).
Radio's Golden Age: Music (250).
World War II: Music (600); news/commentary (40); sports (5).
The Cold War Radio: Music (400).
The Cold War Television: News/commentary (260).
Television's Golden Age: News/comm. (500); commercial messages (5).

Korean War Era: Music (800); comedy (3); talk entertainment (20); talk information (25); news/commentary (300); politics (5).

Vietnam War Era: Music (600); comedy (4); talk entertainment (10); talk information (15); news/commentary (800); politics (10); sports (6).

Contemporary Programming: Comedy (3); news/commentary (100); politics (15).

V. Related Manuscript Materials

Some scripts are available for radio programs, especially in the Gordon McLendon Collection. Raw film footage is available for many of the documentary productions. Manuscript collections (personal papers) can be found on many of the oral history interviewees and some media collections. A small percentage of the oral histories have been transcribed. All are inventoried and abstracted.

VI. Special Interests

This is a comprehensive collection of the history and culture of the American Southwest, with a special emphasis on Texas. It also serves as the university archives for Texas Tech.

VII. Accessibility

Research Aids:

Listings: All audiotapes, all cataloged film and video.
Card Catalog: All oral histories.
Index: News/commentary currently on videotape.
Computer access: In progress.

"Use" Conditions:

On-site facilities are available; restricted access on a few items; tape availabilities, fees, exchange policies, etc., are on-site, no exchanges. **Hours:** 8 a.m. to 5 p.m., Monday, Wednesday, Thursday, Friday; 8 a.m. to 7 p.m., Tuesday; 9 a.m. to 3 p.m., Saturday.

VIRGINIA

I. Organizational Information

Echoes of the Past
The Best of Radio's Golden Age
P.O. Box 9593
Alexandria, VA 22304

Individual to Contact

Ronald C. Barnett

Phone

(703) 751-3238

II. General Formats

Audiotape: 9,000+ programs on open reel tape.

III. General Program Types

Radio's Golden Age: Many programs in each category.

VI. Special Interests

Big band; comedy; rare programs; nostalgia.

VII. Accessibility

For sale by open reel; average price is $10 per reel (4-6 hours).

WASHINGTON

I. Organizational Information

Western Washington University
Center for Pacific Northwest Studies
High Street
Bellingham, WA 98225

Phone

(206) 676-3125

Profit/Nonprofit

Nonprofit

II. General Formats

16mm film; videotape.

III. General Program Types

Information and news, public and current affairs.

V. Related Manuscript Materials

Manuscripts with photos; production materials, personal papers, oral histories re Rogan Jones, pioneer broadcaster, who started radio/KVOS-TV.

VI. Special Interests

Rogan Jones Collection — manuscripts — and papers of pioneer Northwest broadcasters. KVOS — current affairs/news.

VII. Accessibility

Inventories for film — not converted. On-site facility use and charges on a case-by-case basis. **Hours:** Monday through Friday, 8:30 a.m. to 12 p.m. and 1:30 to 4:30 p.m.

WASHINGTON

I. Organizational Information

J. Elroy McCaw Memorial Film Collection
Instructional Media Services
Washington State University
Pullman, WA 99164-5602

Individual to Contact   Lee Fruits

Phone   (509) 335-2716

Profit/Nonprofit   Nonprofit

II. General Formats

16mm film, 466 titles in the collection.

IV. Subject Content Description

WSU has for some time been seriously collecting archival films and within the last few years has received a number of rare movies dealing with local and regional history. It also boasts a collection of rare World War II vintage motion pictures — motivational, informational, and documentary films — from the late 1930s to the early 1950s. It was through a news story about the unique collection, and the work of IMS media resource specialist Gale Franko in cataloging the collection, that the family of the late J. Elroy McCaw learned of WSU's interest in such films.

As a result, in March of 1982, Washington State University received a valuable collection of RKO Radio Pictures films from the family of the late broadcasting executive and station owner J. Elroy McCaw. The donation was handled by a son, Mr. Bruce McCaw through the WSU Foundation. J. Elroy McCaw, a 1934 graduate of WSU, was a former student manager of KWSU radio and began his broadcasting career with ownership of station KELA in Centralia, Washington. He acquired many radio and TV stations throughout the country, but retained a personal interest in his alma mater's radio station, KWSU, making frequent trips to the campus until he passed away in 1969.

The McCaw Memorial Collection consists of 436 RKO feature length films and 27 World War II documentaries, all produced between the years 1930 through 1953. The only other collegiate film archives with comparable RKO film material is at the University of Wisconsin in Madison, Wisconsin. This generous alumni donation represents perhaps the largest feature film donation ever given to a university by an individual or family and is presently valued in excess of half a million dollars.

These ongoing programs represent Washington State University's efforts to preserve much of the rich cultural heritage that is so frequently lost due to lack of knowledge or concern for archival materials. WSU's Instructional Media Services endeavors to make these materials accessible to the public through the technology of video and audio restoration/preservation techniques. IMS seeks to continually develop this collection of historically significant materials. They represent another unique resource of the Libraries in support of the University's dual missions: teaching and research.

VII. Accessibility

Research aids include listings, card catalog, index (on the WW II Collection), and complete descriptions of titles. On-site facility use preferred; availabilities, fees, etc., on a case-by-case basis due to condition. **Hours:** Monday through Friday, 8 a.m. to 5 p.m. year round.

WASHINGTON

I. Organizational Information

Educational Media Collection/
Milo Ryan Phonoarchive
Instructional Media Services
23 Kane Hall
University of Washington
Seattle, WA 98195

Individuals to Contact

Leon W. Hevly

Mary Nelson

Phone

(206) 543-9906 or
(206) 543-9915

Profit/Nonprofit

Nonprofit

II. General Formats

Audiotape: 5,000+, 7 1/2 and 3 3/4.

III. General Program Types

Variety (500 recordings/programs); news/commentary (4,500).

IV. Subject Content Description

Radio's Golden Age: Variety, 500 programs/recordings.
World War II: News/commentary, 4,500.

VI. Special Interests

The Milo Ryan Phonoarchive is a collection of World War II radio broadcasts by the Columbia Broadcasting System. It includes news broadcasts, addresses by important public figures, discussions, documentaries, and some entertainment.

The Milo Ryan Phonoarchive is a valuable collection of early radio broadcasts primarily produced by the Columbia Broadcasting System. Spanning the years from 1939 to 1962, it includes news broadcasts, addresses by important public figures, discussion, documentaries and entertainment programming. This is one of the most extensive archives of such recordings available to scholars and the general public. A Catalog of the Phonoarchives is available for use in the Preview/Reference Offices of Instructional Media Services located in the basement of Kane Hall on the University of Washington campus. A descriptive listing is also contained in the book *History in Sound*, Milo Ryan (Seattle: University of Washington Press, 1963).

VII. Accessibility

Research Aids:

Listings: Alphabetical and chronological listing by reporter.
Other: Book: *History in Sound* by Milo Ryan.

"Use" Conditions:

On-site facilities; primarily for scholarship and research (does not include broadcast rights); minimal charge for labor and materials. **Hours:** 8 a.m. to 5 p.m.

Copies of broadcasts are available on audiocassettes. Because these recordings are irreplaceable, each request for use or study will require transfer from the masters. A nominal service charge will be assessed for duplication and tape stock. One week advance notice is required for the use of these materials. Apply to the Reference Office (206) 543-9906.

Editor's Note: To facilitate research, the Milo Ryan Phonoarchive materials were duplicated and housed at the National Archives, Washington, DC and BYU Archives, Provo, Utah. A valuable collection, computerized and easily accessible.

WASHINGTON

I. Organizational Information

Tom Brown
P.O. Box 20425
Seattle, WA 98102

II. General Formats

Disc (LP - 16" ETs or 78s): 3,000
Audiotape: 1,500 reels.

III. General Program Types

Network entertainment, special events.

VI. Special Interests

Columbia Workshop Series.

VII. Accessibility

Listings of the collections; "use" conditions determined on a case-by-case
basis.

WASHINGTON

I. Organizational Information

Eastern Washington State Historical Society
Special Collections Division
2316 W. First Avenue
Spokane, WA 99204

Individual to Contact   Edward W. Nolan

Phone   (509) 456-3931

Profit/Nonprofit   Nonprofit

II. General Formats

Disc (LP - 16" Ets or 78s): 50 recordings.
Audiotape: 750 recordings.
Videotape: 60 recordings.

III. General Program Types

Documentary, 5 recordings/programs; commercial messages, 20; and miscellaneous. **World War II:** Commercial messages 20 programs/recordings and related oral histories.

VII. Accessibility

Index of typed transcripts; on-site facilities. **Hours:** 10 a.m. to 5 p.m., Tuesday through Saturday, by appointment only.

WEST VIRGINIA

I. Organizational Information

James E. Morrow Library
16th Street and 3rd Avenue
Marshall University
Huntington, WV 25701

Individual to Contact

Lisle Brown

Phone

(304) 696-2320

Profit/Nonprofit

Nonprofit

II. General Formats

Million and a half feet of 16mm film/ 500-3/4" videocassettes.

III. General Program Types

Information and news, WSAZ-TV newsfilm and scripts.

VI. Special Interests

WSAZ television, news archives, 1952-1986. Local station news/service tri-state region: Ohio, West Virginia, and Kentucky.

VII. Accessibility

Card index maintained by station year-by-year, topical section and name section. Restricted to on-site use; availabilities, fees, etc., on a case-by-case basis. **Hours:** 8 a.m. to 5 p.m., Monday through Friday, call for appointment.

WISCONSIN

I. Organizational Information   Mass Communication History Collection
State Historical Society of Wisconsin
816 State Street
Madison, WI 53706

Individual to Contact   Harry Miller

Phone   (608) 262-3338

Profit/Nonprofit   Nonprofit

II. General Formats

Disc (LP - 16" ETs or 78s): 12,000. Audiotape: 1/4" wire recordings.
Videotape: 1", 2", and 3" videotape. 16mm film.

III. General Program Types

Papers, documentaries, film clips, music, variety, talk entertainment, and
news (5 million ft of TV news).

IV. Subject Content Description

May be first or second largest collection of mass communication material.

V. Related Manuscript Materials

Scripts, personal papers, and oral histories. David Susskind, extensive
holdings of a variety of radio broadcasters, audio traces of programs.
Papers and communication by pioneers in mass communication. Papers of
H.V. Kaltenborn, very broad collection, radio broadcast discs.

VII. Accessibility

Research Aids: Card catalog; developing a computer index for TV news.
Published Catalog: *Sources for Mass Communication, Film, and Theater
Research: A Guide.* **"Use" Conditions:** On-site facilities; "by and large,"
unrestricted access on-site; some restrictions for on-site. **Hours:** Monday
through Friday, 8 a.m. to 5 p.m.; Saturday, 9 a.m. to 5 p.m. Best to call
concerning use of media materials.

Editor's Note: This is an important collection, the Society folks are helpful and
aggressively pursuing expansion and development.

WISCONSIN

I. Organizational Information

Wisconsin Center for Film and Theater Research
6040 Vilas Communication Hall
University of Wisconsin - Madison
Madison, WI 53706

Individuals to Contact

Donald Crafton
Director

Sandy Stefaniak
Archivist Assistant

Phone

(608) 262-9706/(608) 262-0585

II. General Formats

Film, manuscript, stills, negatives, posters, pressbooks, playbills, clippings, scrapbooks, graphics, and ephemera — several million items in all.

IV. Subject Content Description

Film

The heart of the film holdings is a magnificent gift from the United Artists Corporation, one of the most significant donations ever made to an educational institution. Included in this gift are more than 1,700 feature films acquired by United Artists from Warner Brothers, RKO, and Monogram. The seven hundred films from RKO constitute nearly all the features produced by this major company in the 1930s and 1940s. The Monogram titles are typical of small, low-budget productions during the same period.

The Warner library, with more than 800 features, is unique in that it contains a virtually complete record of the studio's output between 1931 and 1949, from the low-budget pictures to the more prestigious releases. Its comprehensiveness allows the scholar to examine individual films in relation to the studio's overall style and to trace the careers of Warner's contract personnel. The Warner library is also rich in manuscript documentation. Film Scripts, ranging from original treatments to final shooting scripts, are available on almost every title and include works by such influential screenwriters as John Huston, William Faulkner, Robert Bruckner, the Epstein brothers, and Casey Robinson. Pressbooks, stills, and dialogue transcripts show how the films were advertised and exploited.

Legal files containing story purchase agreements and employment contracts with major stars and directors provide important financial information. Rounding out the Warner library are some fifteen hundred Vitaphone short subjects (again with scripts and dialogues) and over three hundred cartoons from Warner's popular Looney Tunes and Merrie Melodies series.

In addition to the films from the United Artists gift, our Center has more than 8,000 features, shorts, and documentaries from the 1890s to the 1980s. To assist scholars in their study of the history of cinema, we hold films by D.W. Griffith, Erich von Stroheim, Robert Flaherty, Luis Bunuel, Ladislas Starevitch, Alfred Hitchcock, Jean Renoir, Francois Truffaut, and many others. The work of contemporary filmmakers is exemplified in the collections of Shirley Clarke, Doris Chase, and Emile de Antonio. De Antonio's Collection includes such prints as *Point of Order* and *In the Year of the Pig*, as well as more than 500 reels of original and stock footage, outtakes, and sound tracks used in the production of his films. Clarke's Collection contains several of her short films and video work as well as outtakes from her features *Portrait of Jason* and *The Connection*. We also have the Amos Vogel Cinema 16 series that chronicles the early development of avant-garde filmmaking in the United States during the 1950s and 1960s, enhanced by Mr. Vogel's personal papers. Features and shorts are included in the collections of Gilbert Cates, Walter Mirisch, Lionel Rogosin, Dore Schary, Walter Wanger, the American Film Institute, and many others.

We have extended our holdings in international cinema by acquiring the David Shepard Collection of 180 films, and 35mm prints of 270 Soviet features and documentaries produced in the 1950s, 1960s, and 1970s. This represents the largest archival collection of postwar Soviet films in the United States. Included are the works of such modern Soviet masters as Andrei Tarkovsky and Sergei Paradjanov.

Dore Schary's Collection provides a look at the workings of another major film company, MGM, where Schary spent several years as vice president in charge of production. Walter Wanger's files contain correspondence, production and financial records of his projects as an independent producer from the 1930s into the 1950s. The Walter Mirisch papers illustrate the activities of his producing organization, and the Kirk Douglas Collection details the operations of the production company founded by this actor-turned-producer.

Television

The impact of television has, in the last 30 years, arguably surpassed that of the Hollywood film. It has become the main source of entertainment and information in the American home, and scholars are just beginning to assess the relationship between this newest mass medium and American culture. As a pioneer collector in the television field, our Center provides the primary source material necessary for that assessment.

Viewing access to the programs themselves is essential to serious research on television, and we have collected and preserved filmed copies of a broad range of programs. ZIV Television Programs, Inc., the most successful producer of popular dramatic programs for first-run syndicated use in the early days of television, is our largest television collection. The ZIV library contains every episode of "Boston Blackie," "I Led Three Lives," "Mr. District Attorney," "Highway Patrol," "Bat Masterson," and 33 other series, a total of almost 2,000 shows produced from 1948 to 1962. Supplementing this vast film collection are scripts and variant drafts for these series. Manuscript materials for 29 more ZIV series is also available. Some 40,000 still prints and negatives illustrate the production and advertising aspects of all the ZIV programs, and several series are represented in the ZIV production files.

The Center is also particularly strong in materials relating to milestones in television documentary production. In 1952 at the NBC network, a team including Richard Hanser, Donald Hyatt, Isaac Kleinerman, and Henry Salomon produced an historic series that was the prototype of compilation documentary: *Victory at Sea*. The individual collections of these men combine to document the production of this award-winning series and include the renowned musical scores by Richard Rodgers and prints of 13 episodes. The team's second effort for NBC, PROJECT XX, is also documented with research material, scripts, publicity, and prints of 34 episodes. The Kleinerman and Burton Benjamin Collections illustrate their work at CBS on "The 20th Century" and "The 21st Century." Included are over 200 prints from these series.

We also hold the collections of two other important producers of television documentaries, Ernest Pendrell and Perry Wolff. Their work, at ABC and CBS respectively, is exemplified by scripts and prints of many of their major productions.

A number of other collections round out the holdings of television prints. Reginald Rose has presented a complete series of films and scripts for the 260 episodes of "The Defenders." The Nat Hiken Collection contains more than 140 films from his successful comedies "You'll Never Get Rich" and "Car 54, Where Are You?" NBC has contributed episodes from each year of the long-running western series "Bonanza" (produced by David Dortort), while the Walter Mirisch Collection contains all 26 episodes of "Wichita Town." Also available are prints of many of the Ed Sullivan variety programs and from MTM Enterprises, a sampling of episodes from "The Mary Tyler Moore Show," "Rhoda," "Bob Newhart," and other MTM series.

The Fred Coe Collection documents this influential producer's involvement in the theater, television, and film. More than half of the material relates to television, reflecting his lengthy association with that medium. Scripts and production information complement original kinescopes from such successful anthology dramas as "Philco Television Playhouse," "Goodyear Playhouse," "Playhouse 90," "Playwrights '56," and "Showcase."

In addition, our collections include films and kinescopes of episodes from television series such as "Studio One," "Electric Showcase," "Person to Person," "Camera Three," "Omnibus," "Climax," "The Martha Raye Show," and many more. 35mm broadcast prints from Paramount Television update our filmed television holdings to the early 1980s. Complete or near-complete runs of series such as "Mork and Mindy," "Taxi," "Happy Days," "Laverne and Shirley," "Mannix," "Mission Impossible," "The Brady Bunch," and "Love American Style" provide a record of American popular tastes of the period.

V. Related Manuscript Materials

The massive manuscript holdings chronicle the history of television from its origins to the present day. The Paddy Chayefsky Collection contains documentation of his landmark drama "Marty," as well as television plays for "Goodyear Theatre" and "Philco Television Playhouse." Reginald Rose has donated scripts from "Studio One," "Playhouse 90," "Alcoa Theatre," and extensive material on "The Defenders." Rod Serling's papers include scripts from his work on "The Kraft Television Theatre" and "The U.S.

Steel Hour," in addition to comprehensive documentation of his "Twilight Zone" series. David Davidson wrote for many of these anthology series, as did Alvin Boretz, Robert Crean, Max Ehrlich, Loring Mandel, Jerome Ross, and Adrian Spies, all of whom have collections at our Center. Gore Vidal, whose "Visit to a Small Planet" firmly established him in early television, has donated a collection covering his entire career as a novelist, essayist, and screenwriter.

The collections document the progression of the television series through the 1960s and early 1970s. The craft of the comedy writer is shown by Nat Hiken, Hal Kanter, Sidney Sheldon, and MTM Enterprises. Comedy series as diverse as "The George Gobel Show," "Car 54, Where Are You?" and "The Mary Tyler Moore Show" are represented. Dramatic series such as "Doctor Kildare," "Mr. Novak," "Owen Marshall," and "Hawaii Five-O," and acclaimed miniseries such as "Roots" and "Inside the Third Reich" are represented in the donations of David Harmon, Ernest Kinoy, Winston Miller, E. Jack Neuman, Jerry McNeely, and Sy Salkowitz. Additional prime-time series are highlighted, and daytime television is represented by such collections as that of Irma Phillips, writer for "The Guiding Light" and "The Brighter Day."

Directors for television include Tom Donovan, who worked on such series as "The Dupont Show of the Month," "The U.S. Steel Hour," and "Studio One"; John Frankenheimer, one of the best known directors to get a start during this period; and Clark Jones, who directed for "The Bell Telephone Hour," "The Perry Como Show," "The Carol Burnett Show," and various specials.

David Susskind's Collection offers extensive information on his activities as producer for "The Armstrong Circle Theater," "The Dupont Show of the Month," "East Side/West Side," and his discussion show "Open End." Hundreds of drawings for "The Bell Telephone Hour" have come from set designer Peter Dohanos. Promotional activities for "The Armstrong Circle Theatre" and several Alcoa-sponsored series are thoroughly documented by theatrical producer and press representative Arthur Kantor.

Production schedules and financial materials so vital to understanding television are also contained in many collections.

Researchers may examine manuscript holdings at the Archives-Manuscripts Reading Room on the fourth floor of the State Historical Society between the hours of 8 a.m. and 5 p.m., Monday through Friday and 9 a.m. to 4 p.m., Saturday. Catalogs, finding aids, reference assistance, copying machines, and microfilm viewers are available there. Because of the uniqueness of the collections, no materials may be removed from the Reading Room, and appropriate registration and security measures are required. We do not charge a fee or require reservations to use paper collections, but researchers are urged to write or telephone in advance of their visit to confirm the availability of specific material.

The Film and Photo Archive, also located on the fourth floor of the Historical Society, has Steenbeck viewing machines for individual screenings of films and kinescopes in the collections, and 3/4" video decks for tape viewing. Access to sound and graphic materials is also provided by appointments. All films, tapes, and viewing equipment must be reserved in advance. The Film Archive is open to researchers from 1 p.m. to 5 p.m., Monday through Friday.

Archives-Manuscripts Reading Room
State Historical Society of Wisconsin
816 State Street
Madison, WI 53706
(608) 262-3338

Film and Photo Archive
412 State Historical Society of Wisconsin
816 State Street
Madison, WI 53706
(608) 262-0585

WISCONSIN

I. Organizational Information

Ron Sayles
4278 North 53rd Street
Milwaukee, WI 53216

Individual to Contact

Ron Sayles

II. General Formats

Audiotape: 6,000 cassette, 50 reel, 100 recordings. Reel 1 7/8, 3 3/4, 7 ips.

IV. Subject Content Description

Radio's Golden Age: Music (approx. 100 programs/recordings); variety (approx. 50); drama (approx. 4,000); comedy (approx. 500); news/commentary (approx. 150); politics (approx. 50); sports (approx. 50); religion (approx 10).
World War II: News commentary (approx. 30).

V. Related Manuscript Materials

Seven old time radio scripts.

VI. Special Interests

Science fiction and Gunsmoke.

VII. Accessibility

Hand-typed catalog; on-site facilities.

WISCONSIN

I. Organizational Information

Special Collections and University Archives
Memorial Library
1415 W. Wisconsin Avenue
Marquette University
Milwaukee, WI 53233

Individuals to Contact

Charles B. Elston
Director

Phillip M. Runket
Catholic Worker Movement

Mark G. Thiel
Native American Records

Phone

(414) 288-7256

Profit/Nonprofit

Nonprofit

II. General Formats

Disc (LP - 16" ETs or 78s): 76 recordings.
Audiotape: 150 cassettes.
Videotape: 200 cassettes.

III. General Program Types

Music, talk entertainment, news/commentary, commercial messages.

IV. Subject Content Description

HOLDINGS OF THE DOROTHY DAY -
CATHOLIC WORKER COLLECTION:

Look Up and Live
Christopher Closeup
Bill Moyers' Journal

Swords and Plowshares
New Heaven/New Earth
Of Cabbages and Kings
Take One
Wisconsin Magazine
Saints Alive: Dorothy Day
Ending the Silence: Civil Disobedience in the Farm Crisis
Capital Edition

Phonodiscs

Sound Recordings of Radio and Television Programs Featuring J.R. McCarthy (also on cassette, with exception of oversize discs)

Meet the Press, NBC, 28 Feb 1947

Broadcast transcriptions of McCarthy for Wisconsin stations, 1949 (23 broadcasts), ca. May 1950 (oversize), 5 Oct 1951 (guests: Herbert Hoover, J. Edgar Hoover, and Senators George D. Aiken, George Malone, Karl Mundt, and John Williams).

Meet the Press, NBC, 7 Aug 1951
Keep Posted, 1 Jan 1952 (w/Philip LaFollette)
American Forum of the Air, NBC-TV, 21 June 1953 (McCarthy and Paul Scott Rankin, Washington bureau chief of Reuters, discussing "The International Effect of McCarthyism").

Audiograph Discs:

Fulton Lewis, Jr. Program
See It Now (reply to Murrow)
Meet the Press
Mike Wallace's Biography

AL McGUIRE FILM & VIDEOTAPE COLLECTION—1977-1988, n.d.

Marquette Basketball, 1/2" and 3/4" videotape, from 1977

THE DON McNEILL COLLECTION, 1928-1969

Includes 110 reels of 16mm black and white films of Breakfast Club simulcasts (1948-1955), Don McNeill's TV Club (1950-1951), and other television shows (ca. 1950-1960) featuring McNeill, 1948-1960.

ST. FRANCIS MISSION (1886-   ) RECORDS

Material pertaining to local church activities is also widely dispersed but includes several well-documented areas. Radio use in ministry is heavily documented by newsclippings (1974, 1979, 1987), proceedings, and radio program audio recordings. Substantial information on the veneration of Kateri Tekakwitha is found in the correspondence (1969-1980), news-clippings (1970-1975, 1980), photographs (1970), local sodality, proceedings, radio scripts (1969), and architectural drawings (n.d.). Limited information on the Catholic Sioux Congress, Tekakwitha Conference, and local sodalities is found in the newsclippings (1936), proceedings, audio recordings, motion pictures, and the papers of Bosch, Luther, and Perrig's diary (1890s). The correspondence further includes letters on baptisms and conversions (1894, 1907) and the newsclippings include reports on lay ministry and the diaconate (1974-1976). Among the photographs are several relating to a youth summer catechism program directed by Lakota sisters (1964), a diaconate ordination (1976), and a variety of bicentennial celebrations (1976).

Sioux for Christ Radio Program (bilingual, English or Sioux, Bible stories and homilies)
ca. 1964-1980, 199 reels
1974-1981, 101 cassettes

Sicangu Chronicle News Chronicle of KINI Radio
1980-1981, 14 reels
1980-1985, 1988-1989, 134 cassettes

WISN-TV: FILMS OF MILWAUKEE AREA NEWS EVENTS, 1956-1961, 1963, n.d.

8.0 cubic feet consisting of 170 rolls of 16mm black and white film.

This collection consists of 16mm black and white film of Milwaukee area news events produced by an outside contractor employed by WISN-TV (Channel 12). Boxes 1-6 contain 71 rolls of film identified by date (May 1956-December 1961), arranged chronologically; in most instances subject content is not identified; the rolls of film vary in diameter from approximately 8-10". Box 7 contains 91 rolls of film identified by subject or title of news feature, arranged alphabetically by subject; dates are not identified; the rolls of film vary in diameter from approximately 3-4" and are stored in 6 containers (labeled 1-6) within the box; if more than 1 roll exists for a subject, the number of rolls included is indicated in parentheses. Box 8 contains 8 rolls of film identified by subject, arranged alphabetically by subject; in most instances dates are not identified; the rolls vary in diameter from approximately 6-12".

NOTE: Films are mounted on spools rather than reels, and, therefore, cannot be shown on a standard film projector.

V. Related Manuscript Materials

Scripts, production materials, and personal papers in the Don McNeill Collection.

VI. Special Interests

The MU Archives collects nationally in the areas of Catholic social action and Native American evangelization.

VII. Accessibility

Listings; on-site facilities; reference copies may be borrowed for cost of postage, several may be purchased "at cost." **Hours:** 8 a.m. to 5 p.m., Monday through Friday; evenings and weekends by appointment.

CANADA

I. Organizational Information

Arthur Makosinski
698 Albert St.
Fredericton, N.B. 83B 2G4 Canada

Phone

(604) 721-6032

Profit/Nonprofit

Nonprofit

II. General Formats

Disc (LP - 16" ETs or 78s): 1,000 78s; 1,000 LPs.
Audiotape: 300 1/4" and 5" reels.
5,000 ft of 16mm original film.

IV. Subject Content Description

The 1920s: One thousand 78s, mostly Henry Burr recordings and early country music.

Vietnam War Era: Two- to three-thousand feet, raw, 16mm color footage of antiwar demonstrations and rallies.

VII. Accessibility

Research Aids: Listings, tape availabilities, etc.

Published Catalog: *Henry Burr — Discography and Biography,* 250 page book available for $50.

CANADA

I. Organizational Information

British Columbia Archives and Records Service
Sound and Moving Images
655 Belleville Street
Victoria, B.C. V8V 1X4, Canada

Individuals to Contact

Derek Reimer
Head

Allen Specht
Archivist

Paul Kneffel
Technician

Phone

(604) 387-6262 and 387-2963

Profit/Nonprofit

Nonprofit

Sponsor

Government of British Columbia

II. General Formats

Disc (LP, 78s, 45s) — ca. 10 broadcasts. **Acetate discs** — 1,100 broadcasts. **Audiotape** — 9,240 recordings. **Videotape** — About 3,000. **Film** — 1,086 T.V. programs.

III. General Program Types

All categories represented, but especially programs of music, variety, drama, public affairs, news, sports, and commercials.

The Sound & Moving Image Unit is responsible for film, videotape and sound recordings. Broadcast recordings form a fair percentage of our total holdings. For example, of an estimated 25,000 audiotapes, about 9,200 are recordings of radio broadcasts. (The others consist of oral history, Debates of the Legislature, music, public events, etc.)

Some of our noteworthy holdings in broadcasting include 1,00 acetate discs of radio programming from 1933 to ca. 1955. These discs contain every type of radio broadcast of the pre-television era, and are mostly from

252

private radio stations in Vancouver. Another is a collection of about 700 hours of public affairs broadcasting (open line and interview shows or "talk radio") from the years 1962 to 1974. It captures many controversies of the "60s." A third is a group of collections from producers of the Canadian Broadcasting Corporation — Pacific Region that emphasized radio documentaries and dramas produced in the 1970s and 1980s. In television we have selectively acquired over 1,000 CBC Vancouver television programs from 1954 to 1970; this was a highly creative period in the production of TV drama and documentaries.

IV. Subject Content Description

Radio:

Depression 1930 to 1939 — about 70 programs, mostly music and variety.
1940 to 1960 — About 200 documentaries and 700 hours of "talk radio."
1970s and 1980s — About 1,700 audiotapes of radio documentaries and drama.

Television:

1954 to 1970 — 1,086 programs (CBC TV) on film and kinescope.
1970s — About 500 newsclips on film from private TV; 2,500 public affairs shows on videotape.
1970s and 1980s — 200 videotapes of TV specials, news, public affairs.

V. Related Manuscript Materials

Includes personal papers, scripts related to audio, video, and film collections. Also several oral history collections related to radio and television collections.

VII. Accessibility

Research Aids: Card catalogs, inventories, lists, indexes, several printed inventories distributed locally.
"Use" Conditions: On-site listening carrels, film viewers, and video monitor. Some restricted access and many copyright. Copies made at cost.
Hours: 8:45 a.m. to 4:45 p.m. plus evening-weekend access to reference room facilities.

CANADA

I. Organizational Information

Collection Radio-Canada (C.B.C.)
Bibliothèque de Musique
Université du Québec à Montréal
C.P. 8889, Succ. A
Montréal, Québec H3C 3P3 Canada

Individual to Contact

C.-P. Gérald Parker

Phone

(514) 987-3934

Profit/Nonprofit

Nonprofit

II. General Formats

Disc (LP - 16" ETs or 78s): About 300 16" ET discs.
Audiotape (audio only): Last count (1986): 11,060 reels.

III. General Program Types

The collection is only partly cataloged, but consists of music, variety (music-centered), and interviews about music. The archive represents the output of the French Network in Montréal (original production or foreign original production aired on C.B.C., **not** "record shows").

VII. Accessibility

Research Aids: Card catalog (unstandardized) in chronological order; some cards converted (pre-1970) to computer data.

Published Catalog: A published catalog on microfiche has been intended, but its likelihood of ever appearing is somewhat doubtful.

"Use" Conditions: On-site facilities (listening); no dubbing without C.B.C. authorization. **Hours:** 9 a.m. to 5 p.m., Monday through Friday.

CANADA

I. **Organizational Information**

Scott Sound Recordings Library
4700 Keele St.
York University
Downsview, Ontario M3J 1P3 Canada

Individual to Contact

J. Stockton

Phone

(416) 736-2100 ext 88,880

Profit, Nonprofit

Nonprofit

II. **General Formats**

Disc (LP - 16" ETs or 78s): 23,000.
Audiotape: 8,500.
Compact discs: 1,000.

III. **General Program Types**

Broadcast music (300 recordings/programs); variety (200); drama (2,000); documentaries (2,000); and other music.

V. **Related Manuscript Materials**

CBC drama scripts.

VI. **Special Interests**

Ethnomusicology; jazz.

VII. **Accessibility**

Special in-house discographies; automated on-line catalog; computer access with "Yorkline" (OPAC); 60 listening stations; user must have library card. **Hours:** 9 a.m. to 9 p.m. weekdays, 12-5 p.m. weekends.

UNITED KINGDOM

I. Organizational Information

BBC Sound Archives
Broadcasting House
London W1A 1AA

Individual to Contact

Sally Hine
Librarian, Archives & Effects

Phone   011-44-71-580-4468
Telex   265781
Cables   Broadcasts, London

II. General Formats

Disc (LP - 12" ETs or 78s) and audiotapes.

III. General Program Types

The collection now numbers over 500,000 separate recordings and covers the whole spectrum of BBC Radio programs.

UNITED KINGDOM

I. Organizational Information

Imperial War Museum
Lambeth Road
London SE1 6HZ

Individual to Contact

Paul Sargent
Deputy Keeper
Department of Film

Phone

011-44-71-416-5000

II. General Formats

Film.

IV. Subject Content Description

The Department of Film's Collection originated when the official films shot by British cameramen during the First World War were transferred to the Museum in 1919, which makes it one of the oldest film archives in the world. The films deposited were of British and Commonwealth military and naval operations on all fronts and included the three major First World War battle documentaries, *The Battle of the Somme, The Battle of the Ancre* and *The Battle of Arras* together with a wide range of short information or propaganda films dealing with the British war effort on the home front. All these were, of course, silent with explanatory titles.

The Department is concerned in a more general way with all film relating to war and its political and social causes and effects. It has a notable collection of German documentary and feature films which was obtained after the Second World War. The large group of Nazi newsreels includes many made in various languages for distribution in occupied and neutral countries. Other foreign collections include Indian newsreels, a partial set of Soviet newsreels from 1941 to 1944, the American propaganda series *Why We Fight*, and smaller Japanese and Italian collections.

The Department continues to collect post Second World War film, including major television series such as *The World At War*, *The Troubles* (Thames), *The Secret War*, *SOE*, and *Task Force South* (BBC). A considerable amount of ITN and BBC news coverage from the Falklands has been acquired.

VI. Special Interests

In keeping with the Department's status as a national archive, special emphasis is given to the acquisition and preservation of British films. The library's present holdings amount to more than 45,000,000 feet of film.

VII. Accessibility

Films may be viewed by members of the public and students with legitimate research interests on application in writing to the Keeper of the Department of Film. The Museum has a cinema, a smaller preview theatre and a number of viewing machines, which are particularly suitable for study purposes. Details of the current rates charged for both types of screening will be quoted on application to the department. A limited loan scheme for 16mm films and videocassettes is in operation for higher educational institutions. It is not possible at present to extend this scheme to schools or other organizations. Details may be obtained from the Loans Officer within the Department. There are regular public showings of films from the collection in the Museum cinema. Special programs can be organized for individuals and specialist groups.

In certain cases copies of films may be sold to individuals strictly for their own personal use. Details may be obtained from the Production Office, Department of Film.

Hours: Department of Film: Monday through Friday, 10 a.m. to 5 p.m., by appointment. Public Galleries: Monday to Saturday 10 a.m. to 5:50 p.m.; Sunday 2-5:50 p.m.

UNITED KINGDOM

I. Organizational Information

The Joe Pengelly Collection
36, Thorn Park
Mannamead, Plymouth PL3 4TE

Individual to Contact

Joe Pengelly
Hon. Research Fellow
Exeter University

Profit/Nonprofit

Profit

II. General Formats

500 plus cylinder recordings. As the result of a Leverhulme grant, I (Joe Pengelly) had built to my specification an electrical cylinder replay machine that will uniquely play any type of cylinder.

Disc (LP - 16" ETs or 78s): 1,000+; audiotape, 1,000; videotape, 10 (including half hour BBC TV program celebrating the centenary of recorded sound); open reel audiotape 7 1/2 and 15 ips; British VHS.

III. General Program Types

Documentaries, 1,000 recordings/programs.

IV. Subject Content Description

The collection specially embraces Cornish mining before 1900 and beyond, the Boer War, the First World War, the Invorgordan Mutiny of 1931, and the Vatican Castrati.

Radio's Golden Age: Religion, half hour BBC program on Cornish Methodism.

V. Related Manuscript Materials

"In the Beginning Was The Spoken Word," paper given at the Plymouth Anthenaum 29th January 1981.

VI. Special Interests

- "The Technical & Subjective Replication of Archival Sound," University of North Carolina, April 1981.
- "The Castrato, Countertenor & Male Alto Voices," Bowling Green State University, Ohio, April 1984.
- Fi If Not Hi Before 1900 The Cylinders of Henri Lioret," Lincoln Center, New York City, April 1986.
- "In the Beginning Was The Spoken Word," George Washington University, Washington, DC, May 1987.

These are all papers with audio illustration given at conferences of the Association for Recorded Sound Collections conferences in the last decade. The text of these papers with sound tracks in audio illustration are in the recorded sound division of the Library of Congress. A cassette I have produced of Richard James Jose is available in illustration of the paper given at NC in 1981 and is additional to it ($10 airmail, world-wide).

VII. Accessibility

By personal application.

UNITED KINGDOM

I. Organizational Information

Northwest Sound Archive
BBC Local Radio/Commercial
Old Steward's Office
Castle Grounds, Clitheroe Castle
Clitheroe, Lancs BB6 9HG

Individuals to Contact

Ken Howarth
Sound Archivist

Andrew Schofield
Assistant

Profit/Nonprofit

Nonprofit

II. General Formats

Audiotape: 17,000.

III. General Program Types

The collections held are BBC Radio Manchester, BBC Radio Lancashire (formerly BBC Radio Blackburn), and Piccadilly Radio, a Manchester-based commercial station.

IV. Subject Content Description

Oral History: The memories and reminiscences of north west people. Special collections include the Bolton Oral History Survey on engineering and textiles, the Macclesfield Silk Industry interviews, the Manchester Ship Canal series, the Strangeways Prison tapes with prisoners and prison officers, the Gas Industry, and the Liverpool Docks Survey. There are other interviews on coal mining, canals, railways, and the textile industry.

Local Radio Programs: The Archive holds probably the largest collection of local radio programs in the UK. There are regular deposits of recordings from BBC Radio Manchester, BBC Radio Lancashire, and Piccadilly Radio. These include recordings of disasters, such as Abbeystead, and news events such as a major series on the Falkland Islands War. Other recordings include the Yorkshire Ripper hoax tape, Voice in the Crowd (an important series on the memories of ordinary people), local news, sport, politics, religion, folk music, local history, geology — in fact an enormous range of subjects.

Special Collections: These include the Solidarity recordings from Poland recorded by the Solidarity workers and Granada TV, deposited with NWSA for safe-keeping. The LS Lowry personal reminiscence tapes are of national importance, as are the Jodrell Bank Radio Astronomy tapes chronicling the rise of radio astronomy and including the first sounds of Sputnik.

A recent deposit by a Manchester collector Philip Sacaloff of over 1,500 mint 78 rpm shellac discs of Hebrew, Yiddish, and western music has greatly enriched the collections of the Archive, other music includes records and cassettes of north west artists.

Frank Dixon and Audrey Kay of Sale have recently deposited their considerable collection of sound recordings with the Archive, including interviews with Arthur Askey and Ted Ray.

Other recordings include children's playsongs, birdsongs, sounds of the region such as weaving sheds and railway locomotives, and important interviews with leading scientists such as Sir Bernard Lovell on radio astronomy and the late Sir Harry Platt on orthopedic surgery.

Dialect: The Archive has taken a special interest in all aspects of Lancashire Dialect. The Lancashire Authors Association works closely with NWSA in recording the work of its members, many of whom are experts in writing and performing the dialect works of 19th century and contemporary dialect writers. These contributions are available for loan or purchase on a series of cassette tapes. In addition, NWSA in co-operation with the Lancashire Library, North West Regional Library System, BBC Television, local radio, and many other bodies, conducted a major regional survey recording dialect words and phrases. The survey resulted in a publication "Sounds Gradely." All the words have been entered on to computer, and the database file is being constantly updated, giving north west people a unique source of dialect words.

The Survey of English Dialects was conducted by Leeds University from around 1938 to the early 1960s. This unique collection is currently being copied by NWSA and will soon be readily available to researchers at the Archive.

Recording Program: NWSA also makes its own recordings on many subjects, such as canals and railways. The Archive also pursues a policy of recording music of high quality, original, sacred, or traditional within the region, especially music which is unlikely ever to be commercially recorded. Examples include the Lancaster Harpers, and the Moravian Church Choir. From time to time the Archive also produces cassettes on different subjects, many of which are available for loan to appropriate bodies.

V. Related Manuscript Materials

Cue-sheet scripts.

VII. Accessibility

Computer access to collection; on-site facilities; some restrictions.
Hours: 9 a.m. to 5 p.m., Monday through Friday.

The main catalog of the Archive is held on computer. There are around 85,000 recordings held at NWSA and to print a catalog would be impossible as it would be equivalent to several volumes of Encyclopedia Britannica. Extracts from the catalogs are published (e.g., railways, World War II, trade unionism, housing, women, health, General Strike 1926, etc.) and are available on request.

Most tapes can be heard at NWSA headquarters at Clitheroe, providing that reasonable notice is given.

SUBJECT INDEX

The following is a compilation of the lists provided by various collectors. It includes radio and television programs, movies, and scripts. The page numbers reference the text page with name of the collection. For example, the programs listed for page 211 are from the Annenberg Television Script Archive.

285

287

H

Hail the Champ, 48
Hail to the Chief, 211
Hal March-Bob Sweeny, 201
Hal Peary, 115
Hal Willard, 115, 201
Half Hour to Kill, 201
Half-Nelson, 211
Hall of Fantasy, 48, 115, 201
    Hall of Fantasy (Utah), 48
Hallcrafters Hour, 115
Hallmark Hall of Fame, 26, 72, 201
Hallmark Playhouse, 38, 48, 115,
    174, 201
Halloween is Grinch Night, 211
Halloween Special, 115, 201
Halls of Ivy, 48, 115, 201
Hamptons, The, 211
Hancock's Half Hour, 201
Hands of a Stranger, 211
Handsome Harry, 211
Hanging by a Thread, 211
Hanna-Barbera, 211
Hansel and Gretel, 38
Hap Hazard, 115
Happily Ever After, 211
Happy, 211
Happy Battles, 211
Happy Birthday, Las Vegas, 211
Happy Days, 211, 243
Happy Endings, 211
Happy Features, 222
Hard Knox, 211
Hard Time on Planet Earth, 211
Hardcase, 211
Hardcastle and McCormick, 211
Hardcopy, 211
Hardesty House, 211
Hardhat and Legs, 211
Hardy Boys, 211
Hardy Family, 115, 201
Harem, 211
Harlem Globetrotters, 211
Harold Turner, 48
Harper Valley PTA, 211
Harris and Company, 211
Harry, 211
Harry Babbitt, 48
Harry James, 48, 115, 201
Harry Lime, Lives of, 38, 115, 192
Harry Nile, 192, 201

Harry Truman, 211, 227
    Funeral of, 227
Harry Von Zell, 48
Harry and Roger, 211
Harry's Hong Kong, 211
Hart to Hart, 211
Hartz Mountain Canaries, 115
Harvest of Stars, 48, 174
Harvey Korman, 211
Hatter Fox, 211
Haunted by Her Past, 211
Haunted House of Song, 48
Haunting Hour, 48, 115, 201
Haunted Trailer, 211
Haunting of Harington House, 211
Haunting Passion, 211
Have I Got a Christmas For You, 211
Have Faith, 211
Have Gun, Will Travel, 38, 48, 115, 201
Have You Ever Been Ashamed of
    Your Parents?, 211
Have You Tried Talking to Patty?, 211
Haven of Rest, 48
Having Babies, 211
Having It All, 211
Hawaii Calls, 48
Hawaii Five-O, 211, 244
Hawaiian Fantasies, 201
Hawaiian Heat, 211
Hawk, The, 48
Hawke Durango, 38
Hawke Larabee, 38, 201
Hawthorne, 48
Hawthorne Thing, 48
Hawthorne's Adventures, 48
Haywire, 211
Hazard of Hearts, 211
Head of the Class, 211
Headline Edition, 48, 115
Health and Happiness Show, 48
Hear Me Cry, 211
Hear No Evil, 211
Hearst and Davies Affair, 211
Heart of a Champion, 211
Heart of the City, 211
Heart Fund, 48
Heart and Soul, 211
Heart Strings, 48
Heart of Show Business, 110
Heartbeat, 211
Heartbeat of Broadway, 48
Heartbeat Theater, 48, 201

I

295

Joe Garagiola, Roast of, 115
Joe Hasel Sports, 115
Joe Louis/Max Schmelling
 Fight (1938), 227
Joe Manning, 48
Joe Palooka, 201
Joe Penner, 115, 201
Joe and the Colonel, 211
Joe and Valerie, 211
John Charles Thomas, 174, 201
John Davidson, 211
John Denver, 211
John Grin's Christmas, 211
John Hickman's 21st Anniversary, 201
John Phillip Sousa Directing
 His Band, 227
John Steele, Adventurer, 115, 201
John Steinbeck, 211
John and Yoko, A Love Story, 211
Johnathon Brixton, 201
Johnnie Mae Gibson: FBI, 211
Johnny Belinda, 211
Johnny Carson, 115
Johnny Chase, 48
Johnny Desmond, 48
Johnny Madero, 38
Johnny Olson, 227
Johnson Family, 48, 115, 192, 201
Johnson Wax Program, 48
Join Up -- Join In, 110
Joke's on Mr. Little, 211
Jones' Jive Joint, 227
Jordan Chance, 211
Joseph, Story of, 48
Joseph Enos, 48
Journey Into Space, 115, 201
Journey Through Baldidreampt, 201
Journeys Behind the News, 61
Joy Boys, 115, 201
Joyce Jordan, M.D., 48
Juarez, 211
Jubilee, 48, 115
Judgement Day, 211
Judy Canova, 38, 48, 115, 201
Jukebox Saturday Night, 211
Julie Andrews, 211
Julie Farr, M.D., 211
Jumping Beans, 48
Jumpstreet, 211
Jungle Jim, 38, 47, 48, 115, 174,
 192, 201
Junior Miss, 48, 115

Just Entertainment, 115
Just a Little Inconvenience, 211
Just Friends, 211
Just a Little More Love, 211
Just Me and You, 211
Just My Luck, 211
Just Pals, 211
Just Plain Bill, 48, 115
Just the Ten of Us, 211
Just in Time, 211
Just Tipsy, Honey, 211
Just You and Me, 211
Justice Delayed:
 The Lenell Geter Story, 211
Juvenile Jury, 115, 201
Juvi, 211

K

Kaleidoscope, 152
Kallikaks, 211
Kaltenborn Edits the News, 218
Kaltenmeyer's Kindergarten, 115
Karen Ann Quinlan,
 In the Matter of, 211
Karen Carpenter Story, 211
Karen's Song, 211
Kate Bliss and the Ticker Tape Kid, 211
Kate Smith, 48, 115, 201
Kathy McCormick, Secret Life of, 211
Katie--Portrait of a Centerfold, 211
Kay Fairchild, Stepmother, 201
Kay Jeweler's Birthday Book, 48
Kay Kyser, 48, 115, 201, 227
Kay O'Brien, 211
Kay Russell, 48
Kaz, 211
Keep It In the Family, 48
Keep Posted, 248
Kenny Baker, 174
Kenny Rogers, 211
Kenny and Dolly, 211
Kent State, 211
Key to Success, 211
KFI's 50th Anniversary, 38
KFSO's Thanksgiving Special, 201
Kicks, 211
Kid with the Broken Halo, 211
Kid on the Corner, 48
Kid from Nowhere, 211
Kid with the 200 I.Q., 211
Kids Don't Tell, 211

M